Slaves to Sweetness

British and Caribbean Literatures of Sugar

T0335110

CARL PLASA

LIVERPOOL UNIVERSITY PRESS

First published 2009 by
Liverpool University Press
4 Cambridge Street
Liverpool L69 7ZU

This paperback edition published 2011

British Library Cataloguing-in-Publication data
A British Library CIP record is available

ISBN 978-1-84631-184-0 cased
978-1-84631-749-1 limp

Arts & Humanities
Research Council

Typeset by Koinonia, Manchester
Printed and bound by Marston Digital

Slaves to Sweetness

British and Caribbean Literatures of Sugar

LIVERPOOL STUDIES IN INTERNATIONAL SLAVERY 1

To the memory of my father
and for Mister E, who couldn't be sweeter

Heavy matters, heavy matters! But look thee here, boy. Now bless thyself;
thou metst with things dying, I with things newborn.
– William Shakespeare, *The Winter's Tale*

Contents

Acknowledgements

I am indebted to Anthony Cond for originally commissioning this book and to the Arts and Humanities Research Council, which supported the project with a research leave grant covering the period from January to April 2007.

I would also like to thank Sean Purchase for his humour and sense of style and John Thieme for generous encouragement along the way. As ever, special gratitude is reserved for Betty, whose suggestions were invaluable and led me in some interesting directions: without her, the book – like so much else – would not have been possible.

An earlier version of chapter 2 appeared in *Atlantic Studies: Literary, Historical and Cultural Perspectives*, 4.2 (2007), 225–43; and of chapter 3 in *Romanticism and Victorianism on the Net*, 50 (May 2008). Chapter 4 was first published, also in slightly different form, in *LIT: Literature Interpretation Theory*, 16 (2005), 285–309.

Introduction

[S]ugar calls up the binary rhythm of law and work, of patriarchal hierarchy, of scientific knowledge, of punishment and discipline, of superego and castration; it is the space ... of production and productivity, of rule and measure, of ideology and nationalism, of the computer that speaks and separates; it is, above all, the signifier that offers itself as center, as origin, as fixed destination, for that which signifies the Other.
    – Antonio Benítez-Rojo, *The Repeating Island*

[T]hey have no leisure for the cultivation of aught but their estates, – & limit the alphabet to 5 letters, S – U – G – A – R.
    – John Anderson, *A Magistrate's Recollections, or St. Vincent, in 1836*

White/Black

Towards the beginning of her autobiography, Harriet Martineau recalls a mysterious dream occurring in early childhood. Given the nature of its content – a return to the domestic space and to the mother – it might be assumed that the dream would engender a sense of well-being, an expectation increased by the additional oneiric presence of the commodity to which all children are automatically drawn: sugar. In the event, however, the dream has the opposite effect, bringing neither comfort nor pleasure, but a chilling disquiet:

> By the time we were at our own door, it was dusk, and we went up the steps in the dark; but in the kitchen it was bright sunshine. My mother was standing at the dresser, breaking sugar; and she lifted me up, and set me in the sun, and gave me a bit of sugar. Such was the dream which froze me with horror![1]

What can explain the young Martineau's unhomely sense of 'horror' here, as she strangely freezes in the 'sun'? And why should it be precipitated by so sweet a thing as a 'bit of sugar', melting on the tongue as it is eaten? The answer is that sugar is not, as it turns out, anything like as innocent as it appears to be, but indissolubly linked to the history of slavery in the Caribbean, to which it was introduced by Christopher Columbus in 1493.[2] While these nightmarish bonds remain unrealized or even unconscious amid the dreamy chiaroscuro of her memoirs, they are openly acknowledged and explored in Martineau's other writings, especially 'Demerara' (1833), a tale composed just before the emancipation of slaves in the British West Indies in 1834. In this text, Martineau advances a powerful if eclectic anti-slavery case by combining arguments derived from political economy with a somewhat less abstract emphasis on the psychological and corporeal sufferings endured by those she calls her 'slave personages'.[3]

The links between sugar and slavery haunting Martineau's dream and confronted in the politically awakened consciousness of her fiction have been the focus for many studies appearing long after the time in which she herself was living, stimulating twentieth-century landmark analyses by Fernando Ortiz, Noël Deerr and Sidney W. Mintz.[4] Such classic contributions explore their subject from perspectives which are principally historical, economic and anthropological and these methodologies retain a vital currency today, as evidenced in Richard Follett's definitive work on the sugar world of antebellum Louisiana.[5] At the same time, other modes of inquiry, largely inspired and informed by developments in postcolonial theory, have emerged, for which the accent falls more firmly on the textual, as critics seek to engage with how sugar has been represented discursively. The most sustained instance of this approach to date is Keith A. Sandiford's *The Cultural Politics of Sugar: Caribbean Slavery and Narratives of Colonialism* (2000), which deals with a body of plantation writings stretching from the era of early colonial settlement in the 1650s to the time of emancipation. For Sandiford, these texts – by Richard Ligon, Charles de Rochefort, James Grainger, Janet Schaw, William Beckford and Matthew Lewis – are marked, each in its different way, by tensions between the desire to legitimate what he calls an 'evolving ideal of Creole civilization', on the one hand, and the anxious recognition, on the other, that the formation of such an ideal is compromised by 'its central relation to slavery and its marginal relation to metropolitan cultures'.[6] While this book is indebted to Sandiford's analysis of how these tensions are negotiated, if not resolved, in the writings of his authorial sextet, its broad aim is to reorientate the critical and historical framework he delineates, differing from his project in several major respects.

The first of the differences is that this book does not restrict its interest just to texts written at (or about) the site of colonial production, but also considers works addressing the question of sugar's consumption at home. This it does by alternating, in its first four chapters, between colonial and domestic spaces, thus allowing each to serve as a context for and counterpoint to the other. The second difference is historical: while Sandiford commences his study in the mid-seventeenth century, at a point when the English Civil Wars (1642–51) have just been concluded and what Ligon calls the 'great work of Sugar-making'[7] is still in its infancy, this inquiry begins in the 1760s, in the aftermath of a much wider conflict (the Seven Years' War of 1756–63), which saw Britain both establish its superiority as an imperial power over France and other European nations and consolidate its status as prime mover in the transatlantic slave trade.[8] As well as beginning at a considerably later historical juncture, the book further differs from Sandiford by moving far beyond the emancipatory threshold at which he halts, extending the debate first into the Victorian period and then the postcolonial present. This leads to what is the third and most important difference: whereas Sandiford concentrates exclusively on white writings, this book addresses black texts too, examining, in its last three chapters, how sugar has been revisited and rewritten by a number of expatriate Caribbean authors, both male and female, from the early 1970s onwards. The main advantage of expanding the critical analysis into the terrain of the postcolonial is that it enables previously unrecognized relationships between white and black saccharographies to be brought to light, providing new insights into the ways in which the black writing of sugar revises the white archive out of which it grows.

Sugar-Works

The book opens with a chapter on Grainger's *The Sugar-Cane* (1764), a work distinguished not only by its founding role in the tradition of Anglophone Caribbean literature but also by the extensive technical knowledge of sugar production which it exhibits. Yet Grainger's text is as much a poem of evasion as of display, consistently censoring the racial and sexual oppression intrinsic to the plantation culture which inspires it. What is significant about *The Sugar-Cane*'s gaps and silences is the parallels they suggest between aesthetic and economic orders, the making of the poem and the making of the sugar it celebrates: Grainger's text excludes from itself those aspects of slavery the genteel reader might find unpalatable, just as the planter whom he repeatedly addresses, and with whom he identifies, refines out from his sugar those things which threaten its purity and hence its profitability also. Despite the poem's discursive vigilance, however, what it seeks to expunge remains stubbornly present, appearing in displaced, distorted and fragmentary forms, which vitiate the saccharine portrayal of slavery its author seeks to uphold.

The analogical relationships between the production of the text and the production of sugar Grainger's poem sets in play are worth highlighting because they initiate a pattern which recurs in a variety of ways across and between the white and black bodies of writing this book considers. That said, there are some significant differences separating the two modes of production which it is well to bear in mind. Not the least of these is that the processes of refinement in which Grainger involves himself are not simply driven by an economic imperative, as might be the case with the planter: they also entail ideological and/or psychological elements, as Grainger customizes for himself and his readers an image of slavery designed to salve national and personal consciences alike.

Chapter 2 traces a shift from colonial margin to metropolitan centre and from the saccharophilia of *The Sugar-Cane* to the saccharophobia of the white abolitionist writings of the early 1790s, looking, specifically, at the abolitionists' construction of the sugar-eater as cannibal. The chapter's starting-point and frame of reference is Olaudah Equiano's *The Interesting Narrative of the Life of Olaudah Equiano, or Gustavus Vassa, the African. Written by Himself* (1789), a text in which, as is often noted, the discourse of cannibalism is appropriated and rewritten, with the colonizing rather than colonized subject invested with anthropophagous tendencies. The rhetorical strategies used in Equiano's slave narrative are taken up and reworked, in turn, by his white abolitionist contemporaries, a point the chapter illustrates in readings of political pamphlets by William Fox and Andrew Burn. For both of these writers, the consumption of sugar is inseparable from the consumption of the enslaved bodies which produce it, accordingly accruing to itself a 'horror' akin to that signalled in Martineau. But the difference between the two writers is that, in Fox's case, the status of consumer as cannibal is purely figurative, while in Burn it is more disturbingly – and more radically – literal.

With chapter 3, the book switches back to the plantation culture with which it begins, analysing the representation of slavery in Matthew Lewis's *Journal of a West India Proprietor, Kept during a Residence in the Island of Jamaica* (1834). Composed in the mid-1810s – after the abolition of the slave trade in 1807 but some time prior to emancipation – the *Journal* occupies a very different historical and political moment to the one in which Grainger writes *The Sugar-Cane*, just as sugar itself is a far less obvious imaginative stimulus or narrative presence in the text than it is in Grainger. Such contrasts between the two works are counterbalanced, however, by their continuities, not the least of these being the way in which Lewis, like Grainger, figures the Caribbean sugar estate as a kind of utopia, purified of all that made slavery so anathema to its opponents. By censoring the violence of white male desire for the black woman and more generally erasing the traces of master–slave violence, Lewis's *Journal* thus echoes the aesthetics of refinement initiated in Grainger, sweetening colonial realities for similarly self-serving purposes.

The next chapter considers George Eliot's 'Brother Jacob' (1864). Set in the 1820s, this novella returns to the issue of sugar's consumption broached by the abolitionists, taking up the seemingly frivolous subject of confectionery in order to show how its delights are seriously compromised by the slavery on which they depend. Yet as well as looking back to the writings of the abolitionists, 'Brother Jacob' engages with a host of other texts, each of which is implicated, to a greater or lesser degree, in the history of Caribbean slavery with which Eliot herself is dealing. These range from William Shakespeare's *Othello* (1604) and *The Tempest* (1611) to Charlotte Brontë's *Jane Eyre* (1847), and also include the colonial romance of Inkle and Yarico, whose story is first told in Ligon's *A True & Exact History of the Island of Barbados* (1657). In Grainger and Lewis, the production of sugar stands as a kind of allegory for the production of the text and a similar parallel characterizes Eliot's narrative: if 'Brother Jacob' is about the art of confectionery, it is simultaneously a striking mid-Victorian instance of the confectionery of art.

The chapters outlined thus far span a century of white sugar-writings from 1764 to 1864, alternating between sites of production and sites of consumption. With chapter 5, however, the book turns its attention towards more recent black works, beginning with a comparative analysis of two collections of poems by Guyanese-born authors: Grace Nichols's *I is a Long Memoried Woman* (1983) and David Dabydeen's *Slave Song* (1984). In the first of these, the utopian portrait of the plantation cultivated in *The Sugar-Cane* is wholly negated, just as the black female and black feminist perspectives informing Nichols's text provide a timely supplement to the androcentrism characterizing the sugar poetry of the early 1970s, as written by Edward Kamau Brathwaite and Faustin Charles. In Dabydeen, the status of the plantation as utopia is also decisively rejected, but the difference from Nichols is that in Dabydeen's collection the black woman (whether slave or free) finds herself once again at the discursive margin rather than the centre, displaced by her canecutting male counterpart. This figure is a disturbing one, represented, in a number of poems, as the would-be rapist of a white colonial mistress who herself appears – equally disturbingly – to crave her own violation.

Despite such differences of emphasis, it is clear that Nichols and Dabydeen are united in a concern to write back to and critique Grainger, challenging the aesthetics of refinement he puts in place with a new aesthetics of contamination. As the final two chapters of the book go on to show, the main purpose of such an aesthetics is to lay bare the extent to which the violence of slavery and the plantation is a sexual violence, directed overwhelmingly at black and mixed-race women. There is in such a counter-stress something not only politically exigent but also partly redemptive: history itself cannot be undone, but it can be rewritten in a way which allows its pain and injustice to emerge and its silences to be broken.

Such processes of revision are powerfully exemplified in Caryl Phillips's *Cambridge* (1991), the text discussed in chapter 6. In this novel, the events on an early nineteenth-century West Indian estate are told and retold from a variety of competing perspectives, with the central narrative conflict unfolding between the accounts given by the middle-class Englishwoman, Emily Cartwright, and the eponymous slave, Cambridge. What is notable about this intratextual exchange is the way in which it functions as a mirror for the novel's intertextual practices, particularly as they relate to Lewis's *Journal*, the primary historical source on which Phillips bases Emily's own planta-tion memoir. Despite his Christian stoicism, Cambridge is, with respect to this memoir, a figure of rebellion: he tells a tale (itself drawing on elements from Equiano) in which the white male sexual violence unspoken by Emily is dramatically articulated in the rape of his own slave-wife (Christiania) by the plantation manager (Mr Brown). Cambridge's subversive counter-statement is simultaneously the vehicle by which Phillips's novel itself rebels against Lewis's text, breaching its silences and polluting its discursive purity.

The book closes with a reading of Austin Clarke's prize-winning but critically neglected *The Polished Hoe* (2002), a novel set on a Barbadian sugar plantation in the early 1950s, more than a decade before the island gained its independ-ence from British colonial rule in 1966. In a parallel with *Cambridge*, this text features a woman (Mary Gertrude Mathilda Paul) abused and tormented since girlhood by another sexually degraded plantation manager (Mr Bellfeels), but the key difference between the two novels is that Mary escapes the condition of silent victim which by and large defines Phillips's Christiania: she both murders and maims Bellfeels with the implement named in the novel's title and gives an expansive confessional account of the interwoven histories of oppression – both individual and collective, female and male – leading to her vengeful act. In Mary's hands, the hoe thus alters from being a tool used in the cultivation of the cane to being a weapon of redemption, a change additionally associating her with a brand of anti-colonial resistance usually gendered as masculine. But in Clarke's hands, it operates as a means by which the novel establishes one more analogical relationship between sugar and text, as tilling and telling, so to speak, are drawn together. Just as the hoe breaks up and turns over the soil in the cane-fields so often the scene of Mary's exploitation, so the narrative she tells disturbs and loosens. Like Clarke's novel overall, it fragments the superficial images of colonial benevolence and racial superiority which a sweet-tongued plantocracy projects, unearthing the bitter truths those images conceal.

Sugar locks oppressor and oppressed into a violent union, whether at a point far beyond emancipation, as in Clarke, or during the period when the slave trade reaches its dreadful meridian, as in Grainger. It also subjects both parties to its rule, tempting the one with visions of wealth, luxury and pleasure, while transforming the other into the instrument enabling such visions to be realized. Equally, though, sugar possesses a certain textual power, compelling white and black authors to tell its story, albeit in ways which are at once very different from one another and yet intimately related.

Notes

1. Harriet Martineau, *Harriet Martineau's Autobiography*, ed. Maria Weston Chapman, 2 vols (Boston: James R. Osgood, 1877), vol. 1, pp. 11–12.
2. Columbus brought sugar from Madeira to Hispaniola in the course of his second voyage to the Americas. For brief accounts of his epoch-making activities and the subsequent early growth of the sugar industry on the island where it was first essayed, see Eric Williams, *From Columbus to Castro: The History of the Caribbean 1492–1969* (1970; New York: Vintage, 1984), pp. 23–29; and Sanjida O'Connell, *Sugar: The Grass that Changed the World* (London: Virgin Books, 2004), pp. 31–34. For a more detailed analysis, see Genaro Rodríguez Morel, 'The Sugar Economy of Española in the Sixteenth Century', in *Tropical Babylons: Sugar and the Making of the Atlantic World, 1450–1680*, ed. Stuart B. Schwartz (Chapel Hill and London: University of North Carolina Press, 2004), pp. 85–114.
3. Harriet Martineau, Preface to 'Demerara', in *The Empire Question*, ed. Deborah Logan, volume 1 of *Harriet Martineau's Writing on the British Empire*, ed. Deborah Logan, 5 vols (London: Pickering and Chatto, 2004), p. 69. Martineau's critique of slavery takes on an additional charge when it is recalled that her family was itself implicated in its circuits of production and consumption: Robert Rankin, her maternal grandfather, was a sugar-refiner in Newcastle.
4. See Fernando Ortiz, *Cuban Counterpoint: Tobacco and Sugar*, trans. Harriet de Onís, with a new Introduction by Fernando Coronil (1940; Durham, NC and London: Duke University Press, 1995); Noël Deerr, *The History of Sugar*, 2 vols (London: Chapman and Hall, 1949–50); and Sidney W. Mintz, *Sweetness and Power: The Place of Sugar in Modern History* (New York: Viking, 1985).
5. See Richard Follett, *The Sugar Masters: Planters and Slaves in Louisiana's Cane World, 1820–1860* (Baton Rouge: Louisiana State University Press, 2005).
6. Keith A. Sandiford, *The Cultural Politics of Sugar: Caribbean Slavery and Narratives of Colonialism* (Cambridge: Cambridge University Press, 2000), p. 3.
7. Richard Ligon, *A True & Exact History of the Island of Barbadoes. Illustrated with a Map of the Island, as also the Principal Trees and Plants there, set forth in their due Proportions and Shapes, drawn out by their several and respective Scales. Together with the Ingenio that makes the Sugar, with the Plots of the several Houses, Rooms, and other places, that are used in the whole process of Sugar-making; viz. the Grinding-room, the Boyling-room, the Filling-room, the Curing-house, Still-house, and Furnaces; All cut in Copper*, second edition (1673; London: Frank Cass, 1976), p. 85.
8. For a useful overview of the Seven Years' War and the problems the British encountered in the years following their military triumph, see Bruce P. Lenman, 'Colonial Wars and Imperial Instability, 1688–1793', in *The Eighteenth Century*, ed. P. J. Marshall, volume 2 of *The Oxford History of the British Empire*, editor-in-chief Wm. Roger Louis, 5 vols (Oxford: Oxford University Press, 1988), pp. 159–67. Britain's history as pre-eminent slave-trading nation is discussed in detail by David Richardson, 'The British Empire and the Atlantic Slave Trade', also in Marshall, pp. 440–64. According to his estimate, the shipment of slaves from Africa to the New World in the 1760s runs at something over 42,000 per year, with the number 'tend[ing]' thereafter 'to level out or decline' (p. 441).

1

'Muse Suppress the Tale': James Grainger's *The Sugar-Cane* and the Poetry of Refinement

It was very common in several of the islands, particularly in St. Kitt's [*sic*], for the slaves to be branded with the initial letters of their master's name, and a load of heavy iron hooks hung about their necks. Indeed, on the most trifling occasions they were loaded with chains, and often other instruments of torture were added. The iron muzzle, thumb-screws, &c. are so well known, as not to need a description, and were sometimes applied for the slightest faults. I have seen a negro beaten till some of his bones were broken, for only letting a pot boil over. It is not uncommon, after a flogging, to make slaves go on their knees, and thank their owners, and pray, or rather say, God bless them.

– Olaudah Equiano, *The Interesting Narrative*

The Muse thinks it disgraceful in a Briton to sing of the Sugar-cane, since to it is owing the Slavery of the Negroes.
– Anonymous, Argument to Part I of *Jamaica, a Poem, In Three Parts*

Muscovado Poetics

After a sustained period of neglect, James Grainger's *The Sugar-Cane* has recently begun to attract a good deal of critical attention and is now generally regarded as a work with a major, if controversial part to play in the initial shaping of the Caribbean literary canon.[1] The recognition of the poem's formative role would certainly have pleased its author, who regularly insists upon the innovative nature of his 'West-India georgic',[2] while at the same time extolling the delights of the colonial periphery on which he writes (the Lesser Antillean island of St Christopher) in preference to the lures of the metropolis. Not quite so gratifying, equally certainly, however, would be the extent to which critics past and present have taken issue not only with the text's overwhelmingly pro-slavery politics, but also with its scandalous linguistic habits. If James Boswell could famously deride *The Sugar-Cane* for camouflaging the lowness of its agricultural concerns in a 'blank-verse pomp',[3] critics of our own postcolonial era have gone one step further. For them, the more urgent problem of the poem's style – elevated and classical, periphrastic and cloying – is that it masks the realities of the plantation world with which it is concerned. In *The Sugar-Cane*, as David Dabydeen puts it, 'the barbaric experience [of slavery] is wrapped in a napkin of poetic diction and converted into civilised expression'.[4]

Neat as it is, Dabydeen's comment provides only a starting-point for critical analysis of Grainger's poem, containing an ironic logic which, to take up his metaphor, invites unwrapping. On the one hand, there is no doubt that the rhetorical strategies Dabydeen highlights – and sets out to reverse amid the brutal energies of *Slave Song*, his own cycle of cane-poems – can be viewed as the sign of a spectacular retreat from facets of slavery Grainger finds highly troublesome: the hardships of black labour and the white violence which attends it, interracial desire and the threat of slave-rebellion. On the other hand, there is a sense in which such strategies at the same time recall the material operations at the heart of the very system they are designed to disavow. The poetic processes transmuting 'barbaric experience' into 'civilised expression' have, that is, an analogical dimension, paralleling those by which the juice extracted from the 'spiry Cane, / Supreme of Plants' (I. 22–23) is transformed into sugar.

How successful, though, is the poem in fulfilling its aims? The type of sugar on which it focuses is 'strong-grain'd muscovado' (I. 29), a relatively crude brownish substance, whose name derives from the Portuguese *mascavado*, meaning 'incomplete' or 'unfinished'.[5] As the observations of John J. McCusker suggest, muscovado's lack stems, ironically, from an excess – in the shape of the impurities it harbours within itself. These need to be removed in the course of a larger cycle of production, culminating in the creation of the more familiar white sugar associated with the rituals of domestic consumption:

> The production of table sugar from sugar-cane juice involves a series of stages during which progressively greater quantities of liquid are purged from the crystallizing sugar. The initial boiling of the cane juice result[s] in both a raw brown sugar called muscavado and a liquid by-product called molasses.[6]

From this perspective, it becomes evident that the analogy between the production of the text and the production of the sugar it honours is less straightforward than it might at first appear and would itself profit from a degree of conceptual refinement. *The Sugar-Cane* clearly projects a saccharine colonial vision designed to fulfil two main functions, the first of which is to cleanse its creator of the moral stain arising from his personal status as a minor slave-holder with aspirations towards 'some small plantation ... / Which he may call his own' (I. 546–47).[7] The second purpose, broader than the first but directly linked to it, is to provide an apologia for the plantocratic regime as a whole, at a time when, still more than twenty years before the formal beginnings of the campaign against the slave trade in 1787, the sugar-planter was already being satirized as the embodiment of moral degeneracy, cultural impoverishment and blind capitalist greed.[8] Despite its best intentions, however, the poem can only go so far and is repeatedly sullied by the refractory presence of the very things it sets out to expel.

First Things First: *The Sugar-Cane* and the Question of Priority

For the epigraph to *The Sugar-Cane*, Grainger selects the verses of a Roman poet who declares himself to be 'the first to attempt to stir with new songs Helicon and its green-topped, nodding woods, bringing strange mysteries, proclaimed by none before' (p. 213). In so doing, he signals more than just a gentlemanly knowledge of classical sources, gesturing also towards a desire for a certain imaginative earliness. This desire becomes more pronounced in the poem's 'Preface', where Grainger alerts the reader to the 'novelty of [his] subject' and revels in the prospect of the 'many new and picturesque images' with which *The Sugar-Cane* is destined to 'enrich' poetic tradition. As he goes on to remark, though, there have been occasions when the discursive silence he wishes to break has already been challenged, as in the contributions of 'Pere Labat, and other French travellers in America', along with Samuel Martin's *An Essay upon Plantership* (1750). As might be expected from a British author writing during the Seven Years' War – in which his nation's principal antago-nist was France – the works Grainger mentions here are suitably hierarchized. Those produced by the 'French travellers' offer only 'scattered hints' on 'the cultivation of the Sugar-Cane' and are in effect disparaged as the work of dilettantes, while Martin's 'pamphlet' – serious, substantial and seminal – is held up as 'an excellent performance', to which Grainger 'own[s]' himself to be 'indebted' (p. 89). Yet it is the sources Grainger does not acknowledge here which are just as important as those he does, at least with respect to any claims to a specifically poetic originality he might make. As Tobias Döring notes, Grainger's is not the first sugar-poem to appear within the field of eighteenth-century Anglophone Caribbean letters, a distinction belonging instead to Nathaniel Weekes's *Barbados: A Poem* (1754),[9] which explores 'The Virtues of the *Cane* ... / The noblest Plant of all the Western Isles!'[10] in some detail in its closing stages. The 'Preface' to *The Sugar-Cane* is thus marked by a logic of refinement similar to that which informs the poem itself: it erases Weekes's text from the genealogical record all the better to assist the later writer's self-promoting purposes.

Despite the nagging if unspoken precedent of *Barbados* in the margins of *The Sugar-Cane*, Grainger begins his poem with a paean to its firstness, combining this with a wider eye to the post-war economic prosperity of the 'native land' (I. 302) he left for St Christopher in 1759. Bidding for election to an eminent company of poets from both classical and modern British eras, Grainger writes, in typically high-flown mode:

> Spirit of Inspiration, that did'st lead
> Th'Ascrean Poet to the sacred Mount,
> And taught'st him all the precepts of the swain;
> Descend from Heaven, and guide my trembling steps
> To Fame's eternal Dome, where Maro reigns;
> Where pastoral Dyer, where Pomona's Bard,
> And Smart and Sommerville in varying strains,
> Their sylvan lore convey: O may I join
> This choral band, and from their precepts learn
> To deck my theme, which though to song unknown,
> Is most momentous to my Country's weal! (I. 7–17)

Here poetic and national self-advancement coincide. Grainger's exploration and development of his 'theme … to song unknown' is designed to increase his own poetic capital and secure him a niche in 'Fame's eternal Dome', but, at the same time, to be of direct benefit to the planter: it will improve the efficiency of the planter's methods, which will in turn improve his profits, together with those of Britain at large.[11] But whether the returns *The Sugar-Cane* generates be poetic or national, they are compromised alike by the slavery which is their basis and which Grainger strives constantly to wish away, as when, with the text just four lines old, he glosses the slaves compelled to tend the cane as 'Afric's sable progeny' (I. 4). Although such a reading would be anachronistic, it is hard not to sense the racial violence Grainger prefers to occult encrypted in the allusion to his 'Country's weal' which ends these lines. Even as 'weal' is, in this context, simply a contracted form of 'wealth', the word looks forward to a less comfortable set of associations: from the early 1820s onwards, it signifies '[the] mark or ridge raised on the flesh by the blow of a rod, lash, etc.' (*OED*).

Grainger's self-fashioning as poetic trailblazer is maintained throughout *The Sugar-Cane*, even incorporating a movement back from 'Caribbe's cane-isles' (IV. 21) towards the 'wilds' (IV. 22) of Africa itself, whose representation obliges the poet not only to embark upon an imaginative reversal of the Middle Passage but also to 'bind [his] sun-burnt brow with other bays, / Than ever deck'd the Sylvan bard before' (IV. 23–24). While the claims Grainger makes with respect to his originality are ultimately overblown, they are important even so, particularly because they suggest something of the colonizing impulse behind his poetic enterprise, with its desire to open up and possess new literary terrains. It is in this light that it seems entirely fitting for Grainger to have composed *The Sugar-Cane* on 'green St. Christopher' (I. 60), given that this 'blest Isle' (I. 67) has a claim to originality of its own to make, being the first Caribbean island to have been settled by the British in 1623. The claim is in fact more properly twofold, since, as Grainger points out in a detailed historical note, St Christopher was named after Columbus, colonial pioneer *par excellence*, who discovered it in 1493 and 'was so pleased with its appearance, that he honoured it with his Christian-name' (p. 169).

Even as 'the great ... Columbus' finds himself reflected in the 'beautiful and fertile island' (p. 169) he captures, narcissistically, in his name, he in turn features as a mirror for the poet, as Grainger's intrepid pursuit of his 'theme unsung' (I. 300) follows the colonizer's heroic movement through an 'ocean, never cut by keel' (I. 110). There is, though, a more immediate double for the poet than Columbus in the text, and this is the planter himself, who engages in his own violent cutting-edge or ground-breaking activities. This textually ubiquitous figure wields both 'biting ax with ceaseless stroke' (I. 33) and 'wounding hoe' (I. 48) in the name of cane and, more particularly, the economic fortune 'the soul of vegetation' (I. 51) will bring him, when, with a violent answering flourish of its own, it 'burst[s] on day' (I. 52). If the seeds of the twinning of poet and planter are first sown in the phrase with which Martin humbly opens the 'Dedication' to his *Essay* ('This little tract'),[12] their flowering is completed in Samuel Johnson's assessment of *The Sugar-Cane* in the *Critical Review*, which closes with a redeployment of the same earthy trope. Grainger, Johnson writes, 'had an untrodden country to clear; and though he may not have entirely subdued the native rudeness of the soil ... he certainly ... opened a delightful tract for future cultivation'.[13]

The resemblances between poet and planter are not just limited to the breaking and cultivation of new ground, metaphorical in the one case and literal in the other, but, as suggested above, extend to include the complex chemistries of refinement involved in the production of sugar. As Book III of Grainger's poem demonstrates with painstaking technical precision, the planter's job is to rid the cane-juice of its 'harsh intruders' (III. 354) – 'acor, oil, and mucilage' (III. 352), amongst others – turning it into a 'nectar'd muscovado' (III. 396), which 'Rings in the cask' (III. 399), just as Grainger himself censors those aspects of slavery which threaten to encroach upon and pollute the purity of his poetic universe. Like his own Muse, sympathetically etched, at the start of Book II, as a 'poor exile' (II. 5), Grainger remained, to the end of his brief life in 1766, outside the lucrative systems of production and exchange to which the role of planter would have granted him access. Though he was intimately connected to the slave-owning Creole elite by virtue of marriage to Daniel Mathew Burt, a plantation heiress from 'the first family in these Islands',[14] he personally possessed neither 'waving crops' (II. 5) nor a 'Negro-band' sufficiently large to cultivate them and 'skim' 'huge foaming coppers' (II. 7) at his behest. None the less, the workings of his poem enact the tasks of the planter he could never afford to become and it is to their more detailed consideration that this chapter now turns.

Black Labour, White Violence: From Cane-Field to Boiling-House

In the 'Preface' to *The Sugar-Cane*, Grainger identifies the source of the 'new … images' the poem puts into circulation as the very novelty of the Caribbean world he has recently entered: because 'the face of [the] country' where he writes is 'wholly different from that of Europe', simply to 'cop[y] its appearances' (p. 89) is to do something original. To imitate is by definition, in this milieu, to innovate.

The language of physiognomy Grainger uses here certainly bears scrutiny in terms of the racial essentialism to which it can so easily be assimilated, but is also notable for how it undercuts the aesthetic of innovative imitation the 'Preface' ushers in, since to equip the landscape of St Christopher with a metaphorical 'face' is already to have moved beyond mere mimesis towards a more dynamic model of representation. While this shift is only implicit in the 'Preface', it becomes overt in the poem itself. Inspired, in Book I, by the sight of slaves preparing the ground for the canes to be planted, Grainger reflects upon the nature of his own labours as poet. In an address to the planter, which modulates rapidly from the general and theoretical to the specific and practical, he writes:

> As art transforms the savage face of things,
> And order captivates the harmonious mind;
> Let not thy Blacks irregularly hoe:
> But, aided by the line, consult the site
> Of thy demesnes; and beautify the whole. (I. 266–70)

Here the role of 'art' becomes transformative rather than mimetic, operating, in a recurrence of the prefatory physiognomic trope, radically to alter 'the savage face of things', just as the planter in turn confers order upon the 'irregularly' toiling bodies of his 'Blacks'. As well as having an aesthetic advantage – it 'beautif[ies] the whole' – the organization of the slaves' labour along the lines advocated is economically prudent, since the precise manner in which their work is directed is, as Martin notes, of considerable consequence to a plantation's efficiency.[15] But if this passage provides a further illustration of how poet and planter function as one another's doubles, it suggests, in addition, an incidental and rather less predictable doubling between the poet and the slaves he beholds. Like the latter, moving in close formation across the planter's land, Grainger himself tries throughout the poem, according to Johnson at least, 'to reconcile the wild imagery of an Indian picture to the strict rules of critical exactitude', and, in the course of his endeavours, 'treads upon unclassic ground', while always 'maintain[ing] a classic regularity'.[16]

As the correspondence between the activities of poet and planter here suggests, the 'savage face of things' which 'art transforms' can be taken as a metaphor for slavery itself, whose features *The Sugar-Cane* sets out to soften and refine, endowing them with a milder look and even, at times, a grotesque charm. These cosmeticizing procedures are writ large towards the end of the poem's first Book, in the narrative Grainger tells about the mysterious figure of the 'good Montano'. Whether or not this self-made 'friend to man' (I. 579) is based on any historically real personage, his career as colonial entrepreneur recapitulates, as John Gilmore notes, 'the ... progress of British colonisation in the Caribbean [as] he begins with subsistence agriculture, experiments with a number of export crops ... and eventually ... accumulate[s] enough capital to move into sugar' (p. 239). To this it can be added that although Montano's story is set in the past, it none the less possesses a prospective element. By the time Grainger's Muse 'pays [its] tribute to [Montano's] fame' (I. 622), and thus complements the monetary wealth already amassed with poetic riches, the acquisitive subject of its praise is long dead: he is buried beneath the very 'Cane-lands' from which he has extorted his fortune and which thus ironically preserve the 'father lost' (I. 646) for whom they mourn. Yet the tale Grainger elaborates is not just a dewy-eyed exercise in nostalgia or a piece of colonial myth-making, but looks forward to and articulates his own business ambitions, providing an idealized model for the 'move into sugar' he himself wished to effect.

Grainger initially couches Montano's career as planter in terms of a biblical language of Fall, as an unspecified 'persecution' (I. 580) drives him from the 'paradise' (I. 586) of a similarly unspecified 'native shore' to become an 'exile' (I. 581) among 'Indian wilds, / ... tropic suns [and] fell barbaric hinds' (I. 586–87). Despite such inauspicious beginnings, however, Montano soon turns his circumstances to account, mastering the region into which he has been thrust and restoring his lost heaven by replicating the benign labour relations over which he once presided at home. In the domestic sphere he has left, Montano is 'own'd' (I. 585) by the 'swain[s]' (I. 584) he employs to be a 'lov'd master [and] protector' (I. 585), just as, in St Christopher, the 'numerous gang of sturdy slaves' (I. 609) he gradually purchases benefits from his philanthropic schemes, its members 'Well-fed, well-cloath'd [and] all emulous to gain / Their master's smile, who treated them like men' (I. 610–11). There is, of course, a violent contradiction in these lines between the humanity with which the smiling master 'treat[s]' his slaves and the insult of their enslavement, with the latter making a nonsense of the former. Such a contradiction is something the text does its best, in a sleight of its grammatical hand, to conceal, precisely at the point when it seems most glaring. As Grainger writes, reprising the methodical expansion of Montano's personal empire:

> At first a garden all his wants supplied,
> (For Temperance sat chearful at his board,)
> With yams, cassada, and the food of strength,
> Thrice-wholesome tanies: while a neighbouring dell,
> (Which nature to the soursop had resign'd,)
> With ginger, and with Raleigh's pungent plant,
> Gave wealth; and gold bought better land and slaves.
> Heaven bless'd his labour. (I. 593–600)

Here the zeugma rendering 'land and slaves' interchangeable troubles the claims to moral probity *The Sugar-Cane* wants to make on Montano's behalf, exposing his implication in a system in which the human metamorphoses into property. Yet Grainger's language works simultaneously to absolve Montano of the guilt which might be expected to ensue from this, since both his plantation and the 'Negroe-train' (I. 616) corralled into working it are bought not by the master himself, but by the impersonal 'gold' which acts as his surrogate.

Guided by 'generous pity' (I. 575) and 'prompt munificence' – whether towards a 'surly dog' (I. 620) or 'surlier Ethiop' (I. 621) – Montano clearly stands apart from his less compassionate peers. These other planters operate according to a false economy, or 'ill-judg'd avarice' (I. 572), which leads them to subject 'their slaves and herds' (I. 573) alike to the extremes of the tropical climate, denying them the protection of 'breezy shade' (I. 574, 627) when 'solstitial beams' (I. 570) shoot 'yellow deaths' across the 'devoted land' (I. 571). But the key difference governing Montano's narrative is not so much between virtuous and vicious slave-holders, as between the master who advertises the cruelty intrinsic to slavery – flaunts it in broad day, as it were – and the master who cloaks it beneath the self-flattering rhetoric of his own benevolence. By the time of his 'latter days' (I. 626), Montano has become fluent in such rhetoric, as the dying words delivered to his son attest:

> 'Be pious, be industrious, be humane;
> 'From proud oppression guard the labouring hind.
> 'Whate'er their creed, God is the Sire of man,
> 'His image they; then dare not thou, my son,
> 'To bar the gates of mercy on mankind.' (I. 630–34)

Here Montano's final wish is that his heir duplicate and so preserve his values – piety, industry, humanity – just as the 'labouring hind[s]' over whose welfare he frets are made in God's 'image'. Despite Montano's elevated conception of his own legacy, though, he arguably sets an even more dubious precedent for his son, in the end, than the slave-masters whom the poem chastises: they, at least, have the merit of making no attempt to obscure the exploitative nature of slavery beneath the patina of 'virtue' (I. 636) he has perfected. From this perspective – where the slave is ironically better guarded from the sort of 'oppression' which is not 'proud' of itself rather than the sort that is – the meteorological motifs playing across the Montano sequence take on a new significance. While the openly vicious planter, blinded by pursuit of profit at any cost, is prepared to set his slaves to work when the sun is at its height, the duplicitous Montano is a creature wedded to shadow. He is introduced into the text in the company of those 'whom shades delight' (I. 576) and who like to 'screen the public way' with 'cool cedars' (I. 578), just as it is beneath the cover of the 'tamarind-vista' (I. 624), which he himself has 'Planted' (I. 625), that he issues his instructions to his 'eldest hope' (I. 629), 'what time the sun / His sultry vengeance from the Lion pour'd' (I. 627–28). Even as his peroration ends with the claim that his 'soul aspires' to 'yon bright sky' (I. 639), the text conversely roots him in dark and sequestered spaces bespeaking the paradoxical shadiness of his own seemingly enlightened philosophy. Nor is it any wonder that Grainger's Muse should also be attracted to the 'breezy shade' Montano likes to occupy – regularly retreating there to 'escap[e] the sun's meridian blaze' (I. 623) – since the poem the Muse produces practises similar deceptions to Montano's, clouding slavery's bleak realities with an array of sunny pictures.

A typical instance of such textual double-dealing occurs in Book III, in the portrayal of the cutting of the cane which is to 'feed' the planter's 'crackling mills / With richest offerings' (III. 103–105) at crop time. Although this phase of the poem begins with Grainger's indolent injunction to his Muse to 'sing' the 'labour' (III. 110) of the slaves, their work tends to be figured as if it is not in fact work at all, but something much closer to play. The 'Negroe-train ... survey / [The planter's] fields ... / And pant to wield the bill' (III. 96–98), engaging with 'willing ardour' (III. 100) in an oxymoronic 'toil' which is not only 'cheerful' and 'light' (III. 101), but also so 'easy' that neither 'laziness' (III. 123) nor 'lameness' (III. 124) can resist its lure and find themselves drawn 'To join the favoured gang' (III. 125). As with Montano earlier, and as so often in The Sugar-Cane as a whole, however, things are not quite what they seem. While there is a sense of freedom and exuberance in Grainger's representation of the sugar-harvest, it is associated less with the slaves than with the canes, which await 'The hour of sweet release' (III. 93) when they are to be 'ease[d]' of their 'sapless burden' (III. 111), their 'stem[s] ... quiver[ing] in [the] hand / With fond impatience' (III. 113–16). For the slaves themselves, whatever liberation Grainger's text can offer is merely symbolic and ironically so at that. As they cut the 'imperial cane' (II. 100) down to size, the slaves might be said to exact a metaphorical revenge upon the white power of which the cane is the living sign. Yet the violence of their actions simply perpetuates the cycle of their oppression, since what they garner from the field immediately becomes a burden, needing to be carried to the mill in 'bundles' (III. 128) on black backs.

As well as hinting at a metaphorical black violence, the scene of labour Grainger describes here contains buried traces of a white violence rather more pressingly literal in its nature. These traces are discernible in the extended simile in which Grainger aligns his Caribbean canecutters with the sheep-shearing farm-workers of John Dyer's *The Fleece* (1757):

> ... As on Lincoln-plains,
> (Ye plains of Lincoln sound your Dyer's praise!)
> When the lav'd snow-white flocks are numerous penn'd;
> The senior swains, with sharpen'd shears, cut off
> The fleecy vestment; others stir the tar;
> And some impress, upon their captives sides,
> Their master's cypher. (III. 130–36)

Despite their superficial resemblances, the two forms of labour the text threads together at this moment are in one vital respect radically discrepant: the canecutters are enslaved, while the 'senior swains' who 'cut off / The fleecy vestment' work freely. But Grainger's simile is notable for reasons other than its wayward parallels. As an allusion to 'pastoral Dyer', it operates, in the first instance, as a reminder of the yearning for poetic recognition announced by *The Sugar-Cane*'s opening lines, yet it is not simply a passive nod towards an esteemed model but an active rewriting of his *oeuvre*. Part of that rewriting relates to location, as Grainger moves his poem's focus from the cane-fields of St Christopher to the 'plains of Lincoln', thus reversing the itinerary of Dyer's text, where the evocation of an English 'shearing-time'[17] follows on directly from considerations of 'the toils of life, / In foreign climes',[18] particularly as they pertain to 'weary Arabs [who] roam from plain to plain, / Guiding the languid herd in quest of food; / And shift their little home's uncertain scene / With frequent farewell'.[19] More important than this aspect of the revision of Dyer, however, is the closing image of the 'master's cypher' 'impress[ed]' upon the 'sides' of the freshly shorn sheep. As Döring notes, this image does not feature in Dyer's poem,[20] even though the terms in which it is formulated hold the key to an understanding of its curious supplementary appearance in Grainger's. In one sense, the image is itself a cipher or zero, as Grainger grafts on to his source the hallucinatory presence of a practice in which captive skins are violently and possessively branded in the name of their owner. At the same time, however, the image is a cipher in the sense that it is a secret writing or cryptogram, albeit one which can be easily enough decoded to reveal a different sort of branding, in this case involving human rather than animal skins, slaves rather than sheep. The image concisely illustrates, in other words, the ways in which *The Sugar-Cane* works to refine out from itself the less agreeable parts of the slave's existence, even as they continue to inhabit the text in distorted or clandestine forms.

Such processes of refinement are also to be observed in the last section to the canecutting sequence, in which white violence once again assumes a spectral status:

> Nor need the driver, Æthiop authoriz'd,
> Thence more inhuman, crack his horrid whip;
> From such dire sounds the indignant muse averts
> Her virgin-ear, where musick loves to dwell:
> 'Tis malice now, 'tis wantonness of power
> To lash the laughing, labouring, singing throng. (III. 141–46)

While the authenticity of the contentment with which Grainger's 'throng' carries out its work may be doubted, such feigned pleasures serve a genuine strategic function, rendering redundant the 'horrid whip', which would otherwise 'crack' across the bodies of the enslaved in a crude bid to increase their productivity. But if the happiness of the 'labouring' slaves is merely a ruse, other claims the poem makes at this juncture are equally questionable. Grainger concludes this passage with the assertion that 'To lash' slaves so clearly at one with their own labour would be 'malice' and 'wantonness of power', but is careful to attribute the possibility of such disgraceful actions to a black rather than white source, invoking the figure of the 'driver, Æthiop authoriz'd', whose blackness, according to a casually racist logic, makes him more 'inhuman' than his white equivalent. Grainger states that it is from the 'dire sounds' emanating from the 'driver''s 'whip' that his 'indignant muse averts / Her virgin-ear', but the suspicion remains that, far from causing offence, such 'sounds' are to be welcomed as a convenient distraction, muffling the acoustics of white violence, towards which the poem's aversion is greater still.

The structure of this passage is that of a palimpsest, with one type of violence (black on black) overwriting another which is ultimately even more 'horrid' for Grainger's delicate 'muse' to countenance (white on black). A fuller and more complex version of such superscription is in evidence at a slightly later point in Book III, as *The Sugar-Cane* switches its attention from external to internal scenes, cane-field to boiling-house:

> And now thy mills dance eager in the gale;
> Feed well their eagerness: but O beware;
> Nor trust, between the steel-cas'd cylinders,
> The hand incautious: off the member snapt
> Thou'lt ever rue; sad spectacle of woe!
> Are there, the muse can scarce believe the tale;
> Are there, who lost to every feeling sense,
> To reason, interest lost; their slaves desert,
> And manumit them, generous boon! to starve
> Maim'd by imprudence, or the hand of Heaven?

The good man feeds his blind, his aged steed,
That in his service spent his vigorous prime:
And dares a mortal to his fellow man,
(For spite of vanity, thy slaves are men)
Deny protection? Muse suppress the tale. (III. 163–79)

As the possessive of 'thy mills' implies, the recipient of the advice imparted in the first five lines of this passage is the planter, and it is his unwary 'hand' which is initially at risk of being dismembered by the 'steel-cas'd cylinders' used to grind the canes. As the passage develops, however, anxieties about the hypothetically wounded white body give way to reflections on its more materially injured black counterpart. In this alternative scenario, the planter's hand suffers no pain whatsoever but becomes an instrument of cruelty in its own right, manumitting those who have been 'Maim'd', either by 'imprudence' or a similarly despotic 'hand of Heaven', and are consequently most in need of 'protection'. But if the disfiguring of the slave leads the planter suddenly to break his links with his former subject, the poem itself performs an equally precipitous act of severance, cutting off the 'tale' of white inhumanity it has only just begun to tell.

Beneath the surfaces of that tale, which Grainger's 'muse can scarce believe' and must 'suppress', there is another narrative the poem is even less keen to articulate, but at the same time cannot quite bring itself to veto:

VER. 168. *Off the member snapt*] This accident will sometimes happen, especially in the night: and the unfortunate wretch must fall a victim to his imprudence or sleepiness, if a hatchet do not immediately strike off the entangled member; or the mill be not instantly put out of the wind.

Pere Labat says, he was informed the English were wont, as a punishment, thus to grind their negroes to death. But one may venture to affirm this punishment never had the sanction of law; and if any Englishman ever did grind his negroes to death, I will take upon me to aver, he was universally detested by his countrymen.

Indeed the bare suspicion of such a piece of barbarity leaves a stain: and therefore authors cannot be too cautious of admitting into their writings, any insinuation that bears hard on the humanity of a people.

Daily observation affords but too many proofs, where domestic slavery does not obtain, of the fatal consequences of indulged passion and revenge; but where one man is the absolute property of another, those passions may perhaps receive additional activity: planters, therefore, cannot be too much on their guard against the first sallies of passion; as by indulgence, passion, like a favourite, will at last grow independently powerful. (pp. 188–89; italics in original)

Here *The Sugar-Cane* becomes as fragmented as the body of the slave it contemplates, as Grainger detaches a phrase originally part of the main text and transplants it into the supplementary regions of a footnote: '*Off the member snapt*'. The note in its turn is marked by the same confused logic as characterizes the original passage from which the phrase is removed. In the poem itself, Grainger ascribes to the 'unfortunate wretch' who loses his hand a certain humanity when he reminds the 'mortal' planter that, 'spite of vanity, thy slaves are men', even as this parenthetical sympathy is ironically undercut by the equine simile advanced in support of it (wounded slave equals 'blind [and] aged steed'). In the note, Grainger's concern for the unnamed 'victim' is analogously qualified by the order in which potential solutions to his distress are proposed: the hard-edged option of the 'hatchet' taken up 'immediately' to 'strike off the entangled member' noticeably precedes the less drastic alternative that the mechanisms of production responsible for the 'accident' in the first place be halted, 'the mill ... put out of the wind'.

As Grainger continues to ponder the gory spectacle of the 'entangled' slave, the sufferings contingent upon the routines of colonial labour open out into yet more disturbing prospects, in which the sugar-mill is tentatively imagined as an apparatus of reprisal, torture and murder: 'Pere Labat says, he was informed the English were wont, as a punishment, thus to grind their negroes to death'. While whatever crimes these pulverized black subjects might have carried out remain unspecified, Grainger goes to considerable lengths to debunk the disciplinary violence with which they meet. One of the ways he does this is by discrediting the sources from which the allegations of violence arise: the first source (Labat's informant) is rendered suspect on the grounds of anonymity, while the second (Labat himself) is made doubtful, in this firmly anti-Gallic poem, by dint of being French. In addition to this, Grainger narrows the scope of the violence he negotiates here by deflecting attention from 'the English' in general to an aberrant 'Englishman' in particular, who himself assumes a criminal identity: he transgresses 'the sanction of law' and indeed comes to be isolated from the rest of his nation, thus loosely paralleling the predicament of the hand sundered from the slave's body. Although, in still another image of fragmentation, the Englishman practises only 'a piece of barbarity', his actions are sufficiently menacing as to oblige Grainger to exercise his own vigilance in response, casting a horrifying narrative of bodily harm into the margins of his text and, in so doing, showing himself to possess an authorial hand just as 'cautious' as that which the slave forfeits is 'incautious'. Despite such textual watchfulness, however, Grainger misses the irony that the literal grinding of slaves to death he chooses to downplay serves as a gruesomely precise metaphor for the effects slavery frequently produces upon its subjects and which *The Sugar-Cane* labours constantly to deny in its main body.

The relationship between that main body and its footnotes can be compared, not altogether fancifully, perhaps, to that between master and slave, with the one appearing on the page in a literally superior position to the other.[21] But what is distinctive about the relationship in this specific case is its discord, as the note neither obediently amplifies nor confirms the text but overturns it, rebelling against the poem's sugary visions by candidly revealing the abusive conditions which underlie them, crystallized into a simple formula: slavery is nothing more nor less than a situation 'where one man is the absolute property of another'. In the course of such subversive operations, the note establishes one more correspondence between poet and planter, consolidating this by means of textual echo. The poet 'cannot be too cautious', for his part, with regard to 'any insinuation' which might challenge the 'humanity of [the] people' on whose behalf he writes, while the planter, equally, 'cannot be too much on [his] guard against the first sallies of passion', which threaten to 'grow independently powerful' and, in another reversal of hierarchies, make him their slave.

'Alien Mixture': Race and Desire

The male slave featured in this note finds himself under threat from planto-cratic 'passions' which express themselves in exorbitant punishments. His female counterpart, on the other hand, faces different dangers, articulated in the form of the violent desires to which the master can always subject her. Yet the signs of these desires remain conspicuous by their absence in *The Sugar-Cane*,[22] not least because the female slave who is their potential object is herself a consistently marginal and fleeting figure. As the note itself suggests, Grainger's Muse is firmly androcentric, training its sympathetic gaze upon Africa's 'sons in fetters bound' (IV. 15), while paying scant attention to its similarly oppressed daughters.

But if desire between white and black is written out of Grainger's text, significant examples of its circulation between subjects located on the same side of the colour-line can be found. Even in this ideologically less troubling form, however, desire figures as a phenomenon strikingly decorous and restrained, as if *The Sugar-Cane* were not only privileging racial purity above racial mixing, but also setting itself against the notion of erotic exchange *per se* – an orientation strangely at odds with the poem's celebration both of the phallic canes, whose 'Long yellow joints ... flow with generous juice' (I. 426) and the fecund Caribbean earth which receives them. This investment in the not entirely complementary ideals of racial and sexual purity first emerges fairly early on in Book I, as Grainger marvels at the beauties, both natural and human, of his adopted land, contrasting them with those available in the realms of European legend:

Such, green St. Christopher, thy happy soil! –
Not Grecian Tempé, where Arcadian Pan,
Knit with the Graces, tun'd his silvan pipe,

While mute Attention hush'd each charmed rill;
Not purple Enna, whose irriguous lap,
Strow'd with each fruit of taste, each flower of smell,
Sicilian Proserpine, delighted, sought;
Can vie, blest Isle, with thee. – Tho' no soft sound
Of pastoral stop thine echoes e'er awak'd;
Nor raptured poet, lost in holy trance,
Thy streams arrested with enchanting song:
Yet virgins, far more beautiful than she
Whom Pluto ravish'd, and more chaste, are thine:
Yet probity, from principle, not fear,
Actuates thy sons, bold, hospitable, free:
Yet a fertility, unknown of old,
To other climes denied, adorns thy hills;
Thy vales, thy dells adorns. (I. 60–77)

At their broadest, these lines exemplify the reordering of geographical and cultural values which it is part of the overall project of *The Sugar-Cane* to effect, as the unsung attractions of the New World exceed those of the Old, whether embodied in 'Grecian Tempé' or 'purple Enna', and the physical charms of St Christopher's 'virgins' far transcend those of the mythical Proserpine, 'Whom Pluto ravish[es]' and carries off to the underworld. Yet the higher appeal of these unspoiled figures is a function not only of outer appearance but also of inner being, since they are 'more chaste' than Pluto's deflowered victim, ravishing the poet precisely because they themselves remain untouched by St Christopher's virtuous 'sons'. But just as the white women of St Christopher surpass the European female in terms of beauty and virtue alike, so, together with their hesitant male admirers, do they represent a kind of racial or indeed epidermal elite within the context of the Caribbean as a whole. As Grainger puts it in his commentary on the text, citing the eyewitness opinion of Sir Hans Sloane: 'The inhabitants of St. Christopher look whiter, are less sallow, and enjoy finer complexions, than any of the dwellers on the other islands' (p. 171).[23] Such dazzling whiteness runs in parallel, in its turn, to the pre-eminence of the sugar manufactured on the plantations those 'inhabitants' own. As the long note keyed to the opening line in this passage proudly boasts, this 'sells for more than the Sugar of any other of his Majesty's islands; as their produce cannot be refined to the best advantage, without a mixture of St. Kitts' muscovado' (pp. 169–70).

Grainger's generalizations about the racial and sexual virtues of St Christopher's 'sons' and 'virgins' are given more personalized expression in the account of Junio and Theana which brings Book II of *The Sugar-Cane* to a close. This macabre but sentimental fiction of an unrequited love between the children of two mutually antagonistic plantation families would appear somewhat out of place at the end of a Book devoted to cataloguing the manifold 'ills' which 'await the ripening Cane' (II. 2) and threaten its destruction – as if Grainger had somehow fallen back into the amatory 'groves / Of myrtle-indolence' (I. 3–6) he claims, at the very start of the poem, to have left behind. On the other hand, though, the story of 'dauntless Junio' (II. 490) and the woman who is his would-be 'Indian bride' (II. 512) – and whose 'charms' characteristically 'triumph … o'er Britannia's fair' (II. 444) – could be regarded as something the poem's second Book in many ways prefigures. This is especially so in terms of the violent and freakish manner of the lovers' deaths. In a cruel rejection of the poet's hopes, 'Hymen' does not 'light his brightest torch' (II. 456) for the couple, leaving them to other fates: Theana is caught in a storm and electro-cuted by 'lightning's awful power' (II. 518) as she awaits her lover's return from England and patrols the 'cool margin of the purple main' (II. 514), while Junio himself is struck dead by grief shortly afterwards. Such melodramatic events look back to the 'all-wasting hurricane' (II. 271), whose terrors – including 'thunder, yok'd with lightning and with rain' (II. 324) – are described with some brilliance at the Book's mid-point and themselves anticipated in the streaming visions of 'red lightning at the midnight-hour' (II. 12) which mark the Book's beginning. At the same time, the events underscore the poem's tendency both to confine desire to an intraracial frame of reference and, within those limits, to ensure that it reaches no fulfilment, transforming the 'happy union' (II. 460) of a prospective marriage into a deathly parody of itself. As Grainger writes in the Book's last two lines, 'One grave contains this hapless, faithful pair; / And still the Cane-isles tell their matchless love!' (II. 552–53).

Desire between black subjects constitutes an even less fully articulated concern in *The Sugar-Cane* than desire between white, but is touched on in one infamous passage located towards the end of Book IV. In this instance, once again, the poem's libidinal charge is as muted as on the two occasions already considered:

On festal days; or when their work is done;
Permit thy slaves to lead the choral dance,
To the wild banshaw's melancholy sound.
Responsive to the sound, head feet and frame
Move aukwardly harmonious; hand in hand
Now lock'd, the gay troop circularly wheels,
And frisks and capers with intemperate joy.
Halts the vast circle, all clap hands and sing;
While those distinguish'd for their heels and air,
Bound in the center, and fantastic twine.
Meanwhile some stripling, from the choral ring,
Trips forth; and, not ungallantly, bestows
On her who nimblest hath the greensward beat,

And whose flush'd beauties have inthrall'd his soul,
A silver token of his fond applause.
Anon they form in ranks; nor inexpert
A thousand tuneful intricacies weave,
Shaking their sable limbs; and oft a kiss
Steal from their partners; who, with neck reclin'd,
And semblant scorn, resent the ravish'd bliss. (IV. 582–601)

This passage constitutes only the second occasion in the entire poem when the existence of female slaves is openly acknowledged. On the first, these elusive figures are linked to 'the labours of the Cane' (IV. 96), which, Grainger contends, they undertake more capably than their spouses, withstanding both the 'unusual toil' (IV. 97) and the 'new severities [which] their husbands kill' (IV. 98). Here, by contrast, however, 'work is done' and the bodies of Grainger's 'slaves' find themselves liberated into a 'choral dance'. As Edward Kamau Brathwaite points out, though, there is a sense in which those bodies lack the very freedom such activity would seem to promise, moving according to the measures of European rather than African and/or black Creole cultural traditions:

> There can be no doubt that Grainger actually saw slaves dance. The wheeling circle is there, the dancers in the centre; [and] the custom of bestowing coins on a favourite is described. But <frisk> and <caper> [*sic*]? The dancers are moving to the wrong rhythm. This really is a Scottish reel or a Maypole dance.[24]

Equally, it could be said that this inauthentic choreography is as much designed to contain the sexuality with which dance is symbolically associated as to put it on display. If there is an 'intemperate joy' here, it is, as Brathwaite suggests, both diluted by the daintiness of words such as 'frisks' and 'capers' and constrained by the sinister image of slaves' hands not just linked but firmly 'lock'd' together. And if the more accomplished dancers 'twine' themselves around one another in 'fantastic' ways in the 'center' of the 'vast circle', the eroticism of their extravagant embraces is subsequently cancelled. This is an effect achieved by the polite reserve with which the 'stripling, from the choral ring, / Trips forth' to signal his approval of their performance, offering a mere 'token' of the infatuation the 'nimblest' of these figures, complete with her 'flush'd beauties', has instilled in him. The sense in which the language of Grainger's poem functions to mask the sexual pleasures it would convey is mirrored in the coded exchange with which the passage ends, as desire is privately enjoyed beneath the public cover of a 'semblant scorn'.

In so far as desire features at all in *The Sugar-Cane*, it is, as this series of examples bears out, a peculiarly modest thing, manifesting itself exclusively in intraracial terms, with the possibility of miscegenation roundly foreclosed. Despite its absence from the text in any literal form, though, miscegenation leaves its shadowy traces none the less, as the racist animus it customarily provokes in the colonizer reappears in other contexts and is displaced, most noticeably, onto the nascent body of sugar itself. This is especially so in Book III, where Grainger's descriptions of sugar-making are at their most meticulous and extensive, revealing, as they unfold, an anxiety about contamination analogous to that which racial mixing stereotypically induces. As Grainger notes, in the fullest expression of this anxiety, the expertise of the slaves themselves is vital if the trauma of such pollution is to be avoided. Arriving at the critical moment when the sugar is struck – when, that is, the boiled cane-juice is emptied out from the tache into the 'coolers' where it concentrates – Grainger writes:

> Encourage thou thy boilers; much depends
> On their skill'd efforts. If too soon they strike,
> E'er all the watery particles have fled;
> Or lime sufficient granulate the juice:
> In vain the thickning liquor is effus'd;
> An heterogeneous, an uncertain mass,
> And never in thy coolers to condense. (III. 427–33)

In this scene of bad production, heterogeneity displaces homogeneity, just as the scene itself stands in for the 'uncertain' mixing of racial identities the poem prefers not to acknowledge.

Agents of Rebellion

The ways in which the issue of miscegenation is refined out of *The Sugar-Cane* are broadly congruent with the poem's censorship of those other aspects of slavery it finds similarly uncomfortable, ranging from the ordeals of slave-labour to the violence the white master perpetrates upon the black body, whether by means of brandings, whippings or recurrent 'blows' (IV. 134, 154, 155, 210). These strategies are in keeping, in their turn, with how Grainger's text negotiates the possibility of rebellion and black revenge: even as several slave-revolts take place during the period when Grainger is writing (most notably, Tacky's Rebellion, occurring in Jamaica in 1760),[25] *The Sugar-Cane* habitually minimizes the signs of racial unrest, together with the punishments it provokes, while at the same time being unable quite, to use one of the poem's favourite words, to quell them.

That the problem of rebellion should be driven into *The Sugar-Cane*'s margins is appropriate, since it is precisely at the peripheries of St Christopher itself that the poem's more renegade subjects are to be found, occupying positions of flight which challenge Grainger's wishful portrayal of the plantation as a locus of inclusion, docility and compliance, populated by 'crouching slaves' who 'attendant wait [their master's] nod' (III. 582). In Grainger's note on 'green St. Christopher', one of those spaces is identified 'In the barren part of the island', below the aptly named Mount Misery, and consists of 'a small Solfaterre and collection of fresh water, where fugitive Negroes often take shelter, and escape their pursuers' (p. 171). In the main text, similarly, 'negro-fugitives … skulk 'mid rocks / And shrubby wilds' (IV. 483–86), though the difference is that these figures are a danger as much to the livelihoods of other slaves as to their oppressors: they move in 'bands' which 'will soon destroy' (IV. 486) the 'honest wealth' (IV. 487) those slaves have accrued by working the provision-grounds the planter grants them on his 'broken land' (IV. 446).

One of the earliest points at which Grainger's poem glances nervously towards the black menace on the fringes of its colonial Eden is in the latter stages of Book I. Here Grainger enumerates the means by which the planter should 'secure [his] Canes' (I. 492) against the threats they face, which stem not only from the obscure domains of the bestial – the 'Goat's baneful tooth' and 'the churning boar' (I. 493) – but also from 'fire or casual or design'd' (I. 494). As Gilmore explains, the arson to which these equivocal words so fleetingly allude 'was a common form of revenge against plantation owners or managers during slavery' (p. 265), eating away at their profits by consuming the natural resources which are their foundation. But if the Promethean figure of the slave as agent of rebellion flickers into view at this juncture, it is left to smoulder for quite some time, as the text turns its attention instead, in Book II, to cataloguing the gamut of natural rather than human forces jeopardizing the planter's 'waving gold' (II. 203): monkeys, rats, weeds, insects, pestilence and, most dramatically, of course, the hurricane itself, as well as the ravages of tropical heat. It is not until Book III that the notion of the slave as rebel is rekindled, albeit briefly and ambiguously once again, as the 'burning calm' (II. 381) which devastates the planter's 'Cane-groves' (II. 389) reappears in the form of fire itself:

> Nor less, ye planters, in devotion, sue,
> That nor the heavenly bolt, nor casual spark,
> Nor hand of malice may the crop destroy.
>   Ah me! what numerous, deafning bells, resound?
> What cries of horror startle the dull sleep?
> What gleaming brightness makes, at midnight, day?
> By its portentous glare, too well I see
> Palæmon's fate; the virtuous, and the wise!
> Where were ye, watches, when the flame burst forth?
> A little care had then the hydra quell'd:
> But, now, what clouds of white smoke load the sky!
> How strong, how rapid the combustion pours!
> Aid not, ye winds! with your destroying breath,
> The spreading vengeance. (III. 52–65)

While the true origins of the blaze this passage describes remain uncertain
– 'casual spark' or 'hand of malice'? – the explanatory bias of Grainger's text
inclines more towards subversion than towards mere mishap or negligence
on the part of those flown 'watches'. This is especially so in the allusion to
'spreading vengeance', a phrase whose implications clash awkwardly with the
Montano-like qualities of the classically named Palæmon who, despite being
'virtuous' and 'wise', yet finds himself in line for retribution. Equally, though,
it could be argued that the 'crackling flames' (III. 68) the poem summons
forth here are not so much the expression of a black revenge as a replacement for it. The fire may be set by a malicious 'hand', but seems to get out of
hand, pursuing its own course with a demonic autonomy as it 'sweeps, with
serpent-error, o'er the ground' (III. 71) and 'bends its way' towards the planter's
'mansion' (III. 77), finally arrogating to itself the uncompromising rage for
which it is supposed only to be the vehicle: as Grainger warns the fleeing
planter, 'Efforts but serve to irritate the flames: / Naught but thy ruin can their
wrath appease' (III. 82–83). If, in other words, the cane-fire can be read as a
sign of insurrection, such an interpretation is one which the poem stubbornly
does its best to extinguish.

In *The Sugar-Cane*'s final Book, by contrast, there are moments when the
slave's rebellious agencies are figured far less equivocally. One of these occurs
in the early stages of Grainger's inventory of the psychological and physical
'difference[s]' (IV. 39) obtaining among the 'jetty African[s]' (IV. 35), making
some more suited than others for the 'toilsome field' (IV. 49) and hence, of
course, a more prudent investment for the planter. Here, as a dismissive Johnson
notes, whatever 'tenderness and humanity' may hitherto have informed the
poem drop away, as Grainger 'talks of [the slave trade] without the least
appearance of detestation; but proceeds to direct [the] purchasers of their
fellow-creatures with the same indifference that a groom would give instructions for chusing a horse'.[26] In the course of these 'instructions', however,
Grainger also draws attention to one group of 'Negroes' whose purchase is to
be discouraged at all costs:

Yet, if thine own, thy childrens life, be dear;
Buy not a Cormantee, tho' healthy, young,
Of breed too generous for the servile field;
They, born to freedom in their native land,
Chuse death before dishonourable bonds:
Or, fir'd with vengeance, at the midnight hour,
Sudden they seize thine unsuspecting watch,
And thine own poinard bury in thy breast. (IV. 81–88)

This passage forges an image of the unmasterable 'breed' to which it refers
fully consistent with earlier literary portrayals of the Koromantyn slave as

rebel, stretching back at least as far as Aphra Behn's *Oroonoko* (1688). But whatever the influences shaping these lines, it is clear that the attractions of corporeal vigour – a body of slaves 'healthy [and] young' – cannot adequately offset a psychological disposition which makes them a dangerous lot, resisting 'dishonourable bonds' by destroying either themselves or their master, whose own weapon is ironically turned against him and 'bur[ied] in [his] breast'.

As the poem moves towards its conclusion, anxieties about rebellion and retaliation no longer remain specifically or exclusively linked to the Koromantyn, but assume a broader compass. As the admonitory coda to the passage on the slave-dance suggests, the coy flirtation between black bodies can rapidly metamorphose, under the right conditions, into something altogether less reassuring, as the thud of a 'drum' (IV. 602) combines with 'vinous spirits' (IV. 603) to inspire 'Fell acts of blood, and vengeance' (IV. 605) committed by slaves 'to madness fir'd' (IV. 603). These unsettling possibilities are given dramatic expression in *The Sugar-Cane*'s last verse-paragraph, as the poem looks beyond its own immediate moment and towards the future, transfiguring the relatively local conflicts around which it has thus far skirted into a full-blown vision of colonial apocalypse:

> Ah me, what thunders roll! the sky's on fire!
> Now sudden darkness muffles up the pole!
> Heavens! what wild scenes, before the affrighted sense,
> Imperfect swim! – See! in that flaming scroll,
> Which Time unfolds, the future germs bud forth,
> Of mighty empires! independent realms! –
> And must Britannia, Neptune's favourite queen,
> Protect'ress of true science, freedom, arts;
> Must she, ah! must she, to her offspring crouch? (IV. 653–62)

With its celestial and temporal conflagrations, this passage completes the fiery image-chain which runs through the poem, while simultaneously elevating the formerly 'crouching slaves' of Book III into positions of power, as 'Britannia' and her 'offspring', metropolitan mother and colonial child, change places. As might be expected from so evasive a poem, however, the revolutionary prospects Grainger's text opens up are removed to a safe distance, in chronological and textual terms alike: as well as occurring at an undefined later point, the 'wild scenes' in question here remain indistinct, both to the reader (despite the injunction to 'See!') and to Grainger's Muse herself, before whom they 'Imperfect swim!' They are also predictably short-lived, as the inverted power relationship between Britannia and her subjects is swiftly returned to the *status quo ante* by the defiantly repeated 'She shall not crouch' (IV. 669, 675).

Transitory and ill-defined though it is, this 'last brain-racking study' (IV. 632) provides the final sign of the contradictions besetting the text, as Grainger attempts to manufacture and maintain a poetic world purged of slavery's more disturbing elements, only to find them persisting in residual forms and besmirching his portrayal of the 'plantation' as a site which is 'blithe' and 'jocund' and full of 'smiles' (III. 414). Yet if even a work so extravagant an homage to sugar as this one is unable fully to dispel such elements, it should not be surprising to find them becoming all the more evident in the anti-saccharite writings of the abolitionists, which begin to appear in the late 1780s. These writings not only elaborate an account of sugar's production far more negative than Grainger's, but also take up the question of the commodity's consumption he does not address.

Notes

1. The current revival of interest in *The Sugar-Cane* can be partly attributed to the growth in postcolonial criticism which has taken place since the mid-1980s, but results, more directly, from the independent efforts of the poem's recent editors. Thomas W. Krise reprints the text in full for the first time since 1836 in his *Caribbeana: An Anthology of English Literature of the West Indies, 1657–1777* (Chicago and London: University of Chicago Press, 1999), pp. 166–260; and John Gilmore showcases the poem in *The Poetics of Empire: A Study of James Grainger's* The Sugar-Cane (London and New Brunswick, NJ: The Athlone Press, 2000). As Karina Williamson puts it, in a rightly favourable review of Gilmore's critical edition, his 'lengthy introduction and notes significantly enlarge the knowledge previously available about the author's life, the history of the text and its reception, and above all about its West Indian context'. See Karina Williamson, 'West Indian Georgic', *Essays in Criticism*, 52 (2002), p. 81. As well as Gilmore's own study of the poem, major readings of *The Sugar-Cane* to have emerged over the last few years include Sandiford, pp. 67–87; Shaun Irlam, '"Wish You Were Here": Exporting England in James Grainger's *The Sugar-Cane*', *English Literary History*, 68 (2001), 377–96; Tobias Döring, *Caribbean-English Passages: Intertextuality in a Postcolonial Tradition* (London and New York: Routledge, 2002), pp. 49–77; Jim Egan, 'The "Long'd-for Aera" of an "Other Race": Climate, Identity, and James Grainger's *The Sugar-Cane*', *Early American Literature*, 38 (2003), 189–212; and Steven W. Thomas, 'Doctoring Ideology: James Grainger's *The Sugar Cane* and the Bodies of Empire', *Early American Studies: An Interdisciplinary Journal*, 4 (2006), 78–111. For other illuminating contributions to the debate on the poem, see David Fairer, 'A Caribbean Georgic: James Grainger's *The Sugar-Cane*', *Kunapipi: Journal of Post-Colonial Writing*, 25.1 (2003), 21–28; and Markman Ellis, '"Incessant Labour": Georgic Poetry and the Problem of Slavery', in *Discourses of Slavery and Abolition: Britain and its Colonies, 1760–1838*, ed. Brycchan Carey, Markman Ellis and Sarah Salih (Basingstoke and New York: Palgrave Macmillan, 2004), pp. 45–62.
2. James Grainger, 'Preface' to *The Sugar-Cane: A Poem. In Four Books. With Notes*, in Gilmore, p. 90. Subsequent references to Grainger's poem (and Gilmore's commentary on it) are incorporated in the text and given in parenthesis after quotations, either by line or by page number, as appropriate.
3. James Boswell, *Life of Johnson*, ed. R. W. Chapman, intro. Pat Rogers (1791; Oxford: Oxford University Press, 1998), p. 698. Ironically, Boswell also mocks the poem for the moments where style precisely fails to conceal substance and circumlocution gives way to the distasteful bathos of plain expression. As he tells it, the most dramatic instance of such rhetorical descents occurs when Grainger read the poem 'in manuscript at Sir Joshua Reynolds's' and 'made all the assembled wits burst into a laugh' by beginning

a 'new paragraph' with 'Now, Muse, let's sing of *rats*' (p. 698; italics in original). For a more detailed discussion of Boswell's remarks on *The Sugar-Cane* and the probably apocryphal nature of the line he cites, see Gilmore, pp. 199–201.

4. David Dabydeen, 'On Writing "Slave Song"', *Commonwealth Essays and Studies*, 8.2 (1986), p. 46.

5. For this etymological insight, see Russell R. Menard, *Sweet Negotiations: Sugar, Slavery, and Plantation Agriculture in Early Barbados* (Charlottesville and London: University of Virginia Press, 2006), p. 75.

6. John J. McCusker, cited in Menard, p. 75. For an additional flavour of these technical procedures, see Donald Jones, *Bristol's Sugar Trade and Refining Industry* (Bristol: Bristol Branch of the Historical Association, 1996), p. 4: 'Muscovado was contaminated with gluten, lime and caramel and it was the task of ... sugar refiners to expel the impurities and produce various grades of pure white crystalline sugar'.

7. Information relating to Grainger's slave-owning activities is sketchy, but can be partially retrieved from his papers. See, for example, the letter to Bishop Thomas Percy of 25 July 1762, where Grainger refers to 'a pretty little Mulatto slave, about five years of age', named John, to whom his own young daughter, Louise Agnes, is so attached that 'she ... immediately burst[s] into tears if [he] is whipped' (cited in Irlam, p. 388). See also a later letter to the same correspondent of 18 April 1763, in which Grainger describes how he has 'converted all [his] money into negroes' (cited in Gilmore, p. 17). Grainger's will dated 17 July 1763 looks back to these transactions in its allusion to an unspecified number of 'Negroes' as part of his 'Real and Personal Estate' (Gilmore, p. 76, note 56).

8. The contemporary construction of the sugar-planter in such negative terms is strikingly illustrated in two sentimental dramas of the period, Samuel Foote's *The Patron. A Comedy in Three Acts* (London: G. Kearsly, 1764) and Richard Cumberland's *The West Indian: A Comedy* (Belfast: Henry and Robert Joy, 1771). As Thomas argues, following Sandiford, this defensive construction is symptomatic of the tensions between a metropolitan 'desire for sugar', on the one hand, and a 'discomfort with the radical otherness of the colonies and the means of sugar production', on the other (p. 100). For an analysis of similar tensions as they inform the period from the 1780s to the 1830s, which saw the development of the campaigns against the slave trade and slavery itself, see David Lambert, *White Creole Culture, Politics and Identity during the Age of Abolition* (Cambridge: Cambridge University Press, 2005).

9. Döring, p. 55. See also Gilmore, p. 22. It is highly likely that Grainger would, at the very least, have been aware of this work by the Barbadian-born Weekes, since, as Döring notes, it was issued by R. and J. Dodsley, who were also the London-based publishers of his own poem (p. 55). At the same time, however, Grainger's comments in the previously cited letter to Percy of 25 July 1762 suggest that his evaluation of Weekes's text may not have been entirely favourable: 'nobody', he writes, with uncharacteristic waspishness, 'can tell me any thing of the Charibbean poetry; indeed, from what I have seen of these savages, I have no curiosity to know aught of their compositions' (cited in Irlam, p. 377).

10. Nathaniel Weekes, *Barbados: A Poem* (London: R. and J. Dodsley, 1754), ll. 843–45 (italics in original).

11. Such indeed is the authoritative nature of the advice and instruction the poem dispenses, that, at one stage in its publishing history, it could even feature as one of *Three Tracts on West-Indian Agriculture, and subjects connected therewith* (Kingston, Jamaica: Alexander Aikman, 1802). The other two works in this collection were Grainger's own *An Essay on the More Common West-India Diseases*, derived from his Notes to *The Sugar-Cane*, and Martin's *Essay*.

12. Samuel Martin, *An Essay upon Plantership, Humbly inscrib'd to all the Planters of the British Sugar-Colonies in America*, second edition (Antigua: T. Smith, 1750), p. i.

13. Samuel Johnson, *Critical Review*, XVIII (October 1764), p. 277.
14. Grainger, letter to Percy, 1 June 1760, cited in Gilmore, p. 13.
15. See Martin's discussion of the preferred technique for cultivating the planter's lands to maximum effect. In order to avoid the counter-productive situation in which 'the very end of hoe-plowing, or losening [*sic*] the soil is much defeated', Martin argues that the 'present method' of husbandry be given a new slant, obliquely underscoring the point in the patterns of his own typography: 'for as the negroes hoe-plow or dig the soil, *directly forward*, so they must necessarily tread the ground as fast as they dig it: whereas by putting the laborers to dig *sideways*, no one puts a foot upon the soil after it is dug' (p. 24; italics in original).
16. Johnson, p. 273.
17. John Dyer, *The Fleece, in Four Books*, in *Poems. By John Dyer* (London: J. Dodsley, 1770), I. 566.
18. Dyer, I. 551–52.
19. Dyer, I. 526–29.
20. Döring, p. 73.
21. The notes to *The Sugar-Cane* were originally positioned at the foot of the page but in Gilmore's edition are moved to the end of the text. As Williamson points out, this change has the advantage of making for 'a tidier page and easier continuous reading', but the greater drawback of 'obscuring the character of the poem' (p. 81) and, in particular, its discursive heterogeneity, which sees Grainger's generally elevated poetic voice pitched against those other voices which appear in his prose – botanical, medical, historical and classical, among others.
22. It is worth contrasting the absence of interracial desire in *The Sugar-Cane* with the prurient centrality of its role in Isaac Teale's 'The Sable Venus; An Ode', a poem originally written in 1765, but not printed until nearly thirty years later, when it was included in Bryan Edwards's *The History, Civil and Commercial, of the British Colonies in the West Indies*, 2 vols (London: J. Stockdale, 1793), vol. 2, pp. 27–33. Yet despite the antithetical emphases the two poems give to the topic, they enjoy a surprising degree of formal overlap, with Teale's text obscuring the violent realities of miscegenation just as much as Grainger's obscures those of slavery *per se*: 'At the heart' of 'The Sable Venus', as Marcus Wood has observed, 'is the mechanism whereby disempowerment is presented as its opposite', especially with regard to the female slave, whose sexual and racial victimhood before her master(s) is perversely figured as if it were a kind of control, and thus disavowed. On this point and for a fuller consideration of Teale's poem, see *The Poetry of Slavery: An Anglo-American Anthology, 1764–1865*, ed. Marcus Wood (Oxford: Oxford University Press, 2003), pp. 30–31. For a concise overview and analysis of miscegenation in the Caribbean during the period in which Grainger is writing, see Robert J. C. Young, *Colonial Desire: Hybridity in Theory, Culture and Race* (London and New York: Routledge, 1995), pp. 150–58. Young's analysis also features a brief discussion of Teale's poem, which he describes as marking 'an early articulation of the sexual economy of desire in the fantasies of race' (p. 153).
23. The passage Grainger cites (with minor inaccuracies) is from Sir Hans Sloane, *A Voyage to the Islands Madera, Barbados, Nieves, S. Christophers and Jamaica, with the Natural History of the Herbs and Trees, Four-footed Beasts, Fishes, Birds, Insects, Reptiles, &c. of the last of those Islands*, 2 vols (London: Printed by B. M. for the Author, 1707–25), vol. 1, p. 46.
24. Brathwaite, cited in Gilmore, p. 55.
25. Other insurrections concurrent to the composition of *The Sugar-Cane* take place in Montserrat (also 1760), Nevis (1761) and Surinam (1763), but, as Trevor Burnard observes, Tacky's 'was the most significant Caribbean slave revolt before the Haitian Revolution of 1791–1804', delivering a 'shock to the imperial system [which] would

not be equaled until the Jamaican rebellions of 1831 and 1865 and the Indian Mutiny of 1857'. See Trevor Burnard, *Mastery, Tyranny and Desire: Thomas Thistlewood and his Slaves in the Anglo-Jamaican World* (Chapel Hill and London: University of North Carolina Press, 2004), p. 170.

26. Johnson, p. 277.

2

'Stained with Spots of Human Blood': Sugar, Abolition and Cannibalism

I was responsible at the same time for my body, for my race, for my ancestors. I subjected myself to an objective examination, I discovered my blackness, my ethnic characteristics; and I was battered down by tom-toms, cannibalism, intellectual deficiency, fetichism [*sic*], racial defects, slave-ships, and above all else, above all: 'Sho' good eatin'.'

– Frantz Fanon, *Black Skin, White Masks*

I am the sugar at the bottom of the English cup of tea.

– Stuart Hall, 'Old and New Identities, Old and New Ethnicities'

Against the Grain

Samuel Johnson's uneasy comments on the blasé evocation of the transatlantic slave trade in Book IV of *The Sugar-Cane* were clearly prescient: within little more than two decades, his remarks were being echoed and expanded in the campaign for the abolition of the trade, which officially began in 1787, but did not finally realize its aims for a further twenty years.[1] This chapter examines some of the writings which emerged in the early phases of the movement, focusing on what might be called the politics of consumption and, in particular, the provocative identification of the sugar-eater as cannibal, a common discursive motif during the period.[2]

Two texts in which this identification is set in play are William Fox's classic anti-sugar pamphlet, 'An Address to the People of Great Britain, on the Propriety of Abstaining from West India Sugar and Rum' (1791), and Andrew Burn's far less familiar response to Fox in 'A Second Address to the People of Great Britain: Containing a New, and Most Powerful Argument to Abstain from the Use of West India Sugar. By an Eye Witness to the Facts Related' (1792). While these brief works might have similar titles, they differ radically from one another in their treatment of the motif they share, with the cannibal consumer in Fox restricted to a merely metaphorical status which, in Burn, becomes disconcertingly literal.[3] Yet the dialogue between the texts does not take place in isolation but is necessarily shaped by the larger discursive network which surrounds it and which includes black abolitionist writings as well.[4] By far the most influential of these is Equiano's *The Interesting Narrative*, a text in which the possibilities of white cannibalism are directly confronted, albeit in the context of the master–slave encounter itself, rather than in the spheres of metropolitan sugar-consumption.[5] Equiano's anxieties concerning these possibilities feed into the work produced by his white abolitionist contemporaries, so to speak, even as the work itself is worlds away from the stance adopted by Grainger: despite their differences of emphasis, Fox and Burn unite to put a case against sugar which is just as powerful as the one the earlier writer makes in its favour.

Prologue: Cannibal Imaginings

The link between the Caribbean and the cannibal variously exploited in the work of Equiano, Fox and Burn does not, of course, begin in the abolitionist era, but has a much older history, reaching back, as Peter Hulme has shown, to Christopher Columbus's account of his first voyage to the New World in 1492–93.[6] Despite its longevity, however, such a link emerges from a paradoxically uncertain textual origin, since Columbus's personal record of his travels did not much outlast its composition and is now known only in the secondary shape of the transcript produced by the Spanish historian, Bartolomé de Las Casas, in the 1530s. Even within Las Casas's text, the figure of the Carib as cannibal remains oddly mediated, kept at a distance as much discursive as geographical. This is evidenced in the journal entry for 4 November 1492, in which Las Casas writes:

> [Columbus] showed [the Indians] gold and pearls, and certain old men answered that in a place that they called Bohio [Dominican Republic] there was a vast amount and that they wore it on neck and in ears and on arms and legs; and also pearls. Moreover, he understood that they said that there were big ships and much trade and that all of this was to the southeast. He understood also that, far from there, there were one-eyed men, and others, with snouts of dogs, who ate men, and that as soon as one was taken they cut his throat and drank his blood and cut off his genitals.[7]

With its repeated insistence on what is 'understood', this passage ironically acknowledges the potential for misconstruction between the admiral-colonizer and those seemingly 'certain old men' with whom he palavers and hence, by implication, also opens up the possibility that the cannibals in question here might in fact be apocryphal. Despite their somewhat equivocal status, however, these native monsters powerfully establish themselves in the territories of the colonial imagination, casting their shadows across canonical literary works in which the West Indies come subsequently to feature as provenance. In Shakespeare's *The Tempest*, for example, they are both concealed and revealed in the anagrammatic naming of Prospero's slave as Caliban, while in Daniel Defoe's *Robinson Crusoe* (1719) they appear in Crusoe's fevered visions of 'savage wretches' enjoying 'inhuman feastings upon the bodies of their fellow-creatures'.[8]

In historiographic accounts of the West Indies located towards the end of the eighteenth century, however, the situation alters, as the burden of cannibalism comes to be assumed by the archipelago's diasporic rather than indigenous peoples – the African and black Creole subjects whose presence in the islands is the direct consequence of the slave trade. Two of the most influential contributions to this shifting pattern are Edward Long's *The History of Jamaica* (1774) and Bryan Edwards's *The History, Civil and Commercial, of the British Colonies in the West Indies* (1793). In Long's case, the question of African cannibalism is broached at a point in his text when he delves into 'that part of the … continent' which, in a typically infantilizing phrase, he calls 'Guiney, or Negro-land'.[9] As he moves about this region, Long chronicles the dietary habits supposedly both traditional and current among its denizens:

> Their old custom of gormandizing on human flesh has in it something so nauseous, so repugnant to nature and reason, that it would hardly admit of belief, if it had not been attested by a multitude of voyagers; some of whom affirm to have been eye-witnesses of it, and … by report of Negroes themselves imported from [Africa] into our colonies. The difficulty indeed of believing it to be true, is much lessened when we reflect on the sanguinary, cruel temper, and filthy practices of these people, in other respects; many Negroes in our colonies have been known to drink the blood of their enemies with great apparent relish; and at Benin, Angola, and other kingdoms, they at this day prefer apes, monkies [*sic*], dog's flesh, carrion, reptiles, and other substances, usually deemed improper for human food, although they abound with hogs, sheep, poultry, fish, and a variety of game and wild-fowl; why should we doubt but that the same ravenous savage, who can feast on the roasted quarters of an ape (that *mock-man*), would be not less delighted with the sight of a loin or buttock of human flesh, prepared in the same manner?[10]

The scarcely credible spectacle of Africans 'gormandizing on human flesh' precipitates a disturbance in Long's own bodily economy, manifested as nausea. This gut-reaction to the 'filthy practices' he conjures up places him in the company of Crusoe, similarly 'vomit[ing] with an uncommon violence' as he broods over 'the hellish brutality'[11] of cannibalism displaying itself in the residual form of the 'skulls, hands, feet and other bones of human bodies'[12] strewn across his island-shore. At the same time, Long's text echoes Columbus's journal, both in its piquant allusion to 'Negroes' who 'drink the blood of their enemies with great apparent relish' and, more broadly, in terms of a generalized uncertainty as to the truth of its own ethnographic claims. Despite the invocation of a formidable collective testimony drawn from 'a multitude of voyagers', 'eye-witnesses' and even 'Negroes themselves', Long's African man-eater is largely fabricated out of inference and hearsay and collapses, in the end, into a travesty of himself: this 'ravenous savage' 'feast[s]', after all, only on a '*mock-man*' and can only logically be a mock-cannibal in his turn, just as, in a fastidious sensory recoil, he is 'delighted with the sight', rather than the taste, 'of a loin or buttock of human flesh'.

Edwards's contribution to the construction of the black subject as cannibal is less rabid than Long's, but equally sensationalist. One of the places where it emerges is in an inventory of 'the various African nations in the West Indies',[13] which include the Koromantyn and Ibo. In order to illustrate the 'ferociousness of disposition'[14] of the former, Edwards reprises their role in Tacky's Rebellion. As he notes, the rebellious Koromantyn slaves and their ringleader are not content simply with the achievement of liberation, but desire also to complete their triumph by consuming their oppressors:

> At Ballard's Valley they surrounded the overseer's house about four in the morning, in which eight or ten White people were in bed, every one of whom they butchered in the most savage manner, and literally drank their blood mixed with rum. At Esher, and other estates, they exhibited the same tragedy; and then set fire to the buildings and canes. In one morning they murdered between thirty and forty Whites, not sparing even infants at the breast, before their progress was stopped.[15]

The ecstatic cocktail of 'blood mixed with rum' is doubly sweet, combining, as it does, the bodily fluid of the 'White people' with one of the by-products resulting from the very labour they demand of their assailants. It is perhaps even trebly so, since it implies a vampiric draining of white bodies by black which violently parodies the feeding performed by those sucklings whom the insurgents refuse to 'spar[e]'. Yet if cannibalism is a theatrical flourish in the revolutionary signature of the Koromantyn, it is evidently something more prosaically incorporated into the rituals of daily existence for the Ibo. It is this which makes them 'in fact more truly savage than any nation of the Gold Coast', as they regularly engage in and are 'without doubt, accustomed to the shocking practice of feeding on human flesh', 'frequently regal[ing]' themselves on what Edwards calls 'this horrid banquet'.[16]

Despite their differences, the representations of the Carib and the African as cannibals are marked by a common purpose, working to fashion an image of the racial other as savage and inferior to the civilized white self and so fixing it as a legitimate candidate for colonial subjection. The status of representation as an instrument of colonial power is clearly recognized by Caliban, as might be expected, given that he is one of its victims. It is this insight which informs his conspiratorial exchange with Stephano in *The Tempest*'s third act, as the two ponder the question of how best to terminate Prospero's rule, both over Caliban himself and over his island, which Prospero has appropriated:

> Why, as I told thee, 'tis a custom with him
> I' th' afternoon to sleep. There thou mayst brain him,
> Having first seized his books; or with a log
> Batter his skull, or paunch him with a stake,
> Or cut his weasand with thy knife. Remember
> First to possess his books; for without them
> He's but a sot, as I am, nor hath not
> One spirit to command – they all do hate him
> As rootedly as I. Burn but his books.[17]

The fantasies of the destruction to be visited upon the master during his siesta are of a piece with the 'death and desolation'[18] with which Tacky's Rebellion suddenly dawns upon 'the overseer's house at four in the morning' in Edwards. Equally, though, they are counter-weighted by a precautionary insistence that Stephano 'first seiz[e]', 'possess' and finally 'Burn' Prospero's 'books' before the projected murder can take place. The suggestion, in other words, is that it is the 'books' themselves which define the identities of colonizer and colonized, white and non-white, master and monster, exalting the one at the expense of the other. '[W]ithout them', as Caliban knows, difference melts into likeness: 'He's but a sot, as I am'.

'White Men with Horrible Looks': Cannibalism in *The Interesting Narrative*

Caliban advocates a strategy of resistance to the images of self and other the colonizer puts into circulation which is uncompromisingly crude, but a more sophisticated, if equally incendiary, approach would be to revise the master's 'books' rather than have them consumed in fire, unravelling the ideologically loaded representations they contain. Such an approach is usually associated with the writing of the postcolonial era (to be explored in later chapters), but operates in works produced at a much earlier historical juncture as well, one of which is *The Interesting Narrative*. In this work, the racist stereotype of the man-eating African promoted by Long and Edwards on either side of the text's publication is indulged only in order to be ridiculed. This debunking occurs in the opening chapter, where Equiano provides a description of the customs prevailing in his homeland, reducing cannibalism, as Michael Wiley notes, to 'an empty threat ... used to make fun of people'[19] of irascible disposition: 'We had a saying among us to any one of a cross temper, "That if they were to be eaten, they should be eaten with bitter herbs."'[20] Far from being the mark of an unsurpassed African savagery, as Edwards would have it, cannibalism is, in Equiano's version of things, nothing more than 'a joking matter'.[21]

But there is another way in which, to cite Wiley once again, *The Interesting Narrative* 'reconfigure[s] imperialist representations of African cannibalism'[22] and this involves a reversal of roles, as Equiano invests the white subject with the man-eating tendencies it would rather attribute to its black counterpart. The most notable instance of this discursive turnaround occurs in Equiano's famous evocation of the Middle Passage, in his text's second chapter:

> The first object which saluted my eyes when I arrived on the coast was the sea, and a slave-ship, which was then riding at anchor, and waiting for its cargo. These filled me with astonishment, which was soon converted into terror, which I am yet at a loss to describe. ... When I was carried on board I was immediately handled, and tossed up, to see if I were sound, by some of the crew; and I was now persuaded that I had gotten into a world of bad spirits, and that they were going to kill me. ... When I looked round the ship too, and saw a large furnace of copper boiling, and a multitude of black people of every description chained together, every one of their countenances expressing dejection and sorrow, I no longer doubted of my fate, and, quite overpowered with horror and anguish, I fell motionless on the deck and fainted. When I recovered a little, I found some black people about me, who I believed were some of those who brought me on board, and had been receiving their pay; they talked to me in order to cheer me, but all in vain. I asked them if we were not to be eaten by those white men with horrible looks, red faces, and long hair? They told me I was not.[23]

The primal scene of this encounter with the white master begins with a metaphor which may not provoke 'astonishment' in the reader but is certainly striking for its irony, as the slave is 'saluted' by 'a slave-ship ... riding at anchor', the floating signifier, as it were, of Equiano's disempowerment. This figurative inversion of the true power relations organizing the 'world of bad spirits' into which Equiano has been abducted looks forward, in its turn, to the fantasy of white rather than black cannibalism articulated in the fear that he is 'to be eaten by those white men with horrible looks, red faces, and long hair'. As Equiano learns, such a fantasy is just that. He is not to be consumed by the 'crew', but 'carried to these white people's country to work for them',[24] even though, in another irony, it is just when he arrives 'in sight of the island of Barbadoes [*sic*]' that the fantasy returns. Here Equiano is once again 'examined ... attentively' by 'ugly men' ('merchants and planters') who board the slaver 'anchored ... off Bridge Town', and who seem to want to eat him, instilling 'dread and trembling',[25] just as it is on Barbados itself that the sugary fruits of his labour will feed directly into white patterns of consumption in Britain. Despite its '[un]sound' nature, however, the fantasy remains significant, implicitly questioning the essentialist ideology of racial difference on which slavery and the slave trade are predicated, as eater and eaten, cannibal and cannibalized, black and white change places.

This strategic reversal of roles is complemented by another aspect of Equiano's account of the Middle Passage. It is not just that the white rather than black mouth is identified, albeit erroneously, with cannibalism here, but that the latter is itself repeatedly dissociated from the act of eating altogether. Thrust 'down under the decks' of the slave ship, Equiano at first becomes 'so sick and low that [he is] not able to eat' and 'on ... refusing' food is 'flogged .... severely', just as other 'African prisoners' around him are 'hourly whipped' for the same defiance. Such rejections of food, like the slaves' suicidal attempts to 'leap into the water'[26] – where they will be swallowed up by 'the inhabitants of the deep'[27] – clearly function as collective acts of resistance: the black body chooses to starve itself rather than become the means of the production of the sugar which gratifies the white. At the same time, such acts gnaw away yet further at the shibboleth of the African as cannibal. Rather than exhibiting the frenzied longing for 'human flesh' which nourishes capacious white anxieties, Equiano and his fellow slaves do not eat at all.

Cannibal Consumers: Fox and the Rhetoric of Abolition

In reworking the representations of cannibalism in colonial discourse, Equiano performs a critique of the master's 'books' which parallels while simultaneously refining the more material form of rebellion proposed by Caliban. Yet Caliban is not the only Shakespearean character to whom Equiano may be likened, as is suggested by an anonymous appreciation of *The Interesting Narrative*, appearing in *The General Magazine and Impartial Review* for July 1789: 'This is "a round unvarnished tale" of the chequered adventures of an African, who early in life, was torn from his native country, by those savage dealers in a traffic disgraceful to humanity, and which has fixed a stain on the legislature of Britain'.[28] The phrase cited here is taken from act 1, scene 3 of Shakespeare's *Othello* and is strikingly apposite in view of the broad correspondences between Equiano's own biography and 'the chequered adventures' of the play's eponymous hero – enslavement, the difficult negotiation of white culture, the scandal of intermarriage.[29] The additional relevance of the phrase stems from its dramatic context, which takes the form of a series of exchanges in which Othello defends his elopement with and marriage to Desdemona before a Venetian rather than British 'legislature' including Brabantio, Desdemona's outraged father. As Othello informs the 'good masters'[30] who have summoned him into their presence, the amatory spell he casts over Brabantio's daughter is less the result of 'witchcraft'[31] than of an irresistible narrative power, revealed in his exchanges with her paternal guardian:

[Brabantio] loved me, oft invited me,
Still questioned me the story of my life
From year to year – the battles, sieges, fortunes
That I have passed.
I ran it through, even from my boyish days
To th' very moment that he bade me tell it,
Wherein I spake …
…
Of being taken by the insolent foe
And sold to slavery …
…
And of the cannibals that each other eat,
The Anthropophagi, and men whose heads
Do grow beneath their shoulders. This to hear
Would Desdemona seriously incline,
But still the house affairs would draw her thence,
Which ever as she could with haste dispatch
She'd come again, and with a greedy ear
Devour up my discourse.[32]

These lines underscore the perspicacity of the reviewer's allusion by showing how the cannibalistic concerns of Equiano's text are shared by Shakespeare's. They also distance and distinguish Othello from his mutual man-eaters by casting him in the role of anthropologist rather than anthropophagist, just as Equiano refuses to see himself reflected in the mirror of colonial discourse and indeed reverses its images altogether by reincarnating the black cannibal as white. Yet if this passage suggests parallels with *The Interesting Narrative*, it suggests differences as well, introducing cannibalism as a literal practice only to retreat from it: the eating mouths of Othello's racially unclassified 'Anthropophagi' are transformed into the 'greedy ear' of a domestically obliged white woman, while the substance on which this avaricious organ feeds is Othello's 'discourse', rather than his own black flesh. The movement here, in other words, is from a literal to a metaphorical anthropophagy which, while it may signal a departure from *The Interesting Narrative*, offers a curiously precise prefiguring of the discursive shift which takes place between Equiano's text and Fox's, as the cannibal colonizers of the one give way to the cannibal consumers of the other, and the act of eating sugar comes to stand in for the ingestion of the body of the slave.

Like Othello's exotic 'discourse', avidly 'Devour[ed]' by Desdemona, Fox's text evidently satisfied the hunger of the 'People' to whom it was directed, selling some 70,000 copies within just four months of its initial appearance.[33]

The grand scale on which the pamphlet was consumed by its first readers is fitting because the pamphlet itself is concerned with the phenomenon of mass consumption, in the shape of the national predilection for sugar, on which the slave trade is dependent and against which Fox agitates. As he condemns the exponential growth of 'British luxury',[34] Fox engages in a kind of global housekeeping designed to illustrate just what is at stake in gratifying the collective sweet tooth. In his analysis, the devastations of sugar are not confined to the West Indies – those 'regions of horror'[35] dominated by 'hunger, torture, and extreme labour'[36] – but sweep back across the Middle Passage and into Africa itself:

> So necessarily connected are our consumption of the commodity, and the misery resulting from it, that in every pound of sugar used, (the produce of slaves imported from Africa) we may be considered as consuming two ounces of human flesh ... and spreading inconceivable anguish, terror, and dismay, through an immense continent, by the burning of their villages, tearing parents from their families, and children from their parents; breaking every bond of society, and destroying every source of human happiness. A French writer observes, 'That he cannot look on a piece of sugar without conceiving it stained with spots of human blood:' and Dr. Franklin adds, that had he taken in all the consequences, 'he might have seen the sugar not merely spotted, but thoroughly dyed scarlet in grain.'[37]

Here the notion of the Family of Man implied in Fox's later conventional abolitionist allusion to the 'unhappy Africans' as 'brethren'[38] collapses, as white pleasure battens upon black pain, 'tearing', 'breaking' and 'destroying' at will. Yet if white families visit an insouciant havoc upon their black counterparts, Fox has kindred spirits of his own on whom to call by way of protest, including his unnamed 'French writer' and Benjamin Franklin. As the dissident voices of these anti-saccharite figures blot Fox's page, they offer an ironic textual analogue to the hallucinatory 'spots of human blood' 'stain[ing]' the 'piece of sugar' about which they speak.

As 'sugar' metaphorically turns to 'human flesh' in the mouths of those who crave it, Fox himself turns the literality of Equiano's white cannibalism into figurative form. Yet Fox's text does not confine his consuming subjects to the role of figurative cannibal, but establishes other positions for them as well. In Fox's view, for example, the difference between the consumer and the unholy trinity of 'The slave-dealer, the slave-holder, and the slave-driver' is purely nominal. Identities concertina into one another and 'every distinction is done away [with]' since, as he tersely puts it, 'If we purchase the commodity we participate in the crime'.[39] Even more striking than such explicit identifications between seemingly distant parties, however, are those which remain implicit, crystallizing in moments when the consumer takes the small but consequential step of refusing to consume, casting off complicity for resistance:

The laws of our country may indeed prohibit us the sugar-cane, unless we will receive it through the medium of slavery. They may hold it to our lips, steeped in the blood of our fellow-creatures; but they cannot compel us to accept the loathsome potion.[40]

The rejection of the 'sugar-cane' held up to the consumer's 'lips' not only entails a rejection of the role of figurative cannibal (or perhaps even vampire). It also involves a curious doubling with Equiano, whose account of the Middle Passage includes a refusal of the 'eatables' he is offered by 'two of the white men'[41] who accompany him on the voyage. The context for the consumer's tight-lipped refusal is radically different from that in which Equiano's takes place and results in no bodily punishment beyond the pain of self-denial. It is, none the less, an act of abstention whose consequences are just as subversive, having the potential, if replicated in sufficient number, 'totally [to] prevent the Slave Trade to supply our islands'.[42]

Stamping it Out: Burn and the Abolition of Rhetoric

As well as being 'phenomenally successful in launching the campaign of public abstention'[43] from sugar, Fox's text is important for the sequel to which it gives rise, Burn's 'A Second Address'. Yet Burn looks back to Fox only to look beyond him, replacing the 'sentimental' arguments against sugar and slavery used by his predecessor with those which 'affect the Senses'[44] and correlatively transmuting Fox's figurative cannibalism into its gruesomely literal other. Such shifts in emphasis ultimately align Burn less with Fox – his explicit interlocutor – than with Equiano, reviving and reworking the visceral fantasies of black flesh incorporated by white bodies in *The Interesting Narrative*.

As its 'Preface' suggests, Burn's text is 'A Second Address' not only in the sense that it is intended to supplement Fox's, but also because it rehearses in a public context an abolitionist case first privately advanced 'a few evenings ago' to 'some select friends'. This case is itself marked by a certain secondariness, emerging, as it does, from the initial failure of Burn's implicitly Fox-like 'rhetoric' to persuade his audience 'to abstain from the use of Sugar'. Referring to himself in the third person as the embattled 'Author', Burn recollects how such failure turns to triumph as he is called upon to improvise a new discursive strategy:

Finding that neither motives of humanity nor conscience were sufficient to effect his purpose; he gave the contest up; till one or two of the female part of the company, knowing he had been some time resident on a Sugar Plantation in the West-Indies, begged he would favour them with a short account of the Process of making [sugar]. A request which he instantly complied with; and as he drew near the close of his narrative, describing the manner in which the Negroes stampt it in the Hogshead, he could easily perceive an alteration in the complexion of one of his fair hearers; and as he proceeded, knit Brows, distorted Features, and disgustful Emotions, were visible in all their Countenances; till one, unable to stand it out any longer, exclaimed with the most determined resolution, 'Well! I'll never eat another bit of Sugar so long as I live.' (p. 2)

The 'female part of the company' intrigued by Burn's residency 'on a Sugar Plantation in the West-Indies' recalls Desdemona, similarly eager to learn about the exotic spaces Othello has occupied in the course of his 'travailous history'.[45] Yet these women become sharply differentiated from Shakespeare's heroine when the colonial 'narrative' they 'request' reaches its climax, focusing on the labours of the 'Negroes', treading down the sugar 'in the Hogshead' – themselves downtrodden by their masters. Far from eliciting the fascination which Othello's story sparks in Desdemona, Burn's 'account of the Process' of sugar-making occasions only loathing. This feeling of repulsion causes those who experience it to grow oddly repellent in their turn, as 'fair hearers' become gargoyles, complete with 'knit Brows, distorted Features, and disgustful Emotions ... visible in all their Countenances'.

As it later transpires, the disfiguring of these female faces is provoked by Burn's detailed demonstration of how the act of 'eat[ing]' a 'bit of Sugar' partakes of a literal rather than merely symbolic anthropophagy, which itself constitutes a disfiguring of the rhetorical system used by Fox. Yet if the physiognomic disfiguration is something of a spectacle, its discursive equivalent is not 'present[ed] to ... view' (p. 3) at all at this prefatory juncture. Instead it is compressed into an enigma which, Burn promises, he will duly unravel in the course of the main text itself, 'lay[ing] before the People of England at large, what he found so effectual to gain his purpose among his own acquaintance' (p. 2). As the main text commences, however, it soon emerges that Burn is in no hurry to make this disclosure, spending some four pages appealing to the 'feelings' of his 'Readers', to whom he offers a series of chilling vignettes 'respecting the sufferings of the Slaves in the West Indies' (p. 3) and even stepping beyond 'the circle of his [own] knowledge' (pp. 3–4) to embrace the cruelties of the Middle Passage. In one sense, as Burn himself comments, the scenes of colonial and transatlantic terror with which 'A Second Address' properly begins are a 'digression', leading him away from and deferring the more radical revelations at the heart of his text. The scenes might even be considered a regression, since they are not only depicted from the kind of 'sentimental' perspective characteristic of Fox, but are also marked by an intensity surpassing even the atrocities Fox catalogues. On the other hand, not all of these 'plain facts' (p. 3) represent quite as much of a departure from Burn's central preoccupations as might seem at first to be the case. This is evident, for example, in his account of how the colonial order disciplines and punishes its transgressors:

I have myself seen the poor offending Slave, flogged in such a horrid, cruel manner, as really baffles all description, and immediately after the dreadful operation, fastened with both Legs in the Stocks, for days and nights together; while his raw back has been constantly washed with the strongest brine; putting him to the most excruciating torments. Yet in spite of all this precaution to prevent putrefaction, through the heat of the climate, the vermin has made such deep inroads into his mangled flesh, that to preserve his miserable life a few years longer, other Slaves have been employed to pick out the large Maggots, that had already penetrated to the very bone; and who frequently half eat up their dying victim, before the other half is laid in the Dust. (p. 4)

As this extract suggests, the 'poor offending Slave' is a 'victim' twice over. He is subjected both to the master's crude disciplinary techniques and to the predations of an equally hostile natural world, in which his 'mangled flesh' is not only 'penetrated to the very bone' but also 'half eat[en] up'. Thus transformed into an object to be consumed, the enslaved body located at the site of colonial production assumes a status not wholly dissimilar to that which it possesses in the domestic context, where it is indirectly ingested by those who eat sugar. By the same grim token, the sweet-toothed cannibals of the metropolis are themselves implicitly drawn into unflattering alignment with the 'vermin' and outsized 'Maggots' conniving in the slave's destruction abroad.

The anthropophagous nature of British sugar-consumption, at which Burn's 'Preface' hints and which his 'digression' appears to parody and prefigure, is rendered explicit as he returns to his 'main design' (p. 6):

It is evident beyond a doubt, that the Consumers of Sugar and Rum, innocent or guilty, are actually the first and moving cause of all those torrents of Blood and Sweat, that annually flow from the body of the poor African.

Take away the cause, and we all know the effect will cease. Abstain from Sugar, and Slavery falls. The consequence is as clear as the noon-day Sun; yet how difficult to persuade some, that when they eat Sugar, they figuratively eat the Blood of the Negro. This task I leave for others to accomplish; my business at present is, by plain matters of fact, of which I have frequently had ocular demonstration, to convince the inhabitants of Great Britain, who use Soft Sugar, either in Puddings, Pies, Tarts, Tea, or otherwise, that they literally, and most certainly in so doing, eat large quantities of that last mentioned Fluid, as it flows copiously from the Body of the laborious Slave, toiling under the scorching rays of a vertical sun, mixed with many other savory ingredients, which shall be hereafter mentioned. (pp. 6–7)

Here Burn echoes Fox by identifying 'the Consumers of Sugar and Rum' as the prime movers in the slave trade. At the same time, though, he quite self-consciously deviates from his precursor by categorizing the culinary desires of these consuming subjects as not just 'figuratively' but 'literally' cannibalistic. In so doing, he casts a new and unequivocal light on the grimacing women of the 'Preface', retrospectively revealing how the disgust they come to feel towards sugar is more properly a disgust towards the cannibalism sugar secretes within itself. The 'very uneasy, and disagreeable sensations' (p. 6) these women suffer bear comparison in their turn with two of the responses to cannibalism considered earlier, with Long finding there to be 'something so nauseous [and] repugnant' in the rite that it 'hardly admit[s] of belief' and Crusoe undergoing a physical illness alleviated only when 'Nature discharg[es] the disorder from [his] stomach'.[46] Yet the difference between the loathing for cannibalism as it is felt by the female figures in Burn's 'Preface', on the one hand, and by Long and Crusoe, on the other, is that in the former case, it is also a self-loathing. As consumers of sugar, Burn's women unwittingly perform the very practice they revile, while Long and Crusoe safely hold it at one remove by setting themselves over and against the cannibal as racially different. The women's cannibal credentials seem even to have received a bodily coding, with their twisted faces mirroring the 'horrible looks' of the slave-eating 'white men' who haunt the Middle Passage in Equiano.

Burn grounds his seemingly outlandish claims about the adulteration of the 'Puddings, Pies, Tarts [and] Tea' routinely enjoyed by 'the inhabitants of Great Britain' in the authority of the eyewitness, invoking a notion of 'ocular demonstration' which this time echoes Shakespeare rather than Fox and, in particular, Othello's insistent hunger for the 'ocular proof'[47] of Desdemona's sexual sullying. He also adopts a synecdochic approach to his evidence, choosing not to 'go through the whole Process of making Sugar from the juice of the Cane', but concentrating instead on 'the manner in which it is packed in the Hogshead after it is made' (p. 7). Such a slant on the material realities of colonial production is designed to induce an escalating sense of revulsion in Burn's readership, in the hope that – like his original female auditors – they will 'call [him] ugly names; make wry faces; and nauseate the very idea of Sugar' (p. 9), resolving 'never [to] eat another bit, so long as a slave exists to dance in a Hogshead' (p. 10).

Burn's description of this bittersweet choreography is at its most suggestive – if not necessarily most 'nauseous' (p. 9) – as it begins, when, despite his commitment to the literal, his writing briefly takes on a symbolic dimension. At this point in the text, Burn returns to and develops the issue of sweat, giving a fuller and more graphic insight into how this emission from the toiling bodies of the male slaves – 'two or three stout fellows, nearly, or altogether naked' (p. 7) and 'almost in contact with each other' (p. 8) – comes to pollute the sugar which they 'tread … down with their feet … till the Cask is full' (p. 7). While the aroma created by the 'excessive Perspiration' from these ironically 'dancing Blacks' is described as 'insupportable', it eventually dissipates, even as 'the warm stream from whence it proceeds, is … absorbed among the

Sugar', leaving the mark of its presence in the shape of 'little hard lumps …
of a darker hue than the rest'. What exactly is this 'disgusting moisture'? Is
it simply sweat, or metaphorically linked to other somatic fluids? The latter
possibility would certainly seem to be woven into the language of the text,
as Burn concludes his observations on the sweating slaves by declaring how
'every Hogshead of Sugar thus packed and imported into England from the
West Indies, is more or less impregnated with this liquid from the human
body' (p. 8). This sweeping rhetoric of conception transforms the chemical
reactions the text describes into an allegory of interracial exchange: black
sweat becomes black semen and those more darkly toned 'lumps' standing out
from the soft-bodied whiteness around them take on new meaning in their
turn. These particles are reminiscent of the 'spots of human blood' besmirching
the sugar of Fox's 'French writer', but can be construed, equally, as the shadowy
sign of miscegenation and the 'darker' legacies it leaves.

As much as it contaminates the sugar consumed by the British, the sweat
Burn describes so minutely itself comes to be mixed with 'many other disagreeable ingredients' (p. 8). These understatedly distasteful things are itemized
in equally microscopic detail and include among their number the 'dried
carcases' (p. 9) of the lice shaken sugarwards from the 'reeking locks' of the
slave, 'perspiring at every pore' as he 'jump[s] in the cask with all his might'
(p. 8). They also include an unspecified but 'disgusting fluid' stemming from
'a disorder called the Yaws' (p. 9) and the 'little oozing sores' occasioned by
the removal of a 'small Insect called the Jigger' from 'just under the skin' of
'the poor Negro, few of whom [*sic*] are exempt from this plague' (p. 10). What
becomes evident as Burn pursues his deliberately and increasingly rebarba-
tive anatomy of sugar's ills – if it were not clear enough already – is that the
slaves 'constantly labouring' (p. 7) in the hogsheads paradoxically subvert the
order which oppresses them to the precise extent that they serve it, or at least
have the potential so to do, were the true nature of their activities properly
broadcast: their energies are channelled towards the production of the sugar
the master wishes to turn into capital, even as they go against the grain of
such a desire by being the simultaneous source of the commodity's corruption. In this respect, despite their manifold and frequently extreme afflictions,
Burn's slaves offer a degree of resistance to the colonial system and are figures
with whom Burn himself implicitly identifies, as is suggested by the verbally
echoing terms in which he defines the polemical drift of 'A Second Address' as
a whole, particularly in relation to Fox. Just as the slaves whom the text both
mourns and celebrates 'tread … down' their sugar, so Burn 'tread[s] in a very
different path' from that taken by Fox, rebelliously literalizing the man-eating
tropes of the 'worthy Author' (p. 3) who precedes him.

The sense in which Burn's slaves exact a qualified revenge against their
masters is underscored by considering the shifting representation of the

enslaved body in the text, especially its feet. In his excursus on the Middle Passage, Burn tells a tale of 'unparalleled barbarity', at the centre of which is 'a Slave child, of nine months old', who, like the young bondsman of *The Interesting Narrative*, 'refuse[s] to eat' (p. 5) and, like Equiano again, incurs a series of floggings for its pains. Even in mercurial shipboard moments when such egregious punishment gives way to compassion, bodily injury remains the consequence: 'The ... child having swell'd feet, the captain order'd them to be put into water, *though the ship's Cook told him it was too hot.* This brought off the skin and nails' (pp. 5–6; italics in original). In Burn's account of the preparation of the sugar-casks for export, the slaves' feet endure trials of their own, diseased as they are by the yaws and other 'scrophulous disorders' and infested with subcutaneous fleas. But the difference is that while the agonies endured by Burn's excoriated Middle Passage infant go entirely unredeemed, the debilitations suffered by the slaves who work the sugar are not wholly without purpose: if the 'Negro, who stamps in the hogshead' has a 'disorder in his feet' (p. 9), it is not only in a medical sense, but also in so far as his podiatric complaints pose a threat to the colonial regime which seeks to govern and profit from his movements, making him its saboteur.

Even in death, the slave continues to meddle and disrupt, leading a strange and troubling afterlife carefully logged by Burn as his text draws towards its close and switches the reader's attention from the production and consumption of sugar to rum. Moving for a second occasion outside the parameters of his own experience, Burn 'relat[es]' an 'Anecdote' (p. 11), told to him 'as a fact' (p. 12) by an unidentified source. The tale concerns a 'Wine-merchant' who 'import[s]' a quantity of Rum from Jamaica' only to become puzzled by how 'one Puncheon prove[s] exceeding fine, of a very pleasant and delicious flavour', while the 'rest [is] not ... near so good' (p. 11). The mystery of the discrepancy is resolved with a shock when the cask containing the superior spirit is opened up for inspection and analysis:

> the head [of the puncheon] was knocked out, and behold, the whole body of a roasted Negro lay stretched out, and fastened down in the bilge of the Cask, opposite the bung-hole. At the sight of which, neither the Wine-merchant, nor his customers, wished to have any more of the best sort. Now far be it from me to insinuate ... that any such methods are used to meliorate West India Rum; I will only take upon me to affirm, as a certain fact, that the Carcase of a Dog, Cat, Sheep, Goat, Man or Woman, thoroughly burnt, and put in the bottom of a large vessel, full of Spirits of any kind, will greatly tend to meliorate and soften them. But whether there exist such indelicate wretches, who from avaricious motives are capable of doing this, I leave to my Readers to determine, and to ruminate on what they have read. (pp. 11–12)

If the notion of the colonizer as cannibal explored by Equiano offers one context for the discursive strategies deployed by Burn and Fox, this anecdote suggests something of the debt which abolitionist writings owe to the Gothic, a contemporaneous genre littered with its own secrets, crypts and corpses. The anecdote's Gothic resonance is underlined when the 'body' it features is subsequently accorded a brief but violent biography and turns out to be that of a 'Negro Boy', unintentionally killed in a plantation quarrel with a 'Black Cooper' (p. 12), before being partially incinerated and then finally stowed in the 'bilge of the Cask', which comes to function as impromptu casket. As Burn notes, the 'sight' of the 'roasted Negro ... stretched out' at the bottom of the barrel induces an understandable aversion towards the 'Spirits' which would ordinarily be the cask's solitary and more appealing occupants, with 'neither the Wine-merchant, nor his customers, wish[ing] to have any more of the best sort'. Such an aversion is also, of course, the effect Burn intends his writing to instil in those who peruse it and, as if to hint at this kinship of purposes, the language of his text carries out its own covert operation. While the 'Cooper' anxiously conceals the murdered slave in the 'Puncheon he [is] making' in an attempt to avoid 'punishment' (p. 12) for his crime, Burn secretes something too, cooping up the word 'rum' itself in his parting injunction to his 'Readers ... to *rum*inate on what they have read' (emphasis added).

Gothic and cryptographic at once, this anecdote has an intra- as well as intertextual dimension. On the one hand, in a metamorphosis of insect into human, the charred remains of the 'Negro found in the Rum Cask' (p. 12) reincarnate the 'dried carcases' of the lice which 'fall in among the Sugar' (p. 8) at an earlier point and are unknowingly consumed by the British. On the other, in a second metamorphosis, the remains themselves reappear under a new but similarly disquieting guise in the text's suddenly arrested and arresting last paragraph. Here Burn shifts back from rum to sugar once again and, appealing to anecdote for a third and final time, considers the methods of its metropolitan refinement:

An acquaintance of mine ... who, a very few years back worked in a Sugar House in London, positively affirms, as an undoubted fact, to which he was an eye-witness, that one day, as they started a Hogshead of moist Sugar, they found the Skeleton of a Child in the midst of it; the flesh was mostly eat off the bones, by the corroding nature of the Sugar. (p. 12)

This far-flung sugar-rusted 'Child' is the avatar of the slave sealed up in his drum of rum because his 'body ... [would] not consume fast enough' (p. 12). In the end, however, this young 'Skeleton' cuts a still less accountable figure than its imperfectly cremated fellow, lacking even the most minimal of supporting histories or explanatory narratives, just as its 'bones' are all but stripped of their 'flesh'.

For both Burn's 'roasted Negro' and his skeletal 'Child', the final dispersal comes when their presences are absorbed into the products with which they are respectively associated and whose purity they haunt and compromise: like the farmyard 'Carcase of a Dog, Cat, Sheep [or] Goat' with which it is so pointedly collated, the former 'meliorate[s] and soften[s]' the rum Burn's readers imbibe, while the latter yields up its body to the carnivorous 'Sugar' they eat. These metamorphoses run in parallel to the discursive transformations Burn and Fox carry out upon Equiano. Like the white mouths which consume black bodies, their white texts assimilate and refashion Equiano's black writing for their own different but interrelated purposes, domesticating the image of the colonizer as cannibal by refracting it through the prism of a shared anti-saccharite animus.

While Fox and Burn would both live (unlike Equiano) to see the slave trade brought to an end, the full-scale emancipation of slaves in British colonies was not to take place until 1834, leaving a generous interim for many other writers to travel to the Caribbean and record their encounters with slavery first-hand. Among the most accomplished of these traveller-diarists is Matthew Lewis, who inherited two sizeable Jamaican plantations (Cornwall and Hordley) from his father in 1812, visiting them shortly afterwards in 1815–16 and 1817–18. Lewis gives an account of these two visits in *Journal of a West India Proprietor, Kept during a Residence in the Island of Jamaica*, a text published posthumously in the year of the slaves' emancipation, and it is this work which is considered in the next chapter.

Notes

1. Comprehensive accounts of the movement towards abolition are contained in Robin Blackburn, *The Overthrow of Colonial Slavery, 1776–1848* (London and New York: Verso, 1988), pp. 131–60 and 293–314; Adam Hochschild, *Bury the Chains: The British Struggle to Abolish Slavery* (London: Pan, 2005); and Richard S. Reddie, *Abolition! The Struggle to Abolish Slavery in the British Colonies* (Oxford: Lion, 2007).
2. For earlier readings of abolitionist discourse attentive to such issues, see Charlotte Sussman, 'Women and the Politics of Sugar, 1792', *Representations*, 48 (Fall 1994), 48–69; Deirdre Coleman, 'Conspicuous Consumption: White Abolitionism and English Women's Protest Writing in the 1790s', *English Literary History*, 61 (1994), 341–62; Timothy Morton, 'Blood Sugar', in *Romanticism and Colonialism: Writing and Empire, 1780–1830*, ed. Tim Fulford and Peter J. Kitson (Cambridge: Cambridge University Press, 1998), pp. 87–106; and Mimi Sheller, *Consuming the Caribbean: From Arawaks to Zombies* (London and New York: Routledge, 2003), pp. 88–95.
3. Fox's use of cannibalism as figure finds its echo in numerous works of the period. See Samuel Taylor Coleridge, 'On the Slave Trade' (1795); Robert Southey, 'Poems on the Slave Trade' (1797); and Mary Birkett, *A Poem on the African Slave Trade: Addressed to Her Own Sex* (1792). Fox's text, together with that by Coleridge and the half-dozen sonnets making up the sequence by Southey, are discussed in varying degrees of detail in the essays by Sussman, Coleman and Morton, while Birkett's two-part poem is considered in Elizabeth Kowaleski-Wallace, *Consuming Subjects: Women, Shopping, and*

Business in the Eighteenth Century (New York: Columbia University Press, 1997), pp. 37–51. Burn's more literal understanding of the cannibalistic nature of sugar-consumption puts it, on the other hand, significantly out of step with the trends of its time, just as it has been all but ignored in our own. Sussman is the one critic to acknowledge the importance of his text, though even her reading, restricted to less than two pages, is fairly sketchy. It is also questionable in its initial categorization of the text as the 'paranoid double' (p. 55) to Fox's. This phrase relegates the processes of transatlantic bodily exchange Burn describes to the order of fantasy and delusion, as if the cannibalism for which sugar serves as conduit could only ever be a figurative rather than an actual occurrence.

4. Such an interplay between white writers and black has been the subject of much recent critical analysis concerned, as J. R. Oldfield puts it, to chart 'the exchange of ideas, peoples, and cultures across and within the Atlantic world' (J. R. Oldfield, 'Transatlanticism, Race and Slavery', *American Literary History*, 14 [2002], p. 131). As Oldfield notes, these inquiries are heavily influenced by theoretical models derived from the pioneering work of Paul Gilroy, particularly *The Black Atlantic: Modernity and Double Consciousness* (London and New York: Verso, 1993). For major recent examples of this intercultural and transnational critical approach, see Helen Thomas, *Romanticism and Slave Narratives: Transatlantic Testimonies* (Cambridge: Cambridge University Press, 2000); Marcus Wood, *Blind Memory: Visual Representations of Slavery in England and America, 1780–1865* (Manchester and New York: Manchester University Press, 2000); Alan Rice, *Radical Narratives of the Black Atlantic* (London and New York: Continuum, 2003); and Sarah Meer, *Uncle Tom Mania: Slavery, Minstrelsy, and Transatlantic Culture in the 1850s* (Athens, GA and London: University of Georgia Press, 2005).

5. For recent work on cannibalism in Equiano's text, see Mark Stein, 'Who's Afraid of Cannibals? Some Uses of the Cannibalism Trope in Olaudah Equiano's *The Interesting Narrative*', in Carey, Ellis and Salih, pp. 96–107; and Michael Wiley, 'Consuming Africa: Geography and Identity in Olaudah Equiano's *The Interesting Narrative*', *Studies in Romanticism*, 44 (2005), 165–79. For an earlier and more schematic, though still useful, treatment of the topic, see Alan Rice, '"Who's Eating Whom?" The Discourse of Cannibalism in the Literature of the Black Atlantic from Equiano's *Travels* to Toni Morrison's *Beloved*', *Research in African Literatures*, 29.4 (1998), 106–21.

6. Hulme has written extensively on this link from the mid-1980s onwards. For a brief but representative (and typically nuanced) analysis of the association, see Peter Hulme, 'Columbus and the Cannibals', in *The Post-Colonial Studies Reader*, ed. Bill Ashcroft, Gareth Griffiths and Helen Tiffin (London and New York: Routledge, 1995), pp. 365–69.

7. *The* Diario *of Christopher Columbus's First Voyage to America 1492–1493, Abstracted by Fray Bartolomé de las Casas*, trans. and ed. Oliver Dunn and James E. Kelley, Jr (Norman, OK and London: University of Oklahoma Press, 1989), p. 133 (lineation modified).

8. Daniel Defoe, *Robinson Crusoe*, ed. John Richetti (London: Penguin, 2001), pp. 130–31.

9. Edward Long, *The History of Jamaica. Or, General Survey of the Antient and Modern State of That Island: With Reflections on Its Situation, Settlements, Inhabitants, Climate, Products, Commerce, Laws, and Government. In Three Volumes. Illustrated with Copper Plates* (London: T. Lowndes, 1774), vol. 2, p. 351.

10. Long, vol. 2, pp. 381–82 (italics in original).

11. Defoe, p. 131.

12. Defoe, p. 130.

13. Edwards, vol. 2, pp. 76–77.

14. Edwards, vol. 2, p. 63.

15. Edwards, vol. 2, p. 65.

16. Edwards, vol. 2, pp. 74–75.

17. William Shakespeare, *The Tempest*, ed. Stephen Orgel (Oxford: Oxford University Press, 1987), III.ii.83–93.
18. Edwards, vol. 2, p. 65.
19. Wiley, p. 172.
20. Olaudah Equiano, *The Interesting Narrative and Other Writings*, ed. Vincent Carretta (London: Penguin, 1995), p. 41.
21. Wiley, p. 173.
22. Wiley, p. 173.
23. Equiano, p. 55.
24. Equiano, p. 56.
25. Equiano, p. 60.
26. Equiano, p. 56.
27. Equiano, p. 58.
28. Cited in Equiano, p. 13.
29. See William Shakespeare, *Othello*, ed. E. A. J. Honigmann ([Walton-on-Thames]: Nelson, 1997), I.iii.91. Equiano himself is attracted to the comparison with Othello in a note to the letter 'To the Reader' which appears from the fifth edition of *The Interesting Narrative* onwards, citing the lines from Othello's final speech immediately before his suicide: 'Speak of me as I am. Nothing extenuate, / Nor set down aught in malice' (V.ii.340–41). The letter and the quotation are designed to rebut an 'invidious falsehood' that Equiano has fabricated his own origins and was born in 'the Danish island of Santa Cruz, in the West Indies' (Equiano, p. 5) rather than in Africa. For a superb account of Equiano's life – which persuasively argues that he may in fact have been born in South Carolina and hence fictionalized the experience of the Middle Passage – see Vincent Carretta, *Equiano, The African: Biography of a Self-Made Man* (Athens, GA and London: University of Georgia Press, 2005).
30. Shakespeare, *Othello*, I.iii.78.
31. Shakespeare, *Othello*, I.iii.170.
32. Shakespeare, *Othello*, I.iii.129–51.
33. For these statistics, see the 'Headnote' to Fox's text in *The Abolition Debate*, ed. Peter J. Kitson, volume 2 of *Slavery, Abolition and Emancipation: Writings in the British Romantic Period*, ed. Peter J. Kitson and Debbie Lee, 8 vols (London: Pickering and Chatto, 1999), p. 153.
34. William Fox, 'An Address to the People of Great Britain, on the Propriety of Abstaining from West India Sugar and Rum', in Kitson, p. 156.
35. Fox, p. 158.
36. Fox, p. 159.
37. Fox, p. 156.
38. Fox, p. 160.
39. Fox, p. 156.
40. Fox, p. 155.
41. Equiano, p. 56.
42. Fox, p. 156.
43. Kitson, p. 153.
44. Andrew Burn, 'A Second Address to the People of Great Britain: Containing a New, and Most Powerful Argument to Abstain from the Use of West India Sugar. By an Eye Witness to the Facts Related' (London: M. Gurney, 1792), p. 2. Subsequent references to this work are incorporated in the text and given in parenthesis after quotations.
45. Shakespeare, *Othello*, I.iii.140.
46. Defoe, p. 131.
47. Shakespeare, *Othello*, III.iii.363.

3

'Conveying away the *Trash*': Sweetening Slavery in Matthew Lewis's *Journal of a West India Proprietor, Kept during a Residence in the Island of Jamaica*

> Disguise thyself as thou wilt, still slavery! … still thou art a bitter draught.
> – Laurence Sterne, *A Sentimental Journey*

Sugar as Allegory

In stark contrast to its centrality in both the abolitionists and Grainger, sugar occupies a marginal position in Lewis's *Journal*. Despite the promise conferred on the text by its Byronic epigraph – 'I would give many a Sugar Cane / Monk Lewis were alive again!'[1] – overt allusions to the commodity are fairly lightly sprinkled across what is, generically and thematically, a highly eclectic work. These allusions may even be easily missed in the quick switches between prose and verse and the frequent shifts of tone and focus, as Lewis whirls the reader from playful asides about water-melons and centipedes to serious reflections on the aesthetics of Caribbean landscape and the particularities of slave culture. As Keith A. Sandiford summarizes, Lewis 'exhibits no compelling narrative interest in sugar either as an object of natural history or for its long tradition of engendering metaphysical and aesthetic ideas', making 'references to [it]' which 'are by no means continuous or extensive'.[2]

Yet if Lewis's text says little about sugar, sugar has a lot to say about the text, as can be gleaned from the journal entry for 11 January 1816, written shortly after his arrival at the Cornwall plantation. Here Lewis dwells at unusual length on the subject of sugar, giving a meticulous description of a morning visit to the ingenio (or sugar-works) and the processes of production which go on inside it:

> The ripe canes are brought in bundles to the mill, where the cleanest of the women are appointed, one to put them into the machine for grinding them, and another to draw them out after the juice has been extracted, when

she throws them into an opening in the floor close to her; another band of negroes collects them below, when, under the name of *trash*, they are carried away to serve for fuel. The juice, which is itself at first of a pale ash-colour, gushes out in great streams, quite white with foam, and passes through a wooden gutter into the boiling-house, where it is received into the siphon or 'cock-copper', where fire is applied to it, and it is slaked with lime, in order to make it granulate. The feculent parts of it rise to the top, while the purer and more fluid flow through another gutter into the second copper. When little but the impure scum on the surface remains to be drawn off, the first gutter communicating with the copper is stopped, and the grosser parts are obliged to find a new course through another gutter, which conveys them to the distillery, where, being mixed with the molasses, or treacle, they are manufactured into rum. From the second copper they are transmitted into the first, and thence into two others, and in these four latter basins the scum is removed with skimmers pierced with holes, till it becomes sufficiently free from impurities to be *skipped* off, that is, to be again ladled out of the coppers and spread into the coolers, where it is left to granulate. The sugar is then formed, and is removed into the *curing-house*, where it is put into hogsheads, and left to settle for a certain time.[3]

Echoing numerous earlier set-piece descriptions of 'the business of sugar-making' (p. 58), this passage is characterized by a language of separation and removal, even with respect to the personnel recruited to assist in the labour of sugar's birth. As Lewis fastidiously observes, only the 'cleanest' among the female slaves are 'appointed' to the initial task of handling the 'ripe canes … brought in bundles to the mill', just as the 'juice' 'extracted' from the canes themselves is subjected to the rigours of refinement, its 'feculent' and 'grosser parts' 'drawn off' in favour of those which are 'purer and more fluid'. The irony, though, is that this language of purity and pollution, selection and rejection, is marked by its own 'impurities', clouded by a signifying excess which allows it to be read in not only literal but also figurative terms. It is not simply, in other words, that the *Journal* describes the 'process of sugar-making' (p. 57) at this juncture, but rather that the process provides an allegory for the making of the *Journal*, which consistently portrays Lewis's Cornwall estate (the primary narrative focus throughout) as a milieu from which two of slavery's 'grosser parts' – in the forms of sexual and racial violence – have been siphoned away. Such discursive cleansing is already evident even within this early journal entry, whose final paragraph offers a vision of the master–slave relationship radically at odds with the conventionally adversarial model a reader might expect. Contrasting his first impressions of Caribbean society with the 'repulsive manners' of England, the newly arrived Lewis is in rhapsodies: his 'heart … seems to expand itself … in the sunshine of the kind looks and words which meet [him] at every turn, and seem to wait for [his] as anxiously as if they were so many diamonds' (p. 59).

There is, of course, an ideological dimension to the textual strategies facilitating such moments of glittering cordiality, a politics to accompany the aesthetics. Writing in the transition between abolition and emancipation, Lewis finds himself awkwardly placed, personally implicated in a system not only increasingly contested on moral grounds but also of gradually diminishing importance within Britain's changing imperial economy.[4] By configuring the image of slavery on Cornwall in such clearly sentimentalized terms, as he does so often over the course of the *Journal*, Lewis is able both to legitimate his involvement in the system and to defuse any emancipationist criticisms he might incur. After all, how could objections be raised against a plantation whose master is 'surrounded' not by oppressed and exploited slaves, but by lightsome 'beings who are always laughing and singing, and who seem to perform their work with so much *nonchalance*' that Lewis 'can hardly persuade [him]self that it is really *work* that they are about' (p. 65; italics in original)?

As further consideration of the sugar/text analogy suggests, however, the discursive refinement of slavery's more disturbing aspects is necessarily imperfect, leaving the apparent utopia of existence on Cornwall adulterated by that which it attempts to cast out of itself – a situation establishing a certain continuity between Lewis's *Journal* and Grainger's *The Sugar-Cane*, written just over fifty years earlier. While the passage cited above claims to provide a complete account of how sugar is created, there is a sense in which the story it tells remains unfinished, since the sugar 'left to settle' in those 'hogsheads' would still be in a relatively crude condition at this stage of the cycle taking it from Caribbean 'cane-piece' (p. 217) to the realms of domestic consumption: as opposed to the semi-refined white or clayed sugar manufactured in the French West Indies, the type produced on British plantations such as Lewis's would be muscovado, a substance which (as noted in chapter 1) requires a series of additional treatments in metropolitan sugar-refineries before it is sold to the general public. By the same logic, sexual violence can never be fully expunged from Lewis's representation of slavery on his estate, even as he transforms the often brutal realities of white male desire into the stereotypical fantasy of the black man as rapist, and in turn confines the fantasy to 'The Isle of Devils: A Metrical Tale', the Gothic verse narrative inserted into the *Journal* shortly after its mid-point. Racial violence is something, similarly, which resists wholesale filtration: Lewis attempts to remove it from the portrayal of Cornwall by transferring it into a range of temporal and geographical spaces other to his own, but the success of such self-exonerating strategies is only partial. Traces of white–black conflict linger on as a kind of textual 'scum', working to trouble and contaminate an account of colonial governance which, like Grainger's, would otherwise be impossibly saccharine.

Rewriting White Desire: The *Journal* and 'The Isle of Devils'

As much as the early phases of Lewis's Jamaican sojourn provide him with an insight into the intricacies of sugar-making, they also entail an initiation into a different form of colonial production (or reproduction) as it takes place in the context of interracial desire. Lewis signals his conversancy with how this desire operates by rehearsing its ritualized language in the journal entry for 15 January 1816, written just four days after the visit to the sugar-works:

> The offspring of a white man and black woman is a *mulatto*; the mulatto and black produce a *sambo*; from the mulatto and white comes the *quadroon*; from the quadroon and white the *mustee*; the child of a mustee by a white man is called a *musteefino*; while the children of a musteefino are free by law, and rank as white persons to all intents and purposes. (p. 68; italics in original)

As this passage suggests, it is not just the production of the text which can be approached in terms of the production of sugar, but the production of racial difference as well, with the chromatic patterns marking the one replicated in those of the other. In the first instance, 'molasses' (black) are drained off from muscovado (brown), which itself is in due course turned into domestic table-sugar (white). In the second, the blackness of the slavewoman who gives birth to the 'mulatto' – consistently depicted in the *Journal* with tawny skin – is eventually bleached out in the 'children of a musteefino', who 'rank as white persons'.

By claiming such a status, these exalted scions bring the odyssey of inter-racial desire full circle, assuming the same position in what Thomas Babington Macaulay calls the 'aristocracy of skin'[5] as the 'white man' who is their ancestor. Equally, though, they are an awkward reminder that the very mixing of races slavery enables is also the engine of its destruction, since they 'are free by law'. But in addition to the paradoxes and ironies which see it erasing racial differ-ence, on the one hand, and terminating slavery, on the other, Lewis's litany of types is notable for its terseness and compression, as it skips hurriedly and even promiscuously from one interracial coupling to another. In this respect, it is of a piece with those more intimate textual moments when the mulatto – the first of Lewis's mixed-race 'offspring' – appears *in propria persona*, rather than merely as a cipher in an impersonal racial taxonomy. Mary Wiggins, the female slave whose beauty seems so to dazzle Lewis towards the beginning of the *Journal*, is described, for example, simply as 'born upon Cornwall' (p. 46), while the precise circumstances leading to her birth are not given. The 'young ... carpenter, called Nicholas', whom Lewis notices on 'first arrival' (p. 50) at his estate, is similarly figured as a 'person' who is 'very interesting' because of his 'story', even as the story itself undergoes censorship, with Lewis remarking only that Nicholas is 'the son of a white man' (p. 51). Such blocking of the details of the mulatto's genealogy is symptomatic of a refusal to acknowledge the violence in which white male desire under slavery is necessarily implicated. Yet Lewis's text disavows such violence not just by remaining silent about it, but also by displacing it across racial and generic boundaries, openly producing, in 'The Isle of Devils', a poem which precisely rewrites the historical realities his prose entombs within itself. In this work, the black man rather than the white is cast in the role of rapist, while the white female rather than the black is placed in the position of sexual victim.[6]

Originally published in its own right in Jamaica in 1827, some seven years ahead of the *Journal* as a whole, 'The Isle of Devils' is curiously slow to emerge within the text itself. Although appearing at the point when Lewis is returning to England after the completion of the first trip to his Cornwall plantation, it was in fact written en route to the West Indies, some six months earlier. Lewis explains the poem's genesis in the journal entry for 10 May 1816, at the same time nervously anticipating the hostile response it is likely to provoke:

> During the early part of my outward-bound voyage I was extremely afflicted with sea-sickness; and between eight o'clock on a Monday morning, and twelve on the following Thursday, I actually brought up almost a thousand lines, with rhymes at the end of them. Having nothing better to do at present, I may as well copy them into this book. Composed with such speed, and under such circumstances, I take it for granted that the verses cannot be very good; but let them be ever so bad, I defy any one to be more sick while reading them than the author himself was while writing them. (p. 159)

Even as Lewis calmly announces the existence of the poem to his readers for the first time here, he looks back to the rather more stressful period when his 'lines' were initially 'brought up' in solitude. This turn of phrase is not accidental in the context of a resurfacing memory of extreme 'sea-sickness' and implicitly defines the poem as a kind of textual vomit. At the same time, the phrase ties the poem's composition to the turbulent mayday of 17 November 1815, which finds Lewis 'Off the St Alban's Head. Sick to death!', his 'temples throbbing … head burning … limbs freezing … mouth all fever … stomach all nausea' and 'mind all disgust' (p. 9). Yet if Lewis's prefatory comments make him sound adamant that the feelings of revulsion his poem induces in its 'author' can never be surpassed by those its readers might experience, what underlies this hierarchized sense of sickness seems less definite. Does it arise simply for the aesthetic reason that the 'verses cannot be very good', or because of the nature of the topic with which they deal so directly – the black man's sexual violation of the white female – or perhaps again as a result of the two possibilities combined?

Whatever the precise burden of Lewis's remarks, the 'The Isle of Devils' begins in a way which both obscures and prefigures the fate of Irza, the 'blooming maid' (p. 160) 'Not fourteen years' of age, who suffers the sexual trauma at the poem's melodramatic heart. This paradoxical effect is brought about by the brief Orientalist song Irza performs for Rosalvo, the 'youthful cousin' (p. 162) to whom she is betrothed, as the two voyage back 'From Goa's precious sands to Lisbon's shore' (p. 163) aboard a jewel-laden 'bark', belonging to Rosalvo's father. As a 'Spanish lay' about the 'Moorish love' (p. 160) between Zayde and Zayda, the song is superficially far removed in its concerns from the issue of interracial rape with which the larger poem is preoccupied. At the same time, though, it resonates with Irza's narrative in so far as the mutually desired union between the two lovers is thwarted by Zayda's 'tyrant father', who decrees his daughter marry the rival figure of an 'ancient' but wealthy 'lord'. What occurs in the course of the song, in other words, is an expansion of the dyad of Zayde and Zayda into a triangular relationship in which the 'charms' (p. 161) of the 'lovely maid' (p. 160) come to be 'enjoy[ed]' (p. 161) by a disruptive third presence. This shift is replayed in the poem as a whole, as the virginal Irza is wrested from 'Her promised spouse' (p. 163) by the 'master-fiend', 'black ... as storm' (p. 169), who rules the 'Demon-Isle' (p. 168) and who appropriates her body for the purposes of sexual pleasure and self-reproduction alike.

The poem's prefigurative elements are still more clearly marked in its second 'Song', this time sung by the 'Tempest-Fiend' (p. 166) or personified storm whose machinations result in Irza's shipwreck on 'th' enchanted isle' (p. 179). As the language of the song suggests, the storm does not just embody a sudden transformation of the tranquil meteorological conditions in which Rosalvo and his 'destined bride' (p. 163) begin their journey, but is also an allegory for the rape Irza suffers, on two separate occasions, at the 'ebon hands' (p. 176) of the 'Dark and majestic ... demon-king' (p. 170). Despite the carefree impression created by its 'pennants ... gaily ... stream[ing]', Irza's convention-ally feminized ship is 'well ... armed for resistance', but proves no match, in the end, for the 'tempest', which 'clap[s]' its 'black pinions' and 'extend[s]' the phallic 'wand' (p. 166) of its lightning. Yet although the 'ravage' (p. 167) in which Irza's 'vessel' is engulfed looks forward to the conflict on the island itself, the distinction between allegorical and literal forms of rape is that the one is explicitly dramatized while the other is not. The 'sails' of the ship are 'split' from 'top ... to bottom' and 'rent in shivers' by the storm's 'fury' (p. 166), but the scene of Irza's first subjection to the 'fierce desires' (p. 169) of the 'dark demon' (p. 173) is not represented, secretly occurring instead in the break between the poem's fifth and sixth sections. As if to emphasize this textual invisibility, the rape is preceded by a description of Irza's exhausted arrival at the 'cave' forming her assailant's 'lone abode' in which she seems, ironically, to be her own aggressor, rather than the victim of another: 'there / No more their weight her wearied limbs could bear. / Exhausted, fainting, anguish, terror, thirst, / Fatigue o'erpower'd her frame' (p. 170).

The 'veil of ignorance' protecting Irza from the 'crime' perpetrated during her 'death-like swoon' (p. 173) is not 'rent in twain' (p. 173) until she undergoes the horrified convulsions of labour and is delivered of a son. This pattern of a rape which is textually effaced and brought to light only as a consequence of pregnancy and parturition would seem to be repeated some 'Three months' (p. 174) after the son's birth, when Rosalvo, who has also survived the shipwreck, appears on the 'strange isle', only to be instantly and brutally murdered by Irza's 'infernal gaoler' (p. 175). Rosalvo's death plunges Irza into temporary madness and it is in this trance-like state, occurring between the poem's eighth and ninth sections, that the 'fiend' again 'seize[s] the unguarded hour / To force her weakness, and abuse his power' (p. 177). Like the first rape, Irza's second culminates in a son, even as this latter child ultimately introduces difference as much as repetition into the cycles of its mother's history. Although it shares the same sexually violent origin as its brother and is racially identical, it is welcomed by Irza as a 'cherub elf; / In small the model of her beauteous self' and embraced, especially, for a 'fine skin', 'more smooth and white' 'than down of swans' (p. 177). The older sibling, on the other hand, less resembles its narcissistic white mother than its demonically black father or 'hellish sire' (p. 172), and for this reason is as much the object of Irza's 'disgust' as of her 'love' (p. 173). Such affective tensions are brought out sharply when Irza is called upon to suckle her 'shaggy offspring' (p. 181) for the first time: 'Loathing its sight, she melts to hear its cries, / And, while she yields the breast, averts her eyes' (p. 173).

Irza's animus towards this neonate can in part be explained by the status of its blackness as a visual marker of the sexual wound inflicted upon her by her 'demon-husband' (p. 180), just as the whiteness of her second-born represents a complementary forgetting or erasure of the same trauma. But her feelings are also a reminder of how racial difference is constructed beyond the scope of individual experience, with whiteness culturally equating to beauty and blackness to ugliness. This aestheticized racism or racialized aesthetics is endorsed by the poem's third-person narrator, who likewise curses Irza's first-born as a 'hideous stranger', 'monster child' (p. 172) and 'monster-brat' (p. 174). The *Journal* itself, on the other hand, does not share such short-sighted orthodoxies, as Lewis more flexibly invests both the black and mixed-race slavewomen on whom he periodically gazes with a formidable charm. These women include both the figure of Psyche, the very first of Cornwall's female slaves to capture the master's attention in the journal entry for 3 January 1816 and, perhaps most strikingly of all, the statuesque Mary, encountered two days later, whose beauty far transcends that associated with even the most exquisite European women. While this 'mulatto girl' strongly reminds the well-travelled and cultured Lewis of an Italian opera-star – '[Josephina] Grassini in "La Vergine del Sole"' – the difference in the attractiveness of the two females is finally as great as the gap separating the worlds they inhabit. Mary is 'a thousand times more beautiful' (p. 46) than her European counterpart and, as Lewis goes on to observe, qualifies as one of 'the most picturesque objects that [he has] seen for these twenty years' (p. 47).

It could similarly be argued that the *Journal* at large fails to endorse the stereotype of black male sexuality 'The Isle of Devils' so shamelessly promotes, or even that the poem is a parody of both the stereotype itself and the Gothic conventions used to produce it. Either way, the stereotype is undoubtedly a flamboyant one, functioning to divert attention from the darker truth of the white man as purveyor of sexual violence – a more mundane kind of 'master-fiend', as it were. Lewis's text seems determined to refine out from itself this truth and, for the most part, the processes of censorship and exclusion are highly effective. Even so, traces of the sexual threat the white man poses for the black woman, whether in the form of rape or not, reveal themselves from time to time, working to unsettle Lewis's accounts of slavery, as it exists in Jamaica in general and on Cornwall in particular.

One place where such uncertain traces can be located is in 'The Humming Bird', a short poem which comprises the entire journal entry for 8 March 1816 and tells the tale of a 'sable maid' (p. 128) named Zoë, 'charm[ed] and cheat[ed]' by a 'wild youth', who 'Sip[s]' her 'sweets' and 'break[s] his vow' (p. 129). Another is at the beginning of the entry for 12 January 1816, with its extended flashback to the activities of 'a runaway negro called *Plato*', as they occur in the 'parish of Westmoreland', where Lewis's own estate is situated, in 'the year '80'. Operating from the fastnesses of 'the Moreland Mountains', Plato is clearly a danger to the colonizer – he leads a 'troop of banditti', 'robb[ing] very often, and murder[ing] occasionally' (p. 59; italics in original) and is also 'a professor of Obi' (p. 60) – but the menace he embodies is least of all sexual. As Lewis recalls, Plato dedicates himself to 'gallantry' as 'his every day occupation' and, 'being a remarkably tall athletic young fellow', has 'but few Lucretias' 'among the beauties of his own complexion'. The classical allusion here to Lucretia's rape by Sextus Tarquinius (and her subsequent suicide) is a complex one, designed, in the first instance, to suggest the reciprocal nature of Plato's liaisons with the enslaved black women who flee to his 'retreat in the mountains'. At the same time, though, the allusion inevitably raises questions as to the sorts of relationship which exist between the white man and those black women unable to ascend towards their liberation. As Lewis notes, Plato's sexual magnetism is such that 'Every handsome negress who had the slightest cause of complaint against her master, took the first opportunity of eloping to join [him]'. Yet the flight of these female slaves to 'freedom, protection, and unbounded generosity' (p. 59) cannot wholly disguise the more sedentary predicament of others whose grievances might be less trivial, but whose fate, as in Lewis's classical source, is also far less reassuring.

With 'The Humming Bird', Lewis reduces the sexual violence the white man carries out upon the black woman to vestigial form and subjects it to a kind of generic exile, just as he isolates the figure of the black man as agent of interracial rape in 'The Isle of Devils'. In Plato's narrative, on the other hand, such violence is not only rendered similarly residual but also historically distanced to a period almost forty years prior to Lewis's time in Jamaica and linked to a space close to but distinct from Cornwall. There are moments in the *Journal*, nevertheless, when Lewis's own estate does become a site in which the presence of the white man as sexual monster is discernible, albeit, once again, in an implicit or barely articulated form. This can be seen from a more detailed consideration of Lewis's encounter with the previously mentioned Psyche:

> This morning I went to visit the hospital, and found there only eight patients out of three hundred negroes, and not one of them a serious case. Yesterday I had observed a remarkably handsome Creole girl, called Psyche, and she really deserved the name. This morning a little brown girl made her appearance at breakfast, with an orange bough, to flap away the flies, and, on enquiry, she proved to be an emanation of the aforesaid Psyche. It is evident, therefore, that Psyche has already visited the palace of Cupid; I heartily hope that she is not now upon her road to the infernal regions: but, as the ancients had two Cupids, one divine and the other sensual, so I am in possession of two Psyches; and on visiting the hospital, *there* was poor Psyche the second. Probably this was the Psyche of the sensual Cupid. (p. 43; italics in original)

As with the recollection of Plato's story, so in this description of his 'remarkably handsome Creole girl', Lewis utilizes a classical allusion, though the effect is quite different, as the mythic love between Cupid and Psyche invoked here turns interracial desire into a form of romance, rather than a matter of rape and victimhood. As Lewis notes, however, he possesses 'two Psyches', the second of whom is far less fortunate than the first. While this supplementary figure is presumably confined to Lewis's 'hospital' because she is about to give birth – thus following the example of her namesake – the exact nature of the encounter resulting in her pregnancy is not spelled out. Lewis himself is implicitly unconcerned by the slavewoman's condition, since, as he sweepingly announces at the start of this passage, 'not one' of the 'eight patients' in the hospital is 'a serious case'. Yet the suggestion remains that what is particularly 'poor' about 'poor Psyche the second' is that she has been sexually abused by the white man, grotesquely figured, as he is, as a 'sensual Cupid'.

Lewis's second Psyche cannot clarify her situation because she is given no voice with which to tell her story and does not reappear in the *Journal* beyond this fragmentary cameo. In these respects, she differs once more from the other Psyche, whose narrative is briefly developed, shortly after her introduction to the text, in the scene when Lewis watches her dance alluringly and learns that she has left Nicholas for one of Cornwall's 'book-keepers' or '"white people"', on the grounds that 'he had a good salary, and could afford to give her more presents than a slave could' (p. 52).[7] This disclosure makes Psyche's story seem, in retrospect, less romantic than mercenary, or at least suggests that her beauty enables her to manipulate circumstances to her own advantage rather than be their victim. Yet the opposition between Lewis's two female slaves – the sexual agent and the sexual victim – is not as straightforward as it might look, but is made problematic by the ostensibly innocuous motif of the 'orange bough' and the associations which grow up around it as the *Journal* progresses. In this immediate context, this exotic piece of flora is used by the mixed-race 'emanation' belonging to Psyche the first simply as a means to 'flap away the flies' at 'breakfast', but elsewhere it is heavy with an ominous sexual charge. In 'The Humming Bird', for example, what happens to the bough operates as a natural allegory for Zoë's deflowering, as its 'bells' are 'Drain'd of all their sweets' by 'Wandering bees', leaving the 'feather'd Gem' of the poem's title with nothing on which to feed but 'rifled beauty' – rather than 'cups untasted', replete with 'Many a honied drop' (p. 129). The bough is similarly tied to sexual violation in 'The Isle of Devils', where it is proffered to Irza by her 'savage lord' (p. 178) to 'court her to his cave' (p. 170) directly before her first rape takes place. Psyche's 'little brown girl' may indeed be the product of an interracial exchange which is wholly consensual rather than one-sidedly 'sensual', but the detail of the 'orange bough' has the effect of mixing Lewis's slavewomen together, such that their apparently distinct sexual histories become less easy to tell apart.

Refining Racial Violence

In a typically polymathic moment just after the passage about his 'two Psyches', Lewis reviews the various kinds of snake inhabiting Jamaica, commenting that 'The only dangerous species of serpent is the Whip-snake, so called from its exactly resembling the lash of a whip, in length, thinness, pliability, and whiteness' (p. 45). If the detail of the 'Whip-snake''s 'whiteness' smartly reprimands Lewis's sugar-hungry readers for the cruelties carried out in the West Indies on their behalf, the observation taken as a whole sets up a certain correspondence between natural and colonial orders. Such a correspondence is not absolute, however, but disrupted by the anomalous forms of governance Lewis institutes on his plantation. In contrast to the normative practice of other Jamaican sugar estates, these, it seems, do not include a recourse to the infliction of bodily harm. As Lewis puts it in the journal entry for 19 January 1816:

> I am indeed assured by every one about me, that to manage a West-Indian estate without the occasional use of the cart-whip, however rarely, is impossible … All this may be very true; but there is something to me so

shocking in the idea of this execrable cart-whip, that I have positively forbidden the use of it on Cornwall; and if the estate must go to rack and ruin without its use, to rack and ruin the estate must go. (pp. 75–76)

Lewis's interdiction of the white whip is a measure of which he is clearly proud and to which he repeatedly alludes. In this way, he projects an image of himself as a slave-owner who is humane and enlightened – however much a chimera such a thing may be – and one prepared even to sacrifice pecuniary self-interest to his slaves' corporeal well-being by letting his property slide into 'rack and ruin', should the need arise (even as his text quietly opposes the prospect of such decline with its chiastic poise). There is a sense, though, in which the banning of the whip is as much for Lewis's own benefit as for that of his slaves, since the mere 'idea' of it 'shock[s]' the delicate-minded master – with his 'nerves so fragile, and brain so light' (p. 19) – just as much as the thing itself might scandalize the flesh of the slave on whom it descends.[8]

None the less, the veto placed upon the 'lash' not only sets Lewis's Cornwall apart from the ethos prevailing elsewhere in Jamaica but also distances his estate from its own recent history – specifically the period between the time when Lewis first inherits the plantation and the time of his eventual 'arrival'. As this journal entry makes plain, this is an interval whose realities are very different from how they are portrayed by the 'attorney' who is deputed to run the estate during the years of Lewis's absence and who himself turns out to be far from what he seems. While the attorney writes Lewis letters pulsating with 'the greatest anxiety and attention respecting the welfare and comfort of the slaves' (p. 74) on Cornwall, it transpires that he is in fact neglecting the plantation in pursuit of his own colonial gain, either by 'generally attending to a property of his own, or looking after estates of which also he had the management in distant parts of the island' (pp. 74–75). The results of such neglect prove to be bad for Lewis, but substantially worse for his slaves:

During [the attorney's] absence, an overseer of his own appointing, without my knowledge, was left in absolute possession of his power, which he abused to such a degree, that almost every slave of respectability on the estate was compelled to become a runaway. The property was nearly ruined, and absolutely in a state of rebellion; and at length he committed an act of such severity, that the negroes, one and all, fled to Savannah la Mar, and threw themselves upon the protection of the magistrates. (p. 75)

As this passage indicates, the smooth transmission of colonial 'power' from dead father to son to attorney is disrupted by the unsanctioned figure of the 'overseer', to whose vices Lewis is first awakened 'one morning', during a conversation with one of his slaves, John Fuller, brother to one of the original 'runaway[s]'. But if Fuller's oral testimony contains the 'hint' enabling Lewis subsequently to uncover the 'whole truth' (p. 74) about Cornwall's past, the text itself seems in some sense to remask that 'truth' and thus operate, ironically, in a similar though less deliberately duplicitous way to the attorney's written records: while the overseer's reign culminates in 'an act of such severity' that it sends 'the negroes' into mass flight, the precise nature of the 'act' is not divulged, just as the 'extreme ill-usage' to which Fuller's brother is earlier exposed by 'one of the book-keepers, who "had had a spite against him"' (p. 74), remains undefined. Lewis claims that had he not visited Jamaica in person, he would have lacked even 'the most distant idea' of the offences conducted in his name, but it could be argued that the *Journal* he pens *in situ* keeps its readers at arm's length anyway. As well as being historically displaced from Cornwall's present to its past, the estate's conflicts are muzzled by a language of evasion and take on, in the end, an air of caricature, as Lewis figures his 'negroes' sonorously 'groaning under the iron rod of [a] petty tyrant' (p. 75).

The histories of Jamaican sugar plantations other than Cornwall provide additional temporal zones into which Lewis 'draw[s] off' the material realities of racial violence from the ostensible purity of his own present. At times, the agents of such historically decanted violence are white, as, for example, in the narrative, located 'some thirty years ago', which Lewis briefly weaves around the unappealingly named Bedward, owner of 'an estate in [Lewis's] neighbourhood, called Spring-Garden' (p. 203) and reputed to be 'the cruellest proprietor that ever disgraced Jamaica' (pp. 203–204). On other occasions, though, the perpetrators are black, and responsible for violent outbursts represented far more explicitly than in the case of the unauthorized overseer considered above. This is clearly illustrated in Lewis's journal entry for 21 February 1816, which looks back some 'five years' to the assassination of 'a Mr Dunbar' by a group of slaves led by Dunbar's 'head driver' (p. 112). By way of aftermath to this event, the driver cuts off and 'carrie[s] away' one of Dunbar's ears, acting in accordance with 'a negro belief that, as long as the murderer' takes such an organ from his victim, 'he will never be haunted by his spectre'. But while these prophylactic rituals may stave off the master's ghost, they are no match for the master's law: the slaves are 'all executed' and the driver himself decapitated, with his 'head … fixed upon a pole *in terrorem*' (p. 113; italics in original).

If the body of this unruly slave can be so spectacularly 'fixed', the murder he performs is less easily containable, repeating itself in acts of emulation carried out with varying degrees of success. As Lewis reports, even before the driver is executed, he comes to constitute a model for others, including the female slave on a 'property' adjacent to Dunbar's, who assaults her 'overseer' not only with 'the greatest fury' but also with a cry which both echoes and celebrates the driver's original 'crime': '"Come here! come here! Let us Dunbar him!"'. On this occasion, the 'attack' upon the oppressor is not fatal, despite its 'strength and … suddenness' (p. 113), but the outcome is more decisive in the incident with which Lewis abruptly ends his day's account:

[These events] happened about five years ago, when the mountains were in a very rebellious state. Every thing there is at present quiet. But only last year a book-keeper belonging to the next estate to me was found with his skull fractured in one of my own cane-pieces; nor have any enquiries been able to discover the murderer. (p. 113)

Lewis's specification of the time when the initial events he describes took place – 'about five years ago' – is, strictly speaking, unnecessary, since he has already supplied the same detail in the previous paragraph. It is none the less important precisely for this reason, suggesting an anxious reassertion of the very boundaries between past and present whose collapse is threatened by the unsolved killing of the 'book-keeper', occurring 'only last year'. Such defensiveness is similarly evident in the metonymic slide transposing the energies of past rebellion from human to natural agents, slaves to 'mountains', as if Lewis were somehow perversely trying to disavow black violence in the very midst of its acknowledgement. This violence does not quite penetrate the immediacies of Lewis's colonial incumbency: happening 'last year', it is held at one remove from the present in which he writes, just as the 'book-keeper' who suffers it 'belong[s] to the next estate' to Cornwall, rather than to Cornwall itself. While the exact site of the 'book-keeper''s death remains uncertain, the discovery of his dislocated body 'in one of [his] own cane-pieces' is an obvious warning to the Lewis who notes it in the book he himself is keeping, implying a doubling of identities between victim and scribe, as the one literally appears in the place of the other. Lewis himself, of course, was to die not as the result of a 'skull fractured' by an untraceable slave but from yellow fever contracted shortly before the voyage home from his second Jamaican visit in 1818.[9] As might indeed be expected from his idealization of the interracial relationships on his own estate, the only kind of cranial injury he sustains takes the sublimated and semi-comic form of the 'violent headache[s]' repeatedly caused by the protracted revelry of his slaves, who celebrate the extra holidays their master allots them by 'danc[ing] and shout[ing] till two' in the morning (p. 54).

The removal of black violence into the past is complemented by its projection into a time to come, where it is figured as operating not in terms of the fairly parochial interpersonal conflicts already examined, but on a much more ambitious collective scale. Yet no sooner is the possibility of slave revolt opened up in the text than it is closed down, doubly neutralized by being cast into a future which does not take place:

a plan has just been discovered in the adjoining parish of St Elizabeth's, for [the slaves to give] themselves a grand fête by murdering all the whites in the island. The focus of this meditated insurrection was on Martin's Penn, the property of Lord Balcarras, where the overseer is an old man of the mildest character, and the negroes had always been treated with peculiar indulgence. Above a thousand persons were engaged in the plot, three hundred of whom had been regularly sworn to assist in it with all the usual accompanying ceremonies of drinking human blood, eating earth from graves, etc. Luckily, the plot was discovered time enough to prevent any mischief; and yesterday the ringleaders were to be tried at Black River. (p. 137)

It is no coincidence that the 'focus of this meditated insurrection' should be the 'property of Lord Balcarras', given Balcarras's controversial role, as a former Governor of Jamaica, in suppressing the Maroon rebellion of 1795.[10] But while this detail implies that the mass murder envisaged here has as much to do with the righting of past wrongs as with contemporary discontents, the 'ringleaders' of the 'insurrection' – the so-called 'King of the Eboes' and his 'two Captains' (p. 139) – are unable to prosecute their aims. As it later emerges, their 'plan' is drawn up with the mysterious help of 'a *black* ascertained to have stolen over into the island from St Domingo' (p. 139; italics in original), but they can muster no home-grown complement to the epic rebellion which began on that French colony in 1791 and culminated in its rebirth as the independent black republic of Haiti in 1804.[11] They are instead condemned to a revolutionary drama which can only be scripted but not staged and yet towards which Lewis is noticeably defensive, sweeping the ceremonies of allegiance the conspiring slaves perform into the expedient void of his 'etc.' and reducing 'complete massacre' (p. 139) to the infantile bathos of 'mischief'. The failure of the slaves' 'plot' to grow into anything much more beyond itself than the solitary rebel anthem chanted by the 'Eboe King' (p. 139) is not surprising, though, since it would appear to have been ill-omened from the first. This at least is one way of construing the fact that 'the whole conspiracy' is instigated by a group of 'supposed mourners' meeting under the cover of a 'child's funeral', an 'occasion' (p. 138) when the future could hardly be more like a dead end.

Throughout the *Journal*, Lewis cultivates the impression that racial violence is either a thing of the past or part of an unrealizable future, but in any case altogether alien to the present state of affairs on his own plantation, where all appears largely convivial, harmonious and halcyon. The temporal demarcations he establishes are matched by geographical ones, as the violence informing his own contemporary moment is channelled into territories other than Cornwall itself. On a 'considerable estate in the parish of Clarendon', for example, a slave is 'shot … through the head' by his master for stealing 'a small quantity' (p. 211) of coffee, while, on another unspecified plantation, a fifteen-year-old 'female slave' (p. 246) poisons her owner by 'infus[ing] corrosive sublimate in some brandy and water' (pp. 110–11). But the most notable of the convenient alternative terrains at Lewis's disposal is Hordley, his other colonial property, briefly visited during his second Jamaican residency, where 'whites' and 'blacks' (p. 228) are united only by the enmity between them.

Lewis first alludes to this 'other estate' (p. 100) in the journal entry for 5 February 1816, in which he articulates an 'extreme anxiety' that it, like Cornwall, become a place whose slaves are managed outside the aegis of the 'cart-whip'. Although 'assured' by his 'agent' that the whip is seldom wielded on Hordley and 'then only very slightly' and that it is soon not to be 'employed at all' (p. 101), what Lewis in fact discovers on his final advent at the plantation is a situation thoroughly at odds with the expectations such reports have produced in him. Far from being the 'perfect paradise' he anticipates, Hordley turns out to be a 'perfect hell' (p. 228), regulated by a mutual racial hatred poised to resolve itself in an apocalypse of dismemberment, as 'black devils and white' threaten 'to tear one another to pieces' (p. 229). Such a radical difference from the genial etiquettes to which Lewis is accustomed is given curious symbolic expression in terms of geographical location, with the apparent Arcadia which is Cornwall situated in north-west Jamaica, and the countervailing dystopia which is Hordley positioned towards the island's south-eastern coast. The additional and equally curious significance of the estate's location at Jamaica's 'very furthest extremity' (p. 225) is that it parallels the somewhat belated point in the text at which Lewis introduces his account of it, commencing the narrative only as the *Journal* is reaching its own closing margin and confining his remarks to a single entry. This latter detail suggests an attempt to subject the estate's infernal tensions to a kind of textual quarantine, just as the entry's own formal peculiarity – it consists of one breathlessly unbroken paragraph spread over some twelve pages – appears to re-enact the desire for flight which Lewis's initial encounter with Hordley strikes into him, as the pandemonium he finds there 'nearly turn[s]' his 'brain' and makes him feel 'strongly tempted to set off as fast as [he] c[an]' (p. 229) for home.

The 'system of oppression' operative on Hordley as Lewis arrives there clearly defines the plantation as Cornwall's other, its unspoken underside, corrective double or perhaps even its unconscious. By the time of his departure one week later, however, the two estates have assumed a miraculous resemblance to one another, as Lewis intervenes, like a colonial *deus ex machina*, to put things right on Hordley by 'establish[ing] the regulations already adopted with success on Cornwall' (p. 228), even as he recognizes that such order may only be temporary. But if Hordley is in the end made over in the image of Cornwall's seemingly tranquil present, it is also figured textually with an evasiveness reminiscent of the way in which Lewis describes Cornwall's past in the interregnum immediately following his father's death. Even as Lewis emphasizes the extent to which racial violence is endemic to Hordley's culture, he paradoxically renders it in a language which is more one of suggestion than of statement and works to convey but at the same time obscure the 'odious truths' (p. 229) his 'short stay' (p. 231) discloses to him: slaves are 'maltreated … with absolute impunity' and 'atrocious brutality' (p. 229), yet the particulars of the violence they suffer remain tantalizingly secret. They no more break the surface of the text in this part of Lewis's *Journal* than they do in the section devoted to Cornwall's history.

Remnants and Revenants

Yet there is a striking coda to the sequence on Hordley, which provides a fleeting but visceral insight into what it is that Lewis leaves unsaid about the exact conduct of slavery on his second estate, while at the same time seriously marring the carefully confected image of his first as the apogee of racial concord. This coda takes the form of the late journal entry for 9 April 1818, in which Lewis challenges a cool dismissal of racial violence by mustering some powerful counter-evidence as to its reality. His disputant on the subject is the enigmatic 'Mr Shand' (p. 241), who initially appears at the very beginning of the *Journal* as one of Lewis's travelling companions on the first voyage to Jamaica. In response to this complacent 'planter in the "May-Day Mountains"' (p. 6), in whose 'long experience nothing of the kind has ever fallen under [his] observation' (p. 241), Lewis comments:

> Mr S. then ought to consider *me* as having been in high luck. I have not passed six months in Jamaica, and I have already found on one of my estates [Hordley] a woman who had been kicked in the womb by a white book-keeper, by which she was crippled herself, and on another of my estates [Cornwall] another woman who had been kicked in the womb by another white book-keeper, by which he had crippled the child … and thus, as my two estates are at the two extremities of the island, I am entitled to say, from my own knowledge (*i.e.* speaking *literally*, observe), that 'white book-keepers kick black women in the belly *from one end of Jamaica to the other*'. (p. 241; italics in original)

In this moment of ubiquitous uterine monstrosity, the two estates book-ending Lewis's 'island' become almost identical to one another. All that distinguishes them is the ironic twist defining the violence on Cornwall, supposedly the more decorous of the two plantations, as even 'grosser' than that described on Hordley, as the second of the 'book-keeper[s]' outdoes his womb-kicking twin by assaulting a black woman during pregnancy and 'crippl[ing]' her 'child'.

This is not the only juncture in the *Journal* when Lewis's sugar-coated depiction of slavery on Cornwall comes to be tainted by stubborn traces of violence between white and black. Although it is undoubtedly the most hard-hitting example of such violence, the harm the book-keeper visits upon the slave-mother and her child takes its place alongside three earlier interrelated instances of white aggression, the first of which is to be found in the journal entry for 13 January 1816. Here Lewis records an encounter with an African slave hospitalized as a result of 'having fallen into epileptic fits, with which till then he had never been troubled'. Puzzling over the possible origins of the slave's sudden malady, Lewis writes:

> For my own part, the symptoms of his complaint were such as to make me suspect him of having tasted something poisonous, especially as, just

before his first fit, he had been observed in the small grove of mangoes near the house; but I was assured by the negroes, one and all, that nothing could possibly have induced him to eat an herb or fruit from that grove, as it had been used as a burying-ground for 'the white people'. But although my idea of the poison was scouted, still the mention of the burying-ground suggested another cause for his illness to the negroes, and they had no sort of doubt, that in passing through the burying-ground he had been struck down by the duppy [spirit] of a white person not long deceased, whom he had formerly offended, and that these repeated fainting fits were the consequence of that ghostly blow. (p. 64)

In this passage, the 'symptoms' of the slave's 'complaint' become embroiled in a conflict of interpretations – natural versus supernatural – which is never definitively resolved, remaining precisely suspended in a 'sort of doubt'. In one sense, though, the difference between white and black readings is irrelevant, since both have similar consequences for the status of the racial violence featured here. If Lewis is correct in his prosaic suspicion that the slave's seizures are simply the result of 'having tasted something poisonous', such violence is rendered non-existent, thus absolving the master from any 'part' in the convulsive spectacle of black pain. Equally, however, if the 'negroes, one and all' are right in diagnosing the slave's 'fainting fits' as caused by the 'ghostly blow' delivered by a 'duppy', the slave's fall into suffering can be attributed to the machinations of another world. The suffering itself is material enough, even as it is brought about by a 'spiritually terrific' (p. 64) agent whose true provenance lies elsewhere.

Whether deemed real or not, the white ghost who so antagonizes Lewis's fitting slave would at first glance seem a far cry from Lewis himself. On the other hand, though, there are hints that the relationship between Lewis and the belligerent duppy may have less to do with opposition and antithesis than with doubling and duplication. Throughout the journal entry in which the duppy appears, Lewis shows himself to be much preoccupied with the deaths of others, framing his narrative of bitter revenancy with observations on the high mortality rate of 'negro children' (p. 62), the 'strange and fantastical ceremonies' (p. 63) of black funerals and African beliefs about the afterlife. As the entry concludes, however, Lewis shifts the focus to more intimate reflections on his own demise, offering a short tour of the estate's 'family mausoleum' (p. 66), imagined as a possible location for his final repose. If this edifice constitutes another site for the interment of '"white people"', it is one which possesses some distinct similarities to the superannuated cemetery to which Lewis earlier refers. The first of these is that, like the 'burying-ground' concealed beneath the 'grove of mangoes', Lewis's 'building' is also hidden away. It is sequestered 'in the very heart of an orange grove', whose vital and abundant charms – it is 'in full bearing' – themselves perform a screening function, politely disguising 'all vestiges' of the 'dissolution' (p. 66) death involves, while simultaneously carrying the disturbing sexual resonance noted earlier. The second similarity is that both cemetery and 'mausoleum' are places where the supremacist hierarchies by which slavery legitimates itself are put on display: in the one, a black slave is reportedly laid low by a white ghost, while, in the other, 'a tomb of the purest white marble [is] raised on a platform of ebony' (p. 66). Even to the *Journal*'s very last entry of 2 May 1818, Lewis insists upon a 'real good-will' (p. 251) towards his slaves, and there is textual evidence aplenty to support this claim. His sepulchral musings tell a different tale, however, suggesting an oblique identification with the white spectre who persecutes the epileptic slave, as if the master's benevolence were merely the mask worn by his tyranny.

The second vignette of white violence is structurally akin to the first, combining a certain ambiguity of representation with the ejection from Lewis's estate of a supposed agent of violence, while at the same time entailing a further element of doubling. Tucked away in the journal entry for 30 January 1816, this incident revolves around yet another of the text's faceless 'book-keepers'. The 'man in question' is 'accused of having occasionally struck a negro, of using bad language to them [*sic*], and of being … hasty [and] passionate' (p. 96), but responds with counter-claims of his own:

> The book-keeper had denied positively the charge of striking the negroes, and ascribed it to the revenge of the Eboe Edward, whom he had detected in cutting out part of a boiling-house window, in order that he might pass out stolen sugar unperceived; for, to do the negroes justice, it is a doubt whether they are the greatest [*sic*] thieves or liars, and the quantity of sugar which they purloin during the crop, and dispose of at the Bay for a mere trifle, is enormous. However, whether the charge of striking were true or not, it was sufficiently proved that this book-keeper was a passionate man, and he said himself, 'that the negroes had conceived a spite against him', which alone were reasons enough for removing him. (p. 97)

Here the spectral attack from the previous passage takes on fleshly form, even as its precise ontological status remains just as indeterminate. But the question of whether the 'charge of striking the negroes' is 'true or not' is broached by the text only to be side-stepped, as the book-keeper is anyway cashiered from Lewis's estate on the more nebulous grounds of being merely 'passionate'. At the same time, his expulsion places him in a similar situation to that occupied by the duppy, whose persecutory actions allegedly occur within the sublunary realms of Lewis's plantation, but which itself belongs to another order.

While this passage witnesses the book-keeper's removal from Cornwall to 'another situation' (p. 97), it is also marked by a different sort of absence, making no mention of the second of the three charges at issue here – that the book-keeper uses 'bad language' towards Lewis's slaves. This is a significant omission, not least because such a claim could just as well be levelled at Lewis himself, whose 'language' is 'bad' not only in terms of its apposition between 'them' and 'negro' and the misuse of a superlative ('greatest') instead of a comparative ('greater') when calibrating the slaves' moral failings. As Lewis notes, he dispatches the book-keeper in order both 'to make an example of him' to the 'rest' of Cornwall's staff and to underscore his intolerance of any 'white person on the estate who maltreat[s] the negroes, either by word or deed' (p. 96). Yet as the text demonstrates, Lewis blindly engages in his own stereotypical abuse of the 'negroes', administering a dubious 'justice' as he savours the aporia of whether they are better at theft or lying, while simultaneously upbraiding the lack of economic acumen which causes them to 'dispose' of the sugar they 'purloin' for 'a mere trifle'. It is thus perhaps appropriate that the book-keeper should be rewarded with 'a double salary' on his eventual 'going away', because the verbal if not physical injuries he inflicts make him an ironic double for the master who 'dismisse[s]' (p. 97) him.

Lewis's dismissal of the book-keeper is in theory a sign of resourceful management, since it is intended to ensure that, even in the moment of sacking, he remain 'serviceable to the estate' (p. 96) by becoming an admonitory figure. But the terms of the book-keeper's release are so lenient – as well as receiving his 'double salary', he 'stay[s] out his quarter' (p. 97) on the plantation – that it is not surprising when his story fails to have the desired effect and transgressions similar to those he himself is said to have committed continue to occur. These are reported in the journal entry for 26 February 1816, which provides the last of the three occasions when Lewis overtly dramatizes white violence on his estate, prior, that is, to the atrocious revelations about the womb-wounding book-keeper in his text's final pages:

> this evening another [book-keeper] had a dispute in the boiling-house with an African named Frank, because a pool of water was not removed fast enough; upon which he called him a rascal, sluiced him with the dirty water, and finally knocked him down with the broom. The African came to me instantly; four eye-witnesses, who were examined separately, proved the truth of his ill-usage; and I immediately discharged the book-keeper. (pp. 120–21)

The 'ghostly blow' originally struck by the duppy materializes for a second time here, though, in this instance, it is dispensed in a 'boiling-house' rather than in a former 'burying-ground'.[12] But in contrast to both the duppy's assault and that allegedly performed by the previous 'book-keeper', there can be no 'dispute' at all about the 'truth' of the 'ill-usage' suffered in this particular snapshot of white violence, confirmed as it is by the independent testimonies of 'four eye-witnesses'. As Lewis notes, the slaves go on to celebrate their unequivocal 'triumph over the offending book-keeper' with 'songs and rejoicings' which keep their master 'awake the greatest part of the night' (p. 121). In so doing, they perhaps enjoy a victory all the sweeter for the ironic reversal of power on which it turns: the book-keeper 'knock[s] ... down' the slave because of his inability to clean up 'a pool of water ... fast enough', only to be himself removed from Lewis's plantation with all due expedition when he is 'immediately discharged'.

As this series of examples suggests, when white violence manifests itself within Cornwall's immediate bounds, it tends to do so in fugitive and evanescent forms which are sometimes quite equivocal, and is consistently denied anything approaching an expansive narrative presence. But the appearance of black violence on Lewis's plantation is still more markedly attenuated and, even in its most dramatic expressions, firmly contained. The process of containment is discernible with particular clarity in relation to the most disaffected slave on the estate, the 'negro ... called Adam' (p. 86), whose story is briefly introduced in the journal entry for 25 January 1816 and then amplified some two years later, in a four-page entry for 25 February 1818 exclusively given over to him. As Lewis genteelly understates it elsewhere, Adam is 'a most dangerous fellow' (p. 92), plotting revenge against 'a book-keeper whose conduct had been obnoxious' (p. 86) and 'attempt[ing] to poison [Lewis's] former attorney' (p. 91) when he is 'displaced by [him] from being principal governor' (p. 220). In the end, however, these intrigues come to nothing and turn out, indeed, to pose a threat less to their designated white targets than to the two slaves, Edward and Bessie, who respectively resist and betray Adam's schemes, and who are duly punished by means of his recourse to the arts of obeah: Edward's closest friend is gradually tricked into rejecting him, while Bessie becomes rather more seriously 'cursed' with leprosy and is left to watch 'her poor pickaninies ... all die[ ] away, one after another' (p. 91). But the canalizing of Adam's rebellious energies away from his white oppressors and towards his black peers opens out beyond these individual conflicts into a generalized 'warfare' with his 'companions' (p. 92), whose weapons include not only the 'supernatural powers' (p. 222) concentrated in obeah, but also the 'great bodily strength' (p. 224) Lewis ascribes to him. By the time of Lewis's return to Jamaica, Adam has had 'No less than three charges of assault, with intent to kill ... preferred against him'. He has 'endeavoured to strangle' one fellow-slave 'with the thong of a whip', 'thrown [another] into the river to drown' (p. 220) and, most shockingly of all, attacked 'a poor weak creature called Old Rachael', against whom, quite capriciously, it seems, he has 'taken offence': 'on meeting her by accident he struck her to the ground, beat her with a supple-jack, stamped upon her belly, and begged her to be assured of his intention (as he eloquently worded it) "to kick her guts out"' (p. 221).

The wanton corporeal power articulated here links its agent to the intimidating book-keepers who 'kick black women in the belly *from one end of Jamaica to the other'* and in so doing highlights just how badly misaligned Adam has become as would-be colonial rebel. But whether the threat Adam represents derives from supernatural or physical sources, the containment with which it is met is finally twofold. Even as his actual rather than potential victims are black rather than white, Adam's narrative ends, just for good measure, with transportation, 'probably … to Cuba', and it is on this exilic note that he is simultaneously written out of the text. The only wound he is able to inflict upon his white masters (and Lewis in particular) is financial: in compensation for the loss of Adam's labour, Lewis receives a mere 'one hundred pounds currency', which, as he calculates, 'is scarcely a third of his worth' (p. 224).

The problems Lewis faces throughout his *Journal* are, in the end, though, less to do with the economy of his plantation than with the economy of his text, whose accounts never quite tally. Although it may be easy enough for him to cast a menacing slave or an ill-disciplined book-keeper beyond Cornwall's idyllic thresholds, the task of eliminating the marks of sexual and racial violence from his portrayal of the estate itself proves to be rather more difficult. Such formal limitations are not surprising, given the analogy between the production of sugar and the production of the *Journal* with which this chapter began, and result in what might be called a muscovado textuality, whose main characteristic is the tension between refinement and residue. They also bring to the fore the irony of Lewis's antipathy towards those who try to sweeten the sour truth of slavery with false reports, either about Cornwall's past or about Hordley's present, since it is in the work of these unreliable narrators that the reflections of his own textual practice can be glimpsed.

Like *The Sugar-Cane*, Lewis's *Journal* strives for (without ever quite obtaining) a condition of purity which is the discursive and ideological equivalent of the telos towards which sugar itself aspires, as it travels from the colonial cane-field to the metropolitan spaces of its consumption. Such parallels between text and sugar, literary and material forms of production, are also to be found in George Eliot's 'Brother Jacob', a novella published some thirty years after the appearance of Lewis's work, even as, in this text, they are articulated in a different way.

Notes

1. Byron's epigrammatic lament for Lewis originally appears in the course of his 'Detached Thoughts' (1821–22), just after the description of the deceased as one whose paternal and colonial legacy proves to be the death of him: 'Poor fellow – he died a martyr to his new riches – of a second visit to Jamaica'. See Lord George Gordon Byron, *Byron's Letters and Journals*, ed. Leslie A. Marchand, 13 vols (London: John Murray, 1973–94), vol. 9 (1979), p. 18. The image of Lewis as sugar's eventual victim stands in sharp contrast to the playfully regressive (and perhaps even playfully vampiric) terms in which Byron couches the news of Lewis's first Jamaican voyage in a letter of 4 November 1815 to Thomas Moore: 'Lewis is going to Jamaica to suck his sugar-canes' (Byron, vol. 4 [1975], p. 330).

2. Sandiford, p. 152. Lewis's relegation of sugar to the margins of his text is paralleled by the way in which – with the exception of Sandiford himself – even the most perspicacious critics of the *Journal* have given the topic short shrift. See, for example, Elizabeth A. Bohls, 'The Planter Picturesque: Matthew Lewis's *Journal of a West India Proprietor*', *European Romantic Review*, 13 (2002), 63–76; Maureen Harkin, 'Matthew Lewis's *Journal of a West India Proprietor*: Surveillance and Space on the Plantation', *Nineteenth-Century Contexts*, 24 (2002), 139–50; and Maja-Lisa von Sneidern, '"Monk" Lewis's Journals and the Discipline of Discourse', *Nineteenth-Century Contexts*, 23 (2001), 59–88.

3. Matthew Lewis, *Journal of a West India Proprietor, Kept during a Residence in the Island of Jamaica*, ed. Judith Terry (Oxford and New York: Oxford University Press, 1999), p. 57 (italics in original). Subsequent references to this work are incorporated in the text and given in parenthesis after quotations.

4. Excellent analyses of the various interlocking factors contributing to emancipation are provided in Blackburn, pp. 322–26 and 419–72, and Hochschild, pp. 309–32. As both commentators point out, the growing threat to the slave-owner's position on moral and economic grounds is compounded by the rhythm of unrest marking colonial relations in the British Caribbean during this period, as manifested in major slave rebellions in Barbados in 1816, Demerara in 1823 and Jamaica in 1831–32.

5. Macaulay's phrase appears in a speech on parliamentary reform of 2 March 1831 and is cited in Blackburn, p. 448.

6. Like the other verses which sporadically interrupt the flow of Lewis's prose (at least during his first Jamaican visit), 'The Isle of Devils' has been largely ignored by critics of the *Journal*. But for two important departures from this general pattern, see D. L. McDonald, 'The Isle of Devils: The Jamaican Journal of M. G. Lewis', in Fulford and Kitson, pp. 189–205; and Donna Heiland, 'The *Unheimlich* and the Making of Home: Matthew Lewis's *Journal of a West India Proprietor*', in *Monstrous Dreams of Reason: Body, Self, and Other in the Enlightenment*, ed. Mita Choudhury and Laura Rosenthal (Lewisburg, PA: Bucknell University Press, 2002), pp. 170–88.

7. The numerous 'book-keepers' populating Lewis's text are generally as sinister as they are anonymous. For a fascinating insight into their characteristic role within plantation culture, see Michael Craton, *Searching for the Invisible Man: Slaves and Plantation Life in Jamaica* (Cambridge, MA and London: Harvard University Press, 1978), pp. 255–59. Craton's analysis is based on the life and career of Robert Ellis, employed at Worthy Park, Jamaica, as book-keeper (and briefly later overseer) for some six years split over two periods between 1787 and 1795. It combines archival materials with imaginative reconstruction to produce a portrait which is far from flattering: Ellis himself emerges as 'a promiscuous miscegenator', while the 'young white men' (p. 257) of whom he is the rough type are described as being not only 'ignorant of sugar technology, field husbandry, and slave management' (p. 256) but also 'mutinous, lazy, and drunken' (p. 257). As von Sneidern observes, 'Lewis fires bookkeepers with abandon' and 'At even a hint that his slaves are unhappy with their "situation," … immediately scapegoats some nameless white employee' (p. 79). Yet the last letter Lewis was ever to write breaks dramatically with the seemingly impulsive managerial habits of the *Journal*, displaying a touching personal sympathy for the fate of 'a young Book-keeper on Cornwall, named Blackeston', who is 'wasting away hourly' as a result of a recurrent mental illness, 'and must die, unless He leaves The Island'. See Lewis's letter of 4 May 1818 to T. Hill, cited in Louis F. Peck, *A Life of Matthew G. Lewis* (Cambridge, MA: Harvard University Press, 1961), p. 171.

8. It should also be remembered that Lewis's apparently magnanimous recoil from the 'detestable lash' takes place within the context of the other disciplinary techniques at his disposal, the most effective of which, as he later reveals, is 'confinement, solitary or

otherwise'. It is this, to the crude connoisseur of colonial power, which truly 'make[s] a lasting impression' upon the 'minds' of slaves and is to be cherished as 'the best and easiest mode of governing negroes (and governed by some mode or other they must be)'. It far outclasses the 'lash', whose effects are as weakly epidermal as they are ephemeral, producing an impact which is registered 'but upon [the] skins' of the enslaved and 'lasts no longer than the mark' (p. 238). Ironically, the psychic scarring the whip occasions on Lewis himself refutes the argument he is making here – unless, that is, it were somehow to be conceded that there is, in his pseudo-scientific formulation, 'a very great difference between the brain of a black person and [that of] a white one' (p. 243).

9. On the circumstances of Lewis's death, see Peck, pp. 172–74.

10. For a succinct account of this conflict, see Hochschild, pp. 281–85. The controversy surrounding Balcarras arises chiefly from his enlistment of one hundred bloodhounds from neighbouring Cuba, together with their handlers, in order to put down the Maroons. As Hochschild observes, this tactic provoked some unease among the British, even eliciting the disapproval of no less a personage than King George III, who regarded it as 'improper'. What Hochschild does not mention, though, is the irony shadowing the monarch's outrage: the king condemns the use of these 'tremendous animals' on the basis of their 'ungovernable ferocity', even as the ferocity of the colonial power their deployment is designed to uphold remains unchallenged. See Hochschild, p. 283 (unnumbered note).

11. For the classic analysis of this violent epochal struggle, see C. L. R. James, *The Black Jacobins: Toussaint L'Ouverture and the San Domingo Revolution*, intro. James Walvin (1938; London: Penguin, 2001). See also Blackburn, pp. 213–64; and, most recently, Laurent Dubois and John D. Garrigus, *Slave Revolution in the Caribbean, 1789–1804: A Brief History with Documents* (Boston and New York: Bedford/St. Martin's, 2006). Lewis nervously alludes to this bloody revolutionary history elsewhere in the text, as, for example, in the journal entry for 11 February 1816, in which he frets about 'Wilberforce's intentions to set the negroes entirely at freedom', speculating that the direct consequence of such a step for Jamaica 'would be, in all probability, a general massacre of the whites, and a second part of the horrors of St Domingo' (p. 107).

12. These spaces are, generally speaking, less dissimilar to one another than they might appear, since the slaves assigned to the boiling-house could sometimes lose their lives in the course of their daily routines, a possibility most famously dramatized in James Gillray's abolitionist cartoon, 'Barbarities in the West Indies' (1791), with its harrowing image of a slave submerged in a huge copper filled with boiling cane juice. In the case of Lewis's *Journal*, however, it is in fact Cornwall's 'mill-stream' which comes to be associated with the untimely death of slaves, it being in these waters that a four-year-old slave-girl is accidentally 'drowned before any one [is] aware of her danger' (p. 71) – a fate disingenuously attributed, by implication, to a natural rather than colonial order of things. Cornwall's boiling-house remains a place of peril even so, particularly for those slaves exhausted by late hours. As Lewis puts it, in a breathtaking disavowal of black pain: 'Last night a poor man, named Charles … was brought into the hospital, having missed a step in the boiling-house, and plunged his foot into the siphon: fortunately, the fire had not long been kindled, and though the liquor was hot enough to scald him, it was not sufficiently so to do him any material injury' (p. 58).

4

'Sugared Almonds and Pink Lozenges': George Eliot's 'Brother Jacob' as Literary Confection

The consumer of sugar neither knows nor asks where the product he uses comes from; he neither selects it nor tries it out. … The person with a sweet tooth just asks for sugar, without article, pronoun, or adjective to give it a local habitation and a name. When, in the process of refining, sugar has achieved a high degree of saccharose and of chemical purity it is impossible to distinguish one from the other even in the best-equipped laboratory. All sugars are alike.

– Fernando Ortiz, *Cuban Counterpoint*

Victorian Sugar

As Ligon notes, sugar is not indigenous to the Caribbean, but 'brought thither as a stranger, from beyond the Line',[1] and, like every traveller, it has a tale to tell. This is one version of its story:

Sugar has been happily called 'the honey of reeds.' … Our supplies are now obtained from Barbadoes [*sic*], Jamaica, Mauritius, Ceylon, the East and West Indies generally, and the United States; but the largest supplies come from Cuba. Sugar is divided into the following classes: – Refined sugar, white clayed, brown clayed, brown raw, and molasses. The sugarcane grows to the height of six, twelve, or even sometimes twenty feet. It is propagated from cuttings, requires much hoeing and weeding, giving employment to thousands upon thousands of slaves in the slave countries, and attains maturity in twelve or thirteen months. When ripe, it is cut down close to the stole, the stems are divided into lengths of about three feet, which are made up into bundles, and carried to the mill, to be crushed between rollers. In the process of crushing, the juice runs down into a reservoir, from which, after a while, it is drawn through a siphon; that is to say, the clear fluid is taken from the scum. This fluid undergoes several processes of drying and refining; the methods varying in different manufactories. There are some large establishments engaged in sugar-refining in the neighbourhoods of Blackwall and Bethnal Green, London. The process is mostly in the hands of German workmen. Sugar is adulterated with fine sand and sawdust. Pure sugar is highly nutritious, adding to the fatty tissue of the body; but it is not easy of digestion.

Despite their echoes of the passage from Lewis with which the previous chapter began, these words are not to be found in a plantation journal, but in Isabella Beeton's *The Book of Household Management* (1861), the most famous and comprehensive guide to domestic economy of the Victorian period.[2] Presented to the reader's eye in a diminutive font, and crammed between instructions on how to ice and glaze pastry and a recipe for baked raisin pudding, Beeton's comments might seem as incongruous as the illustration set alongside them, which features a semi-naked male slave toiling among luxuriant sugar-canes, perhaps a denizen of one of those anachronistic 'slave countries' (America and Cuba) still in existence at the time when Beeton was writing.[3] As Beeton's gargantuan tome repeatedly makes clear, however, the passage is no freakish trespass of the colonial upon the domestic, as each sphere is fully implicated in the other. The mainly slave-grown sugar whose protracted path she so expertly follows, from the moment of its first 'propagat[ion]' to its eventual metropolitan refinement, is, after all, a substance essential to most of the recipes her book serves up for its middle-class readership. Indeed, as Beeton marvels, in a coda to the instructions for the pudding, such has been the rate of increase in the daily 'use of sugar', since its initial introduction to 'the civilized world', that now 'there is no household … which can do without it'.[4]

While Beeton displays a detailed grasp of the technology of sugar production here, she is strikingly vague with regard to the racial oppression in which such production is grounded. With Graingeresque finesse, she glosses slavery not as a system of expropriated labour but as a somewhat genteel form of 'employment' provided to 'thousands upon thousands' of black subjects implicitly content in their activities of 'hoeing and weeding'. In this respect, Beeton's colonial vignette not only describes a purificatory ritual in which 'clear fluid' is separated from 'scum', but also effects a filtration of its own: in a pattern now familiar from previous chapters, the text carefully siphons off those portions of sugar's tale which are 'not easy of digestion'.

As illustrated in chapter 2, the morally indigestible nature of sugar which Beeton evades is directly confronted in the political writings of the abolitionists, with their evocations of the consumer as cannibal, whether in a figurative or more troublingly literal sense. It is also addressed, or readdressed, albeit more obliquely, in fictional works produced at the same time as Beeton's *magnum opus*, the signal instance of which is George Eliot's 'Brother Jacob', a novella originally written in 1860 but not published until four years later. In this curious narrative of egotism, imposture and final nemesis, Eliot takes up the unlikely and seemingly trivial topic of confectionery and subjects it to the sort of scrutiny it might elicit from Fox or Burn, debunking the apparently innocent pleasures to be gleaned from the consumption of 'candied sugars, conserves, and pastry'.[5] But 'Brother Jacob' is not just a tardy addendum to the anti-saccharite stance adopted by the abolitionists, despite its mid-Victorian moment and 1820s' setting.[6] As well as recalling abolitionist politics, Eliot's text turns its satirical eye in two further directions, critiquing both the pursuit of profit in the sugar islands themselves and the quest for erotic self-gratification which invariably accompanies it (and about which Lewis is so notably tongue-tied). As it elaborates this critique, 'Brother Jacob' simultaneously enters into dialogue with a series of other works, each differently concerned with the questions of colonialism, race and desire preoccupying Eliot herself and ranging from the early modern period to her own contemporary era. In the course of this dialogue, it becomes evident that, far from being the 'trifle' its author dismissed it as,[7] 'Brother Jacob' constitutes a sophisticated and important exploration of (and addition to) an already extensive colonial archive.[8]

To focus on 'Brother Jacob''s intertextual dimensions is only to highlight what is the novella's most distinctive formal feature. Equally, though, it is to depart from those other postcolonial analyses of the text which have emerged since the early 1990s. Although such analyses are attuned to the highly charged links between sugar and slavery this chapter itself pursues, they remain largely deaf to the kinds of nuanced intertextual exchanges in which Eliot's tale participates.[9] In this respect, they necessarily also miss the oddly performative or self-reflexive aspect of Eliot's story. For if 'Brother Jacob' is a narrative about the art of confection, defined by the *Oxford English Dictionary* as a 'Making or preparation by mixture of ingredients' and a 'compounding', it is at the same time a complex literary enactment of such a process, forged out of the eclectic materials on which it draws.

Entering 'The Sugar Department': From Confectionery to Colony

As his surname suggests, the life of David Faux, 'Brother Jacob''s central protagonist, is bound up with notions of fakery, artifice and insincerity, unfolding, indeed, as a series of false steps (the literal translation of the French 'faux pas'). The first of these occurs in Faux's 'early boyhood' when, 'on a single day', his 'tender imagination' is 'fired' by the alluring 'confectioners' shops' he frequents during a 'visit' to his butler-uncle in the 'brilliant town' of Brigford. Here an implicitly feminized sugar works a seduction at once aesthetic, oral and social,[10] persuading the bedazzled child 'that a confectioner must be at once the happiest and the foremost of men, since the things he made were not only the most beautiful to behold, but the very best eating, and such as the Lord

Mayor must always order largely for his private recreation'. The enduring force of this scene of instruction is such that Eliot's sugar-struck youth duly finds himself 'wedded ... irrevocably to confectionery' as his 'trade', resolving on such a course 'without a moment's hesitation' (p. 49) – as if the confectionery had shaped the confectioner, rather than the other way round. Yet no sooner is this metaphorical marriage underway than it begins to sour. As 'Brother Jacob' opens, the reader meets a Faux left only with the belated recognition that his sweet spouse was never really what she seemed and could never really have made good her early promises:

> Among the many fatalities attending the bloom of young desire, that of blindly taking to the confectionery line has not, perhaps, been sufficiently considered. How is the son of a British yeoman, who has been fed princi- pally on salt pork and yeast dumplings, to know that there is satiety for the human stomach even in a paradise of glass jars full of sugared almonds and pink lozenges, and that the tedium of life can reach a pitch where plum- buns at discretion cease to offer the slightest enticement? Or how, at the tender age when a confectioner seems to him a very prince whom all the world must envy, – who breakfasts on macaroons, dines on marengs, sups on twelfth-cake, and fills up the intermediate hours with sugar-candy or peppermint, – how is he to foresee the day of sad wisdom, when he will discern that the confectioner's calling is not socially influential, or favour- able to a soaring ambition? (p. 49)

Faux's dilemma is the precise mirror-image to that elaborated for the Latimer of Eliot's 'The Lifted Veil' (1859), the text to which 'Brother Jacob' is often critically linked. In Latimer's case, the problem is a prescience so terminal as to enable him even to anticipate the exact moment of his own death. Faux, on the other hand, suffers from a lack of clairvoyance. '[B]lindly taking to the confectionery line', he is unprepared for the moment of dialectical reversal when desire passes into its opposite to become disgust and what is an implic- itly exoticized 'paradise ... of sugared almonds and pink lozenges' turns into a place of exile and expulsion, no longer welcoming to the stodgy 'son of a British yeoman'.

As already suggested, one of the ironies attending Faux's sickening fall from the sugary 'paradise' of his youth is that it is precipitated by a quasi-Satanic yearning for social elevation, the 'soaring ambition' of a 'soul swell[ing] with an impatient sense that [its owner] ought to become something very remarkable'. A second irony is that even as Faux aspires above the confectioner's 'narrow lot' in search of a 'position ... in the highest degree easy to the flesh', he does not, strictly speaking, transcend the limits of what Eliot's narrator calls 'the sugar department'. Rather, he locates himself elsewhere within it, moving from centre to periphery. As if to underscore his unappealing nature and general 'want of knowledge' (p. 50), Faux at first selects America, 'a country where the population was chiefly black', as a convenient site in which to exploit the 'broad and easily recognizable merit of [his] whiteness' (p. 51), before settling upon the West Indies as the alternative guarantor of personal prosperity and status. In thus turning to 'the "Indies"' – a place where the chances of '*not* making a large fortune' are said to be 'improbable' (p. 52; italics in original) – Faux traces a path from the domestic to the colonial, fetishized commodity to raw material, consumption to production, which is beset with ironies of its own. On the one hand, Faux's projected colonial venture suggests a future which is as much a repetition of the past as a break with it, since the sugar-based West Indian wealth he covets is merely a much grander version of the confectioner's income he is already earning. At the same time, the departure from domestic to colonial spaces paradoxically serves only to underline the connections between them. In particular, it casts a new and disconcerting light on that delicious 'paradise of glass jars' with which 'Brother Jacob' first tempts its reader. Despite the 'pleasing illusion' (p. 49) they generate, such 'jars' contain a world far from heavenly when considered from the viewpoint of the slaves upon whose infernal labours their contents depend. In this sense, it is evident that the confectioner's profession in which Faux excels, but which he simultaneously wishes to cast aside, is well named, entailing mixings not just culinary in nature. The sweetmeats he makes, from 'drop-cakes' to 'gingerbread-nuts' (p. 50), 'jujubes' to 'barley-sugar' (p. 53), are, in other words, oxymoronic or hybrid creations, bearing slavery's bitter trace within themselves.

Thus considered as an art of the composite and the amalgam, confectionery functions as a trope for the very yoking of domestic gratification and colonial oppression, white pleasure and black pain which it brings about. The confectioner's art can also be thought of as a figure for the intertextual practice sustaining the narrative in which it features, as Eliot composes, or confects, 'Brother Jacob' out of a variety of other sources, gravitating, in particular, towards works sharing her own colonial and racial emphases. The first of these emerges in the moment when the narrator muses on possible alternative vocations for the protagonist, were he not already launched upon the simultaneously divergent but intersecting paths of confectioner and colonizer:

> If he had fallen on the present times, and enjoyed the advantages of a Mechanics' Institute, he would certainly have taken to literature and have written reviews; but his education had not been liberal. He had read some novels from the adjoining circulating library, and had even bought the story of 'Inkle and Yarico', which had made him feel very sorry for poor Mr Inkle; so that his ideas might not have been below a certain mark of the literary calling; but his spelling and diction were too unconventional. (p. 50)

The 'story of "Inkle and Yarico"' is the first of 'Brother Jacob's colonial intertexts. Initially popularized by Richard Steele in *The Spectator* for 13 March

1711, 'Inkle and Yarico' is a narrative of colonial encounter, telling the tale of a twenty-year-old English merchant, committed, like Faux, to 'improv[ing] his fortune by trade'[11] in the West Indies, and a young Native American woman, whom he meets in the perilous course of his voyages. Like the scene of sugary first contact with which 'Brother Jacob' opens, the story is marked by an abrupt shift from desire to aversion. Rescued by Yarico when he and his shipmates are ambushed by 'a party of *Indians*' during an unscheduled 'search for provisions' in America, Inkle is initially smitten with his 'naked *American*'. He is 'highly charmed' by her 'limbs, features, and wild graces', just as she is 'no less taken with the dress, complexion and shape of an *European*, covered from head to foot',[12] and together the two work to improvise 'a language of their own'[13] which is as much sexual as it is verbal. In the end, though, 'the natural impulses' of Inkle's 'passions' yield to a 'love of gain'.[14] Eventually transported to the West Indies with Yarico by a passing English 'vessel', Inkle callously sells his former lover to a Barbadian slave trader, slyly manipulating her pregnant condition as a pretext on which 'to rise in his demands upon the purchaser'.[15]

This treacherous colonial romance is something 'bought' by the ill-read Faux in more senses than one. As well as purchasing the tale from 'an adjoining circulating library', he buys into it, refracting his own West Indian future through the vision of colonial omnipotence the tale promotes, complete with its effortless accretions of erotic bliss and economic wealth. As Eliot writes:

> Such a striking young man as he would be sure to be well received in the West Indies: in foreign countries there are always openings … It was probable that some Princess Yarico would want him to marry her, and make him presents of very large jewels beforehand; after which, he needn't marry her unless he liked. (p. 57)

In this sense, Faux's identification with Inkle tells only half the story. He could arguably be just as properly identified with Yarico, whom he here imagines as a bountiful 'Princess' and whose credulity he shares. This ironic shift in the doubling between reader and text is made amply clear by the discrepancies between Faux's assumptions about the colonial encounter, derived from a fairly casual 'acquaintance with imaginative literature' (p. 79), and its realities. At the end of 'Brother Jacob''s first chapter, Faux hovers on the tantalizing brink of colonial and sexual adventure: he is 'bound for the Indies' (p. 60), where he will be able to unshackle himself from dependence upon 'the prospective hundred' (p. 52) of 'his father's legacy' and 'where a gullible princess await[s] him' (p. 60). By the beginning of chapter 3, however, such expectations have been crushed. Faux looks forward to 'a brilliant career among "the blacks"', but is dismayed to find that they can in fact offer him 'no princesses' (p. 76), just as he is forced to resume his confectioner's occupation, 'devis[ing] cakes and patties in a kitchen' (p. 77) in Kingston, Jamaica, in order to earn his living.

While Steele is instrumental in giving the tale of 'Inkle and Yarico' its enduring appeal, the version which appeared in *The Spectator* was not the original. This is to be found in Ligon's *A True & Exact History of the Island of Barbadoes*, a text which condenses Yarico's story into something less than two paragraphs. Taken as a whole, however, Ligon's text does not just contain the expeditious prototype for Steele's more extended fiction. It also operates as an important supplement, not least because of the detail and immediacy with which it renders the nature of the labour into which Yarico is thrust. This, of course, is the labour of sugar, evoked by Ligon, at this fledgling stage in the history of British West Indian slavery, as an enterprise fraught with difficulties, frustrations and setbacks. These, it seems, can occur anywhere within the machinery and buildings raised in sugar's name, and at any time. This, for example, is Ligon's portrayal of the unpredictable routines of sugar-mill and boiling-house, evoked in a language as strained and faltering as the processes it describes:

> If any thing in the Rollers, as the Goudges, Sockets, Sweeps, Cogs, or Braytrees, be at fault, the whole work stands still; or in the Boyling-house, if the Frame which holds the Coppers, (and is made of Clinkers, fastned with plaister of *Paris*) if by the violence of the heat from the Furnaces, these Frames crack or break, there is a stop in the work, till that be mended. Or if any of the Coppers have a mischance, and be burnt, a new one must presently be had, or there is a stay in the work. Or if the mouths of the Furnaces, (which are made of a sort of stone, which we have from *England*, and we call it there, high gate stone) if that, by the violence of the fire, be softned, that it moulder away, there must new be provided, and laid in with much art, or it will not be. Or if the bars of Iron, which are in the floor of the Furnace, when they are red hot (as continually they are) the fire-man, throw great shides of wood in the mouths of the Furnaces, hard and carelessly, the weight of those logs, will bend or break those bars, (though strongly made) and there is no repairing them, without the work stand still; for all these depend upon one another, as wheels in a Clock.[16]

Like Steele's distracted trader, finally awakened by his arrival in Barbados to the 'loss of time' and 'money' occasioned by his 'stay with *Yarico*',[17] Ligon emerges here as a particularly fretful witness to the spectacle of sugar's hellish creation, his prose enacting the fear that such a birth simply 'will not be' or, at best, will be grossly overdue, as sentences are repeatedly arrested by a parenthetical 'stop' or 'stay' in the 'work' of his own language. In these anxious interludes, time and money are squandered alike, the 'wheels' in sugar's 'Clock' become jammed and production collapses into a form of inefficient consumption, in which 'the mouths of the Furnaces' are misfed by a careless (or possibly subversive) 'fire-man'.

In whatever version it is recounted, 'the story of "Inkle and Yarico"' opens up one further dimension to the meaning of confectionery as metaphor in

Eliot's text. The culinary processes of mixing and compounding involved in the production of Faux's sweetmeats are not just a figure for the blending of the domestic and the colonial which they betoken or for the kinds of manifold intertextual conversations in which Eliot engages. They also operate as a trope for the very mode of desire 'Inkle and Yarico' explores, in which bloodlines are combined and merged. In Steele, such racial confections are represented with a sentimental irony. The love between Englishman and Native American woman is a 'tender correspondence'[18] and appears to bewitch the tale's narrator, who nostalgically recalls how Yarico 'would sometimes play with [Inkle's] hair, and delight in the opposition of its colour, to that of her fingers'[19] – before, that is, 'the opposition of ... colour' twists into a more sinister sense and the white father condemns his unborn mixed-race progeny to slavery. In Ligon, on the other hand, interracial desire is not only more matter-of-fact but also less certainly mutual, the truth of Yarico's pregnancy being, in a strikingly noncommittal phrase, something of an enigma: 'She chanc'd to be with Child, by a Christian servant',[20] he writes. In Eliot, in a last variation on these patterns, miscegenation is a pure if recurrent fantasy: although Faux claims to have 'become familiar with the most luxuriant and dazzling beauty in the West Indies' (p. 68), the narrator rejects his brag and with it 'that life of Sultanic self-indulgence' (p. 76) to which he lays claim.

Given its economic and sexual failures, Faux's six-year sojourn in Jamaica constitutes the second of his life's false steps, following on from the initial error of succumbing to the lures of the confectionery trade. What exacerbates the situation for Eliot's protagonist is that the process of reaching the scene of his disappointment itself proves to be far from smooth, mainly as a result of the inadvertent meddling of the eponymous Jacob, unceremoniously introduced to the reader as 'a very healthy and well-developed idiot, who consume[s] a dumpling about eight inches in diameter every day' (p. 51). Jacob's unwitting obstruction of his brother's self-seeking schemes is a 'day-mare' (p. 54) taking up well over half of the first chapter of Eliot's text. It is dealt with in a particularly drawn-out sequence, which delays the reader's movement through the narrative much as it retards Faux's progress along the seemingly easy path to colonial and sexual aggrandizement.

Eliot prepares the way for Jacob's intervention by means of some intricate scene-setting. Having tarried at home on the 'ground' of a carefully contrived social engagement, Faux appropriates his mother's 'twenty guineas' one 'Sunday afternoon' when she and other family members are attending church, 'slip[s] them into a small canvas bag' and sets out to 'bury' the money 'in a hole he had already made and covered up under the roots of an old hollow ash', until such time as he can collect his haul without suspicion and take his leave of England. His strategy goes awry, however, when he is surprised by 'the sound of a large body rustling towards him with something like a bellow' (p. 52).

The shock of what turns out to be Jacob's quasi-bovine presence causes Faux to drop his money-bag 'so as to make it untwist and vomit forth the shining guineas', a formulation whose alternating images of implicit perversion and explicit nausea clearly suggest a distaste for Faux's unscrupulousness and the wider purposes it serves. In a bid to divert attention from the stolen coins, Faux offers his brother the 'box of yellow lozenges' (p. 53) he had originally intended as a gift for the woman he is supposedly visiting, Sally Lunn. The pastilles produce a sensational effect upon their recipient, initiating Jacob into a utopian world of tastes not to be found anywhere among a diet of 'dumplings', however prodigious their size:

> with a promptitude equal to the occasion, [Faux] drew out his box of [sweets], lifted the lid, and performed a pantomime with his mouth and fingers, which was meant to imply that he was delighted to see his dear brother Jacob, and seized the opportunity of making him a small present, which he would find particularly agreeable to the taste. Jacob, you understand, was not an intense idiot, but within a certain limited range knew how to choose the good and reject the evil: he took one lozenge, by way of test, and sucked it as if he had been a philosopher; then, in as great an ecstacy at its new and complex savour as Caliban at the taste of Trinculo's wine, chuckled and stroked this suddenly beneficent brother, and held out his hand for more. (p. 53)

Eliot's allusion here is to act 2, scene 2 of Shakespeare's *The Tempest*, though it is not strictly accurate, since Caliban's 'ecstacy' is a condition induced by 'wine' given to him by Stephano, Shakespeare's drunken butler, rather than Trinculo, his jester. The misattribution of actions is certainly noteworthy, but the more important point is that in alluding to *The Tempest*, Eliot carries out a second act of literary confection, invoking a text which enjoys a number of parallels both with 'Inkle and Yarico' and with 'Brother Jacob' itself. *The Tempest*'s points of correspondence with 'Inkle and Yarico' most obviously include a shared early colonial setting, but go beyond this to embrace a mutual concern with miscegenation. This is treated in Shakespeare's text, as in the later tale indeed, according to a mercurial logic of attraction and repulsion, as manifested, for example, in act 1, scene 2. Here, in the space of less than twenty lines, Miranda shifts from being the object of Caliban's violent lust – the unwilling sexual partner through whom he dreams of procreating children in his own image – to being someone whom he loathes and curses with equal violence: 'The red plague rid you', he colourfully exclaims, 'For learning me your language!'[21]

The Tempest's parallels with 'Brother Jacob' have less to do with miscegenation, the mixing of races, than with equivocation, the mixing of meanings. While Jacob has a basic grasp of the difference between 'good' and 'evil', he himself is a figure whose behaviour and general manner seem to confound such straightforward distinctions. At the spot intended for the burial of the maternal nest-egg, Jacob hails Faux with a characteristically semi-articulate "'Hoich, Zavy!'" which is described as 'painfully equivocal' to its guilt-ridden hearer, and brandishes a 'pitchfork' with sufficiently 'equivocal intentions' as to make him 'as well worth flattering and cajoling as if he were Louis Napoleon' (p. 53). If these details contribute to the narrator's assessment of Faux's 'idiot brother' as 'an item of … uncertain and fluctuating … character' (p. 56), they are not arbitrary, but derived from the wine-drinking scene to which Eliot alludes in the passage cited above.

That Eliot's allusion to this scene should be an erroneous one is not altogether inappropriate, since the scene itself is marked by a typically Shakespearean negotiation of questions of mistaken identity and features a Caliban who is arguably a doubly equivocal figure. When Trinculo initially encounters him, Caliban is literally lying low, half-hidden under his gabardine on the ground, seemingly neither 'man' nor 'fish', 'dead' nor 'alive',[22] a 'monster' and 'strange beast' in his own milieu, who would nevertheless, in a suitably ambiguous phrase, 'make a man'[23] in England. When he is subsequently discovered by the intoxicated Stephano, he has been comically joined beneath the cloak by Trinculo, taking shelter from the 'foul bombard'[24] of an oncoming storm, just as Caliban had ironically first fled from Trinculo, thinking him one of Prospero's minions bent on persecution. For Stephano, the two figures fuse into one to form a monstrous hybrid, with 'Four legs and two voices',[25] and it is under this misapprehension that he begins the process of plying Caliban, one part of this illusory double-mouthed creature, with 'celestial liquor'.[26] In so doing, he plans to 'keep him tame'[27] the more easily to transport him back to Europe for marketing as a colonial curio. At the same time, Stephano's action prefigures the resourceful ploys of Eliot's Faux, who uses his 'box of yellow lozenges' as a comparable instrument of control, 'pouring a dozen [sweets] into Jacob's palm' (p. 54) and exploiting their 'new and complex savour' as a means of distracting his brother from the guineas he has pilfered.

As well as linking him to Caliban in a kind of intertextual brotherhood, Jacob's 'equivocal' and 'uncertain … character' is mirrored in the contradictions of the role he plays in Eliot's text. This role is in part that of blocking agent, a 'fraternal demon' (p. 58) and 'ogre' (p. 59) who repeatedly intrudes upon and thwarts Faux's colonial designs. On the other hand, Jacob seems to figure not so much an opposition to the colonial project as a certain complicity with it. In sharp contrast to his brother and his 'lipless mouth' (p. 51), he is associated with a seemingly insatiable orality, driven, above all else, by a desire for sugar. Jacob is indeed sugar's ultimate epicure, melting into a condition of 'thorough abandonment' as he enjoys 'the unprecedented pleasure of having five [of Faux's] lozenges in his mouth at once' (p. 54). Nor, once alive to the regressive raptures to be derived from Faux's confectionery, is he any more willing to leave his brother's side than a 'wasp' would be to vacate a 'sugar-basin' (p. 59).

In these respects, Jacob is less reminiscent of Shakespeare's rebellious curse-mongering Caliban than of the self-indulgent sugar-eater whom the abolitionists critique, though he maintains a crucial difference from the latter figure. For the abolitionists, sugar is seen as human flesh, its consumption a form of anthropophagy. In Eliot, however, the reverse is the case, as, in a frequent metonymic slide, the human takes on the quality of the saccharine and the distinctions between the supplier and his goods begin to erode: Faux is not just 'suddenly beneficent' (or at least apparently so) in Jacob's eyes, but 'sweet-flavoured' (p. 58). Like his own mouth-watering products, he seems good enough to eat:

> Jacob, to whom this once indifferent brother had all at once become a sort of sweet-tasted fetish, stroked David's best coat with his adhesive fingers, and then hugged him with an accompaniment of that mingled chuckling and gurgling by which he was accustomed to express the milder passions. But if he had chosen to bite a small morsel out of his beneficent brother's cheek, David would have been obliged to bear it. (pp. 55–56)

If the flesh in question here is literal – 'a small morsel' bitten from Faux's 'cheek' – it can also be metaphorical. This is suggested by an incident located towards the end of the first chapter, when Jacob finds 'a remnant of sugar-candy in one of his brother's tailpockets' and is consequently compelled, in the narrator's tenaciously anatomical figure, to retain 'his hold on that limb of the garment' (p. 59).

Despite such close attentions, Faux is finally able to escape Jacob's sticky 'grasp' (p. 59), leaving for the West Indies via Liverpool, a city historically steeped in sugar and slavery and the profits to be had from them. In pursuing such a path, Faux follows many others who seek to rectify the injustice of not being 'adequately appreciated or comfortably placed in [their] own country' by turning his 'thoughts … towards foreign climes' (p. 50). His project, in other words, is one of self-reinvention. It is a kind of colonial family romance, at once funded by his 'mother's guineas', designed to make his paternal inheritance seem like a 'trifle' (p. 60), and sustained by fantasies of that elusive black 'princess'. When Faux next appears in the text at the beginning of chapter 2, however, he is not the economically and sexually powerful colonial master of whom he dreams. Rather he is merely what he was before, reluctantly returning to England to take up the confectioner's 'apron' which 'Fate' has 'tied … round him' (p. 77), albeit this time under the ironically 'generous-sounding' (p. 63) alias of Edward Freely.

Alternative Subjections: Colonialism at Home

There is clearly a substantial gap between the 'brilliant future' (p. 57) Faux envisages for himself in Jamaica and the rather less glamorous post he comes to occupy as confectioner in Grimworth, the parish-town to which he returns after the debacle of his colonial detour. Yet the difference between imaginary and actual destinies should not be allowed to obscure their similarities. It could even be argued that the course of Faux's domestic career as Freely offers a kind of parody of the mastery for which he strives abroad. It grants him, that is, both a version of the 'advancing prosperity and importance' (p. 68) his colonial escapades so singularly fail to secure, together with a doubtful sexual charm. In Jamaica, the economic and erotic successes Faux desires are predicated upon the subjection of the black slave, producer of the sugar the colonial system transforms into capital. In the domestic milieu, by contrast, the quest for such things entails the subjection of the middle-class white woman who is sugar's principal consumer.

Faux's return to 'the confectionery line' endows 'Brother Jacob' with a certain degree of narrative déjà vu, as he comes back to his original point of departure. At the same time, however, there is a sense in which such a return involves not only a repetition but also a rewriting of origins. As well as giving himself a new name, Faux in effect re-enacts the scene of his 'early boyhood' with which Eliot's text begins, this time recasting himself not as sugar's ingenuous victim but as its more 'calculating' (p. 66) master. The confectioner's art becomes a means to power, used against others as it had once been used against him. This, for example, is Eliot's description of the 'two windows' in Faux's 'new shop' (p. 62) on the day of its first opening:

> On one side, there were the variegated tints of collared and marbled meats, set off by bright green leaves, the pale brown of glazed pies, the rich tones of sauces and bottled fruits enclosed in their veil of glass – altogether a sight to bring tears into the eyes of a Dutch painter; and on the other, there was a predominance of the more delicate hues of pink, and white, and yellow, and buff, in the abundant lozenges, candies, sweet biscuits and icings, which to the eyes of a bilious person might easily have blended into a faëry landscape in Turner's latest style. What a sight to dawn upon the eyes of Grimworth children! They almost forgot to go to their dinner that day, their appetites being preoccupied with imaginary sugar-plums. (pp. 62–63)

Those 'children' with their 'wide-open eyes and mouths' (p. 63) recall the boyhood Faux, similarly agape at the alluring multiplicity of forms into which sugar can be cast.

'[H]itherto unknown' in dismal Grimworth, such a 'blaze of light and colour' (p. 62) offers a visual feast to its young enthusiasts and even menaces the dietary rituals of family life by displacing the prospect of 'dinner' with 'imaginary sugar-plums'. As in the scene to which Eliot's text here looks back, however, desire is hard to uncouple from aversion, just as the two tend also to be spliced together in the context of miscegenation. This sense of aversion or antipathy is signalled both by the figure of the 'bilious person' who evidently cannot stomach the 'delicate hues' of Faux's confections and by Eliot's painterly allusion to Turner. As Kate Flint has suggested, the invocation of Turner at this juncture is an ironic one, conjuring up not so much any 'faëry landscape' as the 'haunted seascape'[28] depicted in *Slavers Throwing Overboard the Dead and Dying, Typhon Coming On*, Turner's dramatic rendering of the Middle Passage. Ever since its first exhibition at the Royal Academy in 1840, this painting has proved controversial, eliciting a divided critical response, in terms of both aesthetic technique and ideological orientation (is it for or against the slave trade?).[29] Yet however it is read, the painting's submerged presence in 'Brother Jacob' works to remind the reader of the links between the consumption and the production of sugar and how, in particular, the delights of the one and the woes of the other are ineluctably 'blended' together.

Faux is happy to draw 'even the smallest child' into his business, assiduously prising the 'halfpenny [from] its tiny fist' in exchange for the 'just equivalent in "rock"' (p. 63), but his most lucrative customers are Grimworth's middle-class housewives. In directing his commercial attentions to the exploitation of these vulnerable figures, he effects another reversal of his originally passive position as sugar's ingénu, leading the mock-anxious narrator, at the beginning of chapter 2, to liken him to those dangerous 'new-comers' who 'solicit feminine eyes by gown-pieces laid in fan-like folds' (p. 61) and 'fill their windows with mountains of currants and sugar, made seductive by contrast and tickets' (pp. 61–62). This penetration of the domestic market by 'the sallow-complexioned stranger' from 'nobody knew where' (p. 62) parodies the work of the colonizer, as Faux's presence becomes the harbinger and source of a 'gradual corruption of Grimworth manners from their primitive simplicity' (p. 64).

The process of 'corruption' is played out in a variety of ways. These extend beyond Faux's potential subversion of the diets of Grimworth's sugar-hungry 'children' to include his capacity to undermine the traditional patterns of supply and demand, according to which 'the families in Grimworth ... buy their sugar and their flannel at the shops where their fathers and mothers had bought before them' (p. 61). But Faux's corrupting influence is most powerfully felt in the transformations wrought upon Grimworth's middle-class homes and, especially, the practices of the women who run them. Despite the narrator's ironic yuletide conviction that no 'housewife in Grimworth would ... furnish forth her table with articles that were not home-cooked' (p. 63) this is exactly what does happen. '[Y]oung Mrs Steene, the veterinary surgeon's wife', is the first to yield to the 'temptation' (p. 64) of Faux's 'ready-made' (p. 65) 'sweets and pastry' (p. 63). Faced with the task of catering for a 'supper-party' invited by her husband 'for Christmas eve', Mrs Steene graces the festive 'table' (p. 64) with 'a dish of mince-pies from Freely's' (p. 65):

> Mrs Steene sent for the mince-pies, and, I am grieved to add, garbled her household accounts in order to conceal the fact from her husband. This was the second step in a downward course … The third step was to harden herself by telling the fact of the bought mince-pies to her intimate friend Mrs Mole, who had already guessed it, and who subsequently encouraged herself in buying a mould of jelly, instead of exerting her own skill, by the reflection that 'other people' did the same sort of thing. The infection spread; soon there was a party or clique in Grimworth on the side of 'buying at Freely's'; and many husbands, kept for some time in the dark on this point, innocently swallowed at two mouthfuls a tart on which they were paying a profit of a hundred per cent, and as innocently encouraged a fatal disingenuousness in the partners of their bosoms by praising the pastry. … Every housewife who had once 'bought at Freely's' felt a secret joy when she detected a similar perversion in her neighbour's practice, and soon only two or three old-fashioned mistresses of families held out in the protest against the growing demoralization. (p. 65)

As this passage makes plain, Mrs Steene is capable only of cooking the books, 'garbl[ing] her household accounts in order to conceal' her subterfuge. Like the allusions to her own premeditated faux pas – the 'step[s]' in her 'downward course' – this artifice turns the wayward wife into the double of her tempter: she misleads her husband as Faux misleads both her and the community at large by masquerading as Freely.

In succumbing to the convenience of '"buying at Freely's"', the 'misguided' (p. 65) Mrs Steene establishes a precedent rapidly adopted by all but the most conservative of her peers. The emergence of such new patterns of domestic economy is firmly in Faux's favour, as 'money … flow[s] into his pockets' (p. 63) and he makes outrageous 'profit[s] of a hundred per cent' (p. 65). Equally, though, the subjection of 'private families' to the escalating 'work of a special commercial organ' involves an element of female emancipation, as Grimworth's middle-class 'maids and matrons' find 'their hands set free from cookery'. Coming 'to rely on Freely for the greater part of their dinner, when they wished to give an entertainment of some brilliancy', these women are in a position, theoretically at least, 'to add to the wealth of society in some other way' (p. 66). Their liberation is necessarily compromised, however, by its implication in the labours of those whose hands are tied – the West Indian slaves towards whom the text constantly gestures but whom it never openly names.

From this perspective, it is possible to feel the satirical edge to the language of pathology Eliot uses in order to frame the clandestine activities of Mrs Steene and her cohorts. To figure the growing preference for a confectionery 'ready-made' instead of 'home-cooked' as an 'infection', a 'perversion' and a 'demoralization' is a self-consciously ironic gesture, a kind of rhetorical imposture of its own. Whether it be produced professionally or domestically, such confectionery, ranging from 'ratafias and macaroons' (p. 64) to 'cheese-cakes', relies on sugar extracted from the same problematic source. Faux might insinuate 'his way gradually into Grimworth homes', bringing his 'commodities' (p. 66) with him, but the domestic spaces into which his business reaches are themselves already haunted by the spectre of slavery.

The resemblances between Mrs Steene and Faux are not confined to a mutual penchant for imposture but also derive from the manner in which the two figures assimilate colonial literature. In the case of Faux, such literature has a determining effect, dictating his notion of the colonies as a field amenable to the fulfilment of economic and erotic desires. For Mrs Steene, 'rather over-educated for her station in life', colonial texts exert a similar influence. As well as inducing 'a distaste for domestic occupations', they instil in her a 'withering disappointment' with regard to the 'top-booted "vet."' who is her husband. This 'brutal man' (p. 64) falls far short, it seems, of the images of dashing masculinity dominating the Orientalist narrative poems his wife so uncritically reads – Byron's 'The Corsair' (1814) and 'The Siege of Corinth' (1816) and Thomas Moore's 'Lalla Rookh' (1817).

With Faux's second coming as Freely, however, the similarities with Mrs Steene become contrasts. In this incarnation, he is no longer the naive consumer of colonial fictions, but their producer:

> it very soon appeared that he was a remarkable young man, who had been in the West Indies, and had seen many wonders by sea and land, so that he could charm the ears of Grimworth Desdemonas with stories of strange fishes, especially sharks, which he had stabbed in the nick of time by bravely plunging overboard just as the monster was turning on his side to devour the cook's mate; of terrible fevers which he had undergone in a land where the wind blows from all quarters at once; of rounds of toast cut straight from the bread-fruit trees; of toes bitten off by land-crabs; of large honours that had been offered to him as a man who knew what was what, and was therefore particularly needed in a tropical climate; and of a Creole heiress who had wept bitterly at his departure. (p. 67)

Faux's status as colonial raconteur sets him apart from the impressionable Mrs Steene, silently learning 'many passages' from the works of her poetic favourites 'by heart' (p. 64). Yet even as the emergence of such a status creates a difference, it establishes a new parallel, recalling the alteration in Faux's relationship to sugar occurring on his return from the West Indies. In either context – that of colonial story or colonial commodity – Faux's self-refashioning as Freely brings with it, in other words, a shift from passivity to agency: he is the spinner of the colonial yarn rather than its dupe, just as he is sugar's master rather than its prey.

Faux's newfound yarn-spinning capacities entail an intertextual parallel as well as an intratextual one. While he takes up the burden of colonial oracle, telling narratives of 'many wonders' witnessed on 'sea and land', Faux is also, of course, the hero of those narratives, appearing in a range of guises from shark-fighter to the cruel betrayer of a 'Creole heiress' who weeps bitter tears 'at his departure'. Such a doubling of teller and told looks back to the text to which Eliot here explicitly alludes, Shakespeare's *Othello*, and the scene (touched upon in chapter 2 above) when Othello recounts the story of the tales he has told, both to Brabantio and to the woman whom he eventually marries, Brabantio's daughter, Desdemona. Faux's narratives are oral in a double sense. They are spoken rather than written and marked by half-sinister images of bodies eaten alive – the 'monster' poised to 'devour the cook's mate' and 'toes bitten off by land-crabs'. The same is true of Othello's marvellous and frequently death-defying tales, which are communicated by word of mouth, feature 'cannibals that each other eat'[30] and themselves constitute a 'discourse' 'Devour[ed] up' by Desdemona 'with a greedy ear'.[31] Such stories are additionally part of a text which not only concerns itself (like 'Inkle and Yarico' and *The Tempest*) with miscegenation, but also traces out a path from interracial desire to interracial loathing, as Othello's love for Desdemona degenerates into a suffocating and finally murderous jealousy.

Prior to this reversal, however, the telling of the exotic and self-heroizing tales in which Othello indulges is no innocent pastime. It is, rather, a means to an end, and an effective one at that, as he himself recognizes: 'She loved me for the dangers I had passed / And I loved her that she did pity them'.[32] The potential of such tales to elicit female desire is not lost on Faux either, whose starring role in his own implausible colonial dramas works similarly to 'charm the ears' of his female audience and causes 'disengaged hearts [to] flutter a little' (p. 67). One of these 'hearts' belongs to Penny Palfrey, 'second daughter of the Mr Palfrey who farmed his own land' (p. 69). Latter-day Desdemona that she is, this land-owner's daughter is quite swayed by Faux's 'power of anecdote' (p. 70), which acts as a kind of prosthetic device: it imbues him with just the appeal his 'pasty visage' (p. 51) could not otherwise arouse and leads his admirer to compare him favourably with other colonial adventurers. As the narrator comments, with the usual air of weary superiority: 'A man who had been to the Indies, and knew the sea so well, seemed to [Penny] a sort of public character, almost like Robinson Crusoe or Captain Cook' (p. 70).

Faux's evaluation of 'Pretty Penny' (p. 70), on the other hand, is more self-serving than romantic, less driven by 'love' than by 'ambition' (p. 69), a point underscored by the language Eliot uses in order to represent the object of her protagonist's affections. As befits one described by Mr Palfrey as '"that sugar-plum fellow"' (p. 70), Faux sees himself as a 'fastidious connoisseur of the fair sex' (p. 68) and duly regards Penny's 'prettiness', in turn, as 'comparable to the loveliest things in confectionery' (p. 71). This conventional figuration of Penny as sweetheart implies a linkage between women and sugar reflected in 'Brother Jacob''s colour symbolism. Penny's 'yellowish flaxen hair' recalls the yellow lozenges of the novella's opening chapter, just as her own appearance – 'as neat as a pink and white double daisy' (p. 69) – connects her to the enticing 'pink and white jars' (p. 71) in Faux's shop. Yet if Penny's desirability arises from her likeness to Faux's confections, the corollary is that it is not wholly erotic in nature but also economic, since it is out of the sugar from which such confections are made that Faux hopes to gain his fortune, whether in the colonies or at home.

In a doubling of domestic and colonial spaces, Faux would seem finally to have found in Penny a version of the Yarico whose elusive body and dowry of 'large jewels' he expects to be offered in Jamaica, even figuring her docility in terms of racial otherness: 'he judged her to be of submissive temper – likely to wait upon him as well as if she had been a negress'. In the end, however, the 'marriageable' (p. 71) Penny slips through his fingers, just as his colonial Yarico had been a mere figment before her. The reason for this denouement and the concomitant revelation of Faux's masquerade as Freely is the return of Jacob, who seeks out his own 'flesh and blood' (p. 84) with a zeal which proves to be as irresistible as it is characteristic.

Brother Jacob, Sister Bertha: Eliot's Ending and *Jane Eyre*

The truth of Faux's masquerade – the third of his life's false steps – is not officially disclosed until the flashback opening to 'Brother Jacob''s third and final chapter. Here the narrator gives a brief resumé of Faux's colonial career, drawing attention both to the economic and sexual disappointments he sustains in 'the luxurious Indies' (p. 76) and to the anabaptismal act by which he hopes to erase them: 'since a new christening seemed a suitable commencement of a new life, Mr David Faux thought it as well to call himself Mr Edward Freely' (p. 77). To a reader schooled in the conventions of mid-Victorian fiction, of course, Faux's deceit is evident long before it is spelled out by Eliot's playful and well-travelled narrator. In this respect, such a reader enjoys a superior hermeneutic knowledge to that possessed by the inhabitants of Grimworth whom Faux hoodwinks so comprehensively, though there is one exception to this pattern, in the shape of Mr Prettyman, the town's 'highly respectable grocer' (p. 67). Just as the devious Faux gives his female customers 'useful hints about choosing sugars' which cast 'much light on the dishonesty of other tradesmen' (p. 64), so Prettyman seems to have a disquieting insight into the bogus status of the 'good confectioner' (pp. 76–77): "'I'm not fond of people that have been beyond seas, if they can't give a good account how they happened to go'" (pp. 67–68), he remarks, adding that, "'When folks go so far off, it's because they've got little credit nearer home'" (p. 68).

For the competent reader and the sceptical Prettyman alike, Faux's imposture is, it would seem, relatively easy to spot. Yet the closing narrative sequence which makes his ruses plain to 'the Grimworth people' (p. 86) as a whole contains secrets of its own. As befits a tale so heavily enmeshed in other works, these secrets are intertextual in nature and can best be brought to light by considering the moment of Jacob's narrative re-emergence. This is an event which occurs at a point just prior to Faux's marriage to Penny, as the couple endeavour (together with Penny's parents and sister) to finalize the domestic arrangements to be set in place after the wedding. As he hosts an afternoon tea of 'best muffins and buttered buns' (p. 79), Faux finds his tête-à-tête with his prospective wife and in-laws interrupted by the advent of a figure intent on reasserting existing family ties rather than cultivating new ones:

> At this moment an extraordinary disturbance was heard in the shop, as of a heavy animal stamping about and making angry noises, and then of a glass vessel falling in shivers, while the voice of the apprentice was heard calling 'Master' in great alarm.
>
> Mr Freely rose in anxious astonishment, and hastened into the shop, followed by the four Palfreys, who made a group at the parlour-door, transfixed with wonder at seeing a large man in a smock-frock, with a pitchfork in his hand, rush up to Mr Freely and hug him, crying out, – 'Zavy, Zavy, b'other Zavy!'
>
> It was Jacob, and for some moments David lost all presence of mind. He felt arrested for having stolen his mother's guineas. He turned cold, and trembled in his brother's grasp. (p. 80)

Jacob crashes back into the narrative here and exposes Faux – once his kinship claims have been vindicated – as 'a poor sneak' and '"interloper"' (p. 85). In so doing, he brings things full circle, blocking his brother's marital plans, just as he had previously marred his colonial intent.

If Jacob freezes 'Zavy' into a trauma of 'fraternal recognition' (p. 79) at this critical juncture, the narrative resolution he precipitates has its own familiar ring, possessing, as it does, some striking affinities with the melodramas of Charlotte Brontë's *Jane Eyre*. Like Eliot in 'Brother Jacob', what Brontë writes in this text is a narrative in which a return from the colonies, masquerade and thwarted marital ambitions all converge. In Eliot, the returning figure is Faux, the 'white dog' (p. 78) who comes back from Jamaica incognito and attempts to enter into marriage with the innocent Penny. In Brontë, the part of colonial revenant is played by Rochester, who not only returns from the same West Indian island as Faux but also resembles Eliot's protagonist in seeking to marry under false pretences, desiring the eponymous Jane as his bride. In Eliot, Faux's charade is exposed by another return, that of the 'half-witted' (p. 81) Jacob. In Brontë, on the other hand, Rochester's deception is revealed by

Bertha Mason, the 'bad, mad, and embruted partner!'[33] to whom, it transpires, he is already married.

Although its presence in Eliot's story is not openly signalled, *Jane Eyre* has much in common with those other intertexts 'Brother Jacob' explicitly confects into itself at earlier points, offering, in particular, its own version of the inter-racial encounter in which desire turns to loathing. This is located at the start of *Jane Eyre*'s third volume, as Rochester provides Jane with a vivid account of his involvement with Bertha in the West Indies, recalling how he was initially 'dazzled, stimulated [and] excited'[34] by 'Miss Mason ... the boast of Spanish Town for her beauty',[35] only to find himself repelled by her, shortly after their marriage, as 'a wife at once intemperate and unchaste'.[36] As his own 'Creole heiress', the source of the 'thirty-thousand pounds'[37] Rochester takes back with him to England, Bertha is, as Susan Meyer notes, 'clearly imagined as white' in Brontë's text, and it might consequently be argued that Rochester's movement from desire to disgust lacks the interracial element it possesses in 'Inkle and Yarico', *The Tempest* or *Othello*. As Meyer also notes, however, Bertha's white-ness is far from fixed in *Jane Eyre*, suffering a curious disfigurement as Brontë's tale proceeds: 'when she actually emerges as a character in the action of the novel', Meyer writes, 'the narrative associates Bertha with blacks, particularly with the black Jamaican antislavery rebels, the maroons. In the form in which she becomes visible in the novel, Bertha has *become* black'.[38] 'Brother Jacob''s concluding turn to *Jane Eyre* is thus consistent with the intertextual practice governing the novella as a whole.

While 'Brother Jacob' takes the cue for its denouement from *Jane Eyre*, the two texts are in other ways quite dissimilar. This is no more so than in terms of sugar itself, the substance out of which – via the base alchemy of slavery – Rochester forges his 'English gold'.[39] In Brontë's text, sugar is in fact less substance than spectre, reduced, like slavery, to the status of a ghostly 'underpresence'[40] throughout the course of the narrative. In Eliot, by contrast, sugar supersaturates the text. It materializes everywhere, foisting itself upon the reader constantly, from the opening allusion to 'the confectionery line' to the valedictory image of the child-like Jacob clasping 'a bag of sweets in his hand' (p. 86), as he and the disgraced Faux leave Grimworth. It is this aspect of the text – sugar's status as narrative overpresence, so to speak – which not only sets 'Brother Jacob' in such sharp contrast to *Jane Eyre* (and Lewis's similarly sugar-shy *Journal*) but also makes it so vital to an understanding of how white texts, from the mid-1760s to the mid-1860s, have engaged with and been shaped by the commodity. In the three chapters which follow, the book turns its focus from white writings to black, moving beyond Eliot to explore the place sugar occupies in texts by a range of expatriate Caribbean poets and novelists. As might be expected, these postcolonial writers produce an account of sugar (and of the slavery with which sugar is largely synonymous) very different from that which characterizes the work of their white predecessors. At the same time, though, the black imagining of sugar reveals itself to be not only indebted to the white saccharographic tradition but also marked by its own internal conflicts.

Notes

1. Ligon, p. 85.
2. See Isabella Beeton, *The Book of Household Management; Comprising Information for the Mistress, Housekeeper, Cook, Kitchen-maid, Butler, Footman, Coachman, Valet, Upper and under house-maids, Lady's-maid, Maid-of-all-work, Laundry-maid, Nurse and nurse-maid, Monthly, wet, and sick nurses, etc. etc. also, sanitary, medical, & legal memoranda; with a history of the origin, properties, and uses of all things connected with home life and comfort* (1861; Lewes: Southover Press, 2003), p. 671. As the encyclopædic sweep of its title suggests, this work is a text whose ambitions far exceed the genre of the recipe-book to which it is commonly boiled down.
3. The abolition of slavery in America was shortly to be secured, of course, following the onset of the Civil War, by the Emancipation Proclamation of 1863 and the Thirteenth Amendment of 1865. In Cuba, on the other hand, slave-liberation did not come until as late as 1886.
4. Beeton, p. 672.
5. George Eliot, 'Brother Jacob', in *The Lifted Veil; Brother Jacob*, ed. Helen Small (Oxford and New York: Oxford University Press, 1999), p. 50. Subsequent references to this work are incorporated in the text and given in parenthesis after quotations.
6. On the dating of the narrative, see Small, 'Introduction' to Eliot, *Lifted Veil*, p. xxxiii.
7. For Eliot's comment on her own fiction, see *The George Eliot Letters*, ed. Gordon S. Haight, 9 vols (New Haven and London: Yale University Press, 1954–78), vol. 4, p. 157.
8. Together with these operations, Eliot's multi-tasking text anticipates recent critical interest in the cultural value and cultural history of confectionery. See Wendy A. Woloson, *Refined Tastes: Sugar, Confectionery, and Consumers in Nineteenth-Century America* (Baltimore and London: Johns Hopkins University Press, 2002); and Tim Richardson, *Sweets: A History of Temptation* (London: Bantam Books, 2003).
9. See Susan de Sola Rodstein, 'Sweetness and Dark: George Eliot's "Brother Jacob"', *Modern Language Quarterly*, 52 (1991), 295–317; Melissa Valiska Gregory, 'The Unexpected Forms of Nemesis: George Eliot's "Brother Jacob," Victorian Narrative, and the Morality of Imperialism', *Dickens Studies Annual*, 31 (2002), 281–303; and Nancy Henry, *George Eliot and the British Empire* (Cambridge: Cambridge University Press, 2002), pp. 80–88. 'Brother Jacob' is also briefly but suggestively discussed by Kate Flint in 'Spectres of Sugar', in *White and Deadly: Sugar and Colonialism*, ed. Pat Ahluwalia, Bill Ashcroft and Roger Knight (Commack, NY: Nova Science Publishers, 1999), pp. 87–88. For an intertextual analysis of the novella which conversely underplays its colonial dimensions in favour of a feminist perspective, see Rebecca Mackay, 'Women and Fiction in George Eliot's "Brother Jacob"', *George Eliot Review*, 31 (2000), 31–36.
10. The association of sugar with the feminine is a traditional one, dating back to the early modern era. For an illuminating discussion of the link, see Kim F. Hall, 'Culinary Spaces, Colonial Spaces: The Gendering of Sugar in the Seventeenth Century', in *Feminist Readings of Early Modern Culture: Emerging Subjects*, ed. Valerie Traub, M. Lindsay Kaplan and Dympna Callaghan (Cambridge: Cambridge University Press, 1996), pp. 168–90.

11. Richard Steele, '*The Spectator*, no. 11', in *English Trader, Indian Maid: Representing Gender, Race and Slavery in the New World, An Inkle and Yarico Reader*, ed. Frank Felsenstein (Baltimore and London: Johns Hopkins University Press, 1999), p. 86.
12. Steele, p. 87 (italics in original).
13. Steele, p. 88.
14. Steele, p. 87.
15. Steele, p. 88.
16. Ligon, p. 56 (italics in original).
17. Steele, p. 88 (italics in original).
18. Steele, p. 88.
19. Steele, p. 87.
20. Ligon, p. 54.
21. Shakespeare, *Tempest*, I.ii.363–64.
22. Shakespeare, *Tempest*, II.ii.23–25.
23. Shakespeare, *Tempest*, II.ii.29–30.
24. Shakespeare, *Tempest*, II.ii.21.
25. Shakespeare, *Tempest*, II.ii.85.
26. Shakespeare, *Tempest*, II.ii.112.
27. Shakespeare, *Tempest*, II.ii.74.
28. Flint, p. 88.
29. For a useful overview of the conflicting interpretations to which Turner's painting has given rise, together with his own contribution to this evolving critical history, see Wood, *Blind Memory*, pp. 41–68. The ghostly, or ghastly, presence of *Slave Ship* somewhere beneath the surfaces of Eliot's text is further suggested by the curious parallels between the respective reactions of Eliot's 'bilious person', appalled by the pigments characterizing the confectionery Faux displays in his shop-window, and Mark Twain's singularly hostile response to Turner's picture when it made its American debut at the Boston Museum of Fine Arts in 1875. As the highly visceral language of his diaries indicates, Turner is for Twain an artist whose technique is truly sickening. In *Slave Ship*, as in his work as a whole, Turner offers, to Twain's eye, 'splendid conflagrations of colour [which] have the effect of nauseating the spectator' and induce 'the belly ache' (cited in Wood, p. 42).
30. Shakespeare, *Othello*, I.iii.144.
31. Shakespeare, *Othello*, I.iii.150–51.
32. Shakespeare, *Othello*, I.iii.168–69.
33. Charlotte Brontë, *Jane Eyre*, ed. Margaret Smith (Oxford: Oxford University Press, 1998), p. 306.
34. Brontë, p. 322.
35. Brontë, p. 321.
36. Brontë, p. 323.
37. Brontë, p. 321.
38. Susan Meyer, *Imperialism at Home: Race and Victorian Women's Fiction* (Ithaca and London: Cornell University Press, 1996), p. 67 (italics in original). Extreme as it can sometimes be, the textual slippage of Bertha from whiteness to a stereotypical blackness is not wholly surprising, given the ambiguity intrinsic to her designation as 'Creole' (Brontë, pp. 304, 328). As the *OED* points out, this is a term which, in its nineteenth-century context, refers equally to persons born and naturalized in the West Indies of either European or African descent, having 'no connotation of colour'. It is a category, in other words, in which white and black are, as it were, confected together.
39. Brontë, p. 146.
40. Flint, p. 83.

5

'Cane is a Slaver': Sugar Men and Sugar Women in Postcolonial Caribbean Poetry

Slavery is terrible for men; but it is far more terrible for women. Superadded to the burden common to all, they have wrongs, and sufferings and mortifications peculiarly their own.

    – Harriet Jacobs, *Incidents in the Life of a Slave Girl*

Black Sugar

At the end of 'Brother Jacob', Eliot bids farewell to her duplicitous anti-hero by consigning him to prospects whose exact nature is unclear. Shortly after the unmasking of the imposture at the heart of the text, the narrator notes how 'the shop in the market-place was again to let, and Mr David Faux, *alias* Mr Edward Freely, had gone – nobody at Grimworth knew whither'. The obscurity of the future into which the discredited Faux is cast accords Eliot's tale a neat symmetry by balancing out the vagueness of the past from which he emerges into Grimworth in the first place: 'he had absconded with his mother's guineas', the narrator continues, adding, 'who knew what else he had done, in Jamaica or elsewhere, before he came to [the parish]'.[1] Yet Faux's mysterious disappearance has an import which resonates well beyond the parochial limits of Eliot's novella, prefiguring the literary fortunes of the very commodity from which he hopes to profit: while sugar is central to 'Brother Jacob' itself, it is not, for some considerable time to come, a subject with which subsequent texts in Eliot's literary tradition are inclined to engage to any great degree. Like the Faux moving into his disconcertingly blank new life, sugar starts, after Eliot, and exactly a century on from Grainger, to fade from view, as if it were somehow being refined out from the white British literary imagination altogether.

This trend is not significantly reversed until the appearance of Barry Unsworth's *Sacred Hunger* (1992), a historical novel which assumes a suitably epic scale in order to critique the transatlantic slave trade during the mid-eighteenth-century period when *The Sugar-Cane* is written and published.[2] But while Unsworth's text signals a belated revisiting of the question of sugar in the white British literary tradition, the sort of project it represents is already discernible in the somewhat earlier and very different context of the black Caribbean poetry produced in the decades after the Second World War, when many formerly colonized territories (including Jamaica, Trinidad and Tobago, Barbados, Guyana, Antigua, Dominica and St Christopher) finally gain independence from their so-called British motherland.[3] The emancipation of slaves in the British West Indies in 1834 might be adduced as one reason for the relative scarcity of white writings on sugar in the protracted period which follows, as the substance comes inevitably and increasingly to lose its cachet as a symbol of moral iniquity and racial oppression. Conversely, the processes of post-war Caribbean decolonization not only define another epochal moment in the liberation of black peoples from white power, but also bring about a discursive renaissance in the texts those peoples create, as sugar is reworked from the perspective of the slave rather than the master, and the dominant system of representation comes to be reconfigured in the name of a postcolonial counter-memory.

Early instances of such reconfiguration are to be found in the poetic output of Edward Kamau Brathwaite and Faustin Charles, whose meditations on sugar are featured in Andrew Salkey's influential *Breaklight: The Poetry of the Caribbean* (1971). Both of these writers implicitly look back, in their different ways, to the idealized version of slavery elaborated by Grainger, but, as befits their outright rejection of the plantocratic order the earlier poet embraces, their writing is governed by aesthetic and ideological principles radically different from those informing his. As suggested in chapter 1, the production of Grainger's poem can be compared to and understood in terms of the production of the sugar in which it so delights: *The Sugar-Cane* is animated, that is, by the desire – albeit never quite met – to refine slavery's image into sanitized form. For Brathwaite and Charles, on the other hand, the opposite is the case, as the brutal historical truths Grainger prefers to evade assume a new prominence, with the accent falling less on discursive cleansing than on discursive contamination. Even so, these two writers are not above practising their own kind of censorship, most noticeably in relation to the black woman, whom they tend (like the androcentric Grainger) to marginalize in favour of a focus on the predicaments of her male counterpart.

The rewriting of sugar initiated by Brathwaite and Charles is developed on a much more ambitious scale and with even greater sophistication in Grace Nichols's *I is a Long Memoried Woman* (1983) and David Dabydeen's *Slave Song* (1984), both of which won the Commonwealth Poetry Prize in their respective years of publication.[4] Like the more modest works preceding them, these innovative, challenging and frequently disturbing texts are written against Grainger, but at the same time exist in a marked tension with one another. Adopting a black feminist perspective, Nichols is primarily concerned to give voice to the figure of the female slave whose presence is barely acknowledged in the poetry of her immediate male forerunners. This is something she achieves by drawing attention to the slavewoman's body as it is subjected to extremes of suffering – whether in the defile of the Middle Passage, labour in the cane-field or the context of sexual exploitation – before ultimately becoming an instrument of resistance and revenge. Dabydeen's *Slave Song* strives, for its part, to reconcile these opposed perspectives by encompassing both black male and black female experience, whether under slavery itself or in the post-emancipation era of the late twentieth century. Yet even as *Slave Song* thus constitutes a significant progression beyond the blinkered though formative visions of Brathwaite and Charles, it too remains caught up in the play of censorship, particularly with regard to the sexual violence which, historically speaking, has largely defined the white man's relationship with the black woman. Together with its silence on the Middle Passage, the evasiveness of Dabydeen's text towards such violence is one of its principal differences from Nichols's and suggests a disavowal of historical realities. This is all the more striking when it is recalled that *Slave Song* is a text clearly preoccupied, not to say obsessed, with interracial rape as it occurs in other forms.

Early Sugar Men: Brathwaite and Charles

As well as engaging critically with *The Sugar-Cane* in his comments on the evocation of the slave-dance in Book IV of Grainger's poem, Brathwaite offers an imaginative response to the text in 'Labourer', the penultimate poem in the *Breaklight* anthology. As its title suggests, what draws Brathwaite to Grainger, and what he sets out to rewrite, is the earlier poet's account of the work entailed in sugar's production and, more specifically, the supercharged image of the hand which carries it out. *The Sugar-Cane*'s characteristic tendency is to idealize such work, as when it praises the 'swarthy sires' of 'young negroes' for the 'ardent gladness' with which they 'wield the bill' in order to expedite the completion of the 'crop'.[5] None the less, the poem is unable entirely to avoid acknowledging the perils and the pains of the slave's labours, which creep back into its margins from time to time and kink its surfaces. In Book II, for example, Grainger ponders the problem of the 'cow-itch', a tropical weed which contains medicinal properties but is stinging to the touch. While his advice is that the planter wear 'thick gloves'[6] when handling this equivocal plant, the note attached to the main text fails to exhibit the same pragmatic concern for the welfare of the slaves more likely to encounter it in their daily rounds, and indeed suggests that the true worry posed by 'This extraordinary vine' is less physical than economic: the cow-itch, Grainger warns, 'should not be permitted to grow in a Cane-piece; for Negroes have been known to fire the Canes, to save themselves from the torture which attends working in grounds where it has abounded'.[7]

The botanical agonies the slave risks amid the cane-field anticipate the potential sufferings incurred in the boiling-house where the canes are crushed into juice and, in a passage previously discussed in some detail in chapter 1, the 'hand incautious' can also be easily 'snapt' off by 'steel-cas'd cylinders'.[8] In 'Labourer', however, the links between cane and pain are not only echoed and amplified with a rather greater compassion than anything mustered by Grainger, but also given a subtle new twist:

> Look at his hands,
> cactus cracked, pricked,
> worn smooth by the hoe,
> limestone soil's colour;
> he has lost three fingers
> of his left hand, falling
> asleep at the mill;
> the black crushing grin
> of the iron tooth'd rachets,
> grinding the Guinep Hill cane,
> has eaten him lame;
> and no one is to blame;
>
> the crunched bone was juicy
> to the iron; there was no difference
> between his knuckle joints
> and ratoon shoots: the soil
> receives the liquor cool and sweet;
> three fingers are not even worth
> a stick of cane; the blood
>
> mix does not show; the star-
> gaze crystal sugar shines
> no brighter for the cripple blow.[9]

It is not clear, strictly speaking, whether the damaged 'hands' depicted in these lines belong to a *bona fide* slave or to a black man working at an unspecified point after emancipation, since Brathwaite's poem lacks any obvious historical markers, even as the topographic allusion to Guinep Hill explicitly situates the scene in Jamaica. Yet the poem's use of number goes some way to countering this sense of indeterminate historical location, while also investing the accident it describes with the first of several ironies. Throughout the poem, Brathwaite's mutilated black man appears melancholy and abandoned: he is

'lame' and the victim of 'a cripple blow', with literally 'nothing more to show /
for thirty years' spine / curving labour'[10] than the gap where his 'three fingers'
should be. In symbolic terms, however, the loss of those three digits is far from
accidental, pointing towards the historical personage of Three-fingered Jack
(or Jack Mansong), an escaped slave and folk hero whose rebellious activities
brought him a brief period of fame in Jamaica in 1780.[11] This contrast between
the impotent finality of defeat and the vigorous possibilities of rebellion is
underscored in the final stanza of Brathwaite's text, which consigns the black
man to the bleakest of outlooks, as words splinter and whirl around him:
'name- / less days in the burnt cane- / fields without love'. In Grainger's
note, the burning of the cane-fields is frowned upon as a regrettable means
of self-defence, even as, elsewhere in the poem, it is linked to anxieties about
slave revolt. In 'Labourer', conversely, the signifiers of insurgency have been
extinguished: the blaze is out and the 'crack of … / loud trash' and 'spinn- / ing
ashes'[12] merely herald the moment of harvest and hence the perpetuation of
the cycle of oppression. As Dabydeen explains in his own note to 'Love Song',
one of the poems in his collection: 'before cutting takes place the fields are set
on fire to burn away the unwanted leaves of the caneplant. The canecutter is
therefore steeped in ash as he chops away'.[13]

But what is genuinely innovative about these lines is how they take up and
develop the violent orality latent to the language of the intertextual scene to
which they return. In Brathwaite, the black man's fingers are not just 'snapt'
off (as is the slave's hand in *The Sugar-Cane*), but become a 'juicy' meal to be
'eaten' and 'crunched' by 'iron tooth'd rachets' which fail, in the poem's second
irony, to discriminate between 'knuckle joints' and the 'ratoon shoots' from
which fresh canes will grow. By setting in play such associations between the
black body, consumption and sugar, 'Labourer' similarly adds something new
to the discourse of the abolitionists examined in chapter 2. In its claim that the
black man's blood lives on invisibly in the 'star- / gaze crystal sugar' enjoyed by
white subjects, Brathwaite's text itself bears the traces of the radical arguments
put forward by Burn, for whom the consumption of sugar is always potentially
a literal act of cannibalism. Yet where Brathwaite's text distinctively supple-
ments the abolitionists is in its figuration of the production of sugar as itself
a form of consumption, with the hungry mill assuming a cannibalistic guise,
complete, in a final ironic turn, with a 'crushing grin' which is not white but
'black'.

If 'Labourer' is a text in which black blood is swallowed up by white sugar
in such a way as to render it imperceptible, it is also one into which all sign
of black female oppression is invisibly absorbed. A similar effacement is
performed by Charles's deceptively transparent 'Sugar Cane Man'. This poem
begins with a speaker positioned in the present and yet drawn back to the past
in a bid to unravel the riddle of his own identity:

Who am I,
black,
with my woolly, plaited hair,
my thick lips,
my rich, red blood
and my tall, muscular body?

My generation worked in the cane-fields,
its labour gone in vain,
in somebody else's service,
for somebody else's profit;
there was no gratitude, no sharing;
there was only Massa,
on his puppet throne;
his whip reminded us of our existence.[14]

These opening two stanzas are more elusive than they might appear to be at first glance. Although the speaker is emphatically defined as 'black' by the phenotypical clichés of 'woolly, plaited hair' and 'thick lips', and as stereotypically male by his 'muscular body', these exterior signs of identity remain somehow insufficient to resolve the question of who he really is and, more particularly, the question of the historical moment he occupies, which proves, in fact, to be even more uncertain than that inhabited by the black man in 'Labourer'. As the movement between the stanzas indicates, the poem's speaker does not simply look back towards the time of slavery in order to establish a sense of self, but has been actively involved in the scenes he describes: if it is his 'generation' which 'worked in the cane-fields', then he must once have belonged to it, suffering the 'whip' of the puppet-'Massa' whom he berates. What is the logic of this? The common-sense answer would be to say that Charles's sugar-cane man is simply an ex-slave narrating the poem in the immediate wake of emancipation. But the more radical possibility is that the persona is a kind of corporeal ghost or fleshly revenant, positioned on the other side not just of slavery but of 'existence' itself.

Whatever the persona's precise historical location and ontological status, the emphasis of the narrative he tells is placed squarely on collective experience, with 'our', 'we' and 'us' woven throughout the text. Yet there is one point when this grammar of inclusion comes up against its own limits and the differences between male and female forms of enslavement stubbornly obtrude themselves:

We had no names,
only borrowed tags,
hand-me-down misfits,
or numbers,

Massa's cast-off family features,
and always the branding iron.[15]

The replacement of an original African name by a 'borrowed' (and often mock-ingly ironic) European alternative might well be, like the perpetual incandes-cence of the 'branding iron', something with which male and female slaves must commonly contend. But this sense of shared experience founders on the periphrasis of 'Massa's cast-off family features', with its throwaway allusion to the white man's everyday rape of the female slave, from which, of course, he reaps both sexual pleasure and economic reward, in the form of the additional slaves his acts of violation produce as children. While the poem acknowledges the distinctiveness of the slavewoman's situation – her double oppression on the grounds of race and sex – it allows her no space in which to make her sufferings known, no language for her pain. Despite the earlier recognition of the disturbances slavery produces in the slave's 'state of mind',[16] Charles's poem stops far short of any insight into what the psychological effects of white male sexual violence might be upon the female slave, or even, for that matter, the psychological dilemmas confronting the mixed-race subjects who spring from the lusts of the father-master.

Rather than pursue such a course, the poem directs its attention towards the strategies of resistance at the slave's disposal, ranging from end-stopped dreams of marronage – 'We, often, felt like running away. / But where could we go, and / who would take us in?'[17] – to physical violence. Yet as the speaker points out, for slaves to embrace this latter strategy is to indulge in 'a paraphrase of cruelty',[18] ironically mimicking the original treatment the master himself prescribes for them, just as the racial hybrid mirrors the master's look by inher-iting his 'cast-off features' (and Charles himself inherits the gender-blindness of Grainger, his adversarial literary master). All that is left to the slaves, in the end, is not so much a paraphrase as a parody of cruelty, as the energies of black reprisal are bathetically expressed in ersatz forms: 'We killed a white rooster / against a white-washed wall; / and we watched the blood flow / along the out-house gutter'.[19]

Out from the Margin: Nichols's Sugar Women

In Nichols's 'Among the Canes', the female slave confronts the possibility of her own historical oblivion, crying 'O who will remember me? / Who will remember me?', as she 'stumbl[es] blindly' 'across the fields'.[20] The answer to the question is, of course, Nichols herself, whose text not only performs the act of remembrance the slave desires but also breaks up the silence in which black women are encrypted in Brathwaite and Charles. Yet *I is a Long Memoried Woman* does not restrict its interventions just to the 'little sugar island[s]' (p. 26) which make up the Caribbean, but extends them back beyond these realms to encompass the dislocation and diaspora of the Middle Passage itself, as, for example, in 'One Continent / To Another', the poem with which Nichols's volume begins:

Child of the middle passage womb
push
daughter of a vengeful Chi
she came
  into the new world
birth aching her pain
from one continent / to another

moaning

her belly cry sounding the wind

after fifty years
she hasn't forgotten
hasn't forgotten
how she had lain there
in her own blood
lain there in her own shit

bleeding memories in the darkness

how she stumbled onto the shore
how the metals dragged her down
how she thirsted. (p. 5)

As if to presage the gynocentric orientation of the text in general, these lines not only focus on one of the 'daughter[s]' of the Middle Passage, but also represent her intercontinental transit in terms of the female body, likening the voyage to a 'womb' from which a 'Child' is eventually 'push[ed]' out. Such a comparison is striking, not least for the irony with which it sets the warmth and protection associated with the interior space of the mother's body against the unhomely environment of a slave ship. In this light, it seems that the 'Chi' to whom the poem alludes – a kind of personified fate in Igbo belief – is indeed 'vengeful', abandoning the slave to a place where all she can lay claim to are the corporeal excretions in which she languishes – 'her own blood' and 'her own shit' – rather than the amniotic fluid surrounding the foetus prior to birth.

The glimpse into the hold of a slaver at the outset to this poem reveals a nightmare world which continues to hold sway over the woman at its centre. This is suggested both by the stuttering repetition in 'after fifty years / she hasn't forgotten / hasn't forgotten' and by the ways in which temporal distinctions seem to dissolve, as the bloody exudations of the originally captive body are transformed into and paralleled by a haemorrhage of recollections in the present: 'bleeding memories in the darkness'. The sense of traumatic fixation upon the Middle Passage is more broadly mirrored in the first Part of *I is a Long Memoried Woman* as a whole, which returns to the experience on a number of occasions and from a variety of perspectives. In 'Each Time They Came', the figure who initially 'stumble[s] onto the shore' in 'One Continent / To Another' relives the moment of her faltering Caribbean debut as she watches a mix of fresh slaves being delivered into the 'new world' (p. 6), reeling out a litany of recognitions: 'Igbo / Yoruba / Ashanti / Fanti / Mane'. As she bears witness to these 'new arrivals' and quietly chants a 'dreaming / kind of prayer' for their liberation, she also implicitly underscores how the slaves' bodies are striated by the traces of the global rupture in which they are caught, as the signs of African tribal custom and European violence compete and clash upon the flesh: 'faces full of old / incisions / calves grooved from / shackles / ankles swollen / from the pain' (p. 15). In 'Web of Kin', on the other hand, the poem's speaker does not simply pray for the victims of the Middle Passage, but imagines herself engaging in more elaborate rituals, designed at once to honour, cleanse and aestheticize:

> even in dreams I will submerge myself
> swimming like one possessed
> back and forth across that course
> strewing it with sweet smelling
> flowers
> one for everyone who made the journey. (p. 9)

The irony of the speaker's self-figuration as 'one possessed' is clear enough in this context, as is the totalizing ambition of the watery ceremony she envisages. In 'Eulogy', however, the memory of the Middle Passage becomes more selective, concerning itself with those who not only fail to complete the 'journey' from Africa to the Caribbean but do so deliberately, either by 'plunging wildly to the waters' or by 'swallowing [their] tongues / cold and still on [their] chains'. As the sign of a collective resistance to slavery, these suicidal acts – spectacular, heroic and sublime – demand a difficult acclaim, even as the deaths they entail oblige the speaker to be equally resourceful in the forms of commemoration she devises: 'How can I eulogise / their names?', she wonders, adding, 'What dance of mourning / can I make?' (p. 17).

'One Continent / To Another' ends with the woman whose tale it tells 'stoop[ing] / in green canefields / piecing the life she would lead' (p. 7), an image which shifts the focus of Nichols's text away from memories of the Middle Passage and a lost African motherland and towards the material realities of oppression in the Caribbean itself, particularly the work involved in the cultivation of the cane. As the image implies, this is a topic Nichols approaches, like so much else in the text, from an almost exclusively female rather than a male viewpoint, replacing the sugar men favoured by Brathwaite and Charles with her own sugar women. One of the most sinister of these emerges in the shape of the crone in 'Like Clamouring Ghosts', whose superannuated and disfigured body defines her as a direct complement to the mutilated male of Brathwaite's 'Labourer'. With her 'skin' marked by 'stripes / of mold where the whip fall / hard' (p. 40), a 'missing toe' and 'jut-out / hipbone' resulting from an accident 'way back … when' (p. 41), this female grotesque offers none of the spiritual and emotional uplift traditionally associated with the figure of the ancestor in slave cultures. Instead she herself needs to be supported by the very instrument which is the sign of her oppression:

I see the old dry-head woman
leaning on her hoe
twist-up and shaky like a cripple
insect

I see the pit of her eye

I hear her rattle bone laugh
putting a chill up my spine. (p. 41)

In these lines there is not only disfigurement but also prefigurement, as the 'dry-head woman' provides an unnerving vision of what the poem's speaker may in turn become. Such a doubling of self and other, young slave and old, is written into the poem's language here and made evident in terms of both the play of homonymic reflections between the poem's 'I' and the 'eye' into which she peers, and the way in which the 'rattle bone laugh' the speaker hears seems to infiltrate and unsettle her own physique: it 'put[s] a chill up [her] spine', just as the woman who makes the sound possesses a posture 'twist-up and shaky'.

The figure of the labouring female slave appears in a number of other poems in the text, three of which – 'Days That Fell', 'We the Women' and 'Waterpot' – are clustered together to form a brief sequence early on in Part One. What is distinctive about these poems is how the cane-fields in which they are set themselves come to be imaginatively exploited by Nichols, providing analogical resources with which she is able to illuminate aspects of black female experience under slavery. In the first poem, for instance, the weeds which threaten the cane's growth are compared to the torments the slave must face on a daily basis, the irony being that the latter prove far more difficult to eradicate than the former: as the poem puts it, 'the cutlass in her hand / could not cut through / the days that fell / like bramble' (p. 10). This analogical pattern is developed in 'We the Women', where, despite the importance of their contribution to the economy of the plantation on which they 'cut / clear fetch dig sing', the female slaves of the poem's title are held of no account by the master and likened to the cane-trash it is their job to strip away: 'we the women / ... / whose deaths they sweep / aside / as easy as dead leaves' (p. 12). The pattern is extended in the vignette of 'Waterpot', a poem in which the female slave attempts to challenge the dehumanized condition to which she and her peers are reduced – 'always being hurried / along / like like ... cattle', as they move to and from the cane-fields – only to end up becoming a figure of ridicule. She 'trie[s] hard to walk / like a woman' as she returns from her labours in 'the evenings', and even assumes the stately air of the plant whose sovereign power demeans her in the first place, 'holding herself like royal cane' (p. 13) as she carries her water container atop her head. Yet far from investing the woman with gravitas or 'dignity', this culturally specific practice is derided as a 'pathetic display' by the white overseer who beholds it and whose ignorant response the poem parrots: 'O but look / there's a waterpot growing / from her head' (p. 14).

The analogical relationships between the female slave and the cane she works are something to which this chapter will return at a later point. What requires more immediate consideration is the rape to which the enslaved black woman is subjected by the unalluring 'buckra man' who 'come over de sea / with him pluck-chicken skin' (p. 44). Together with the Middle Passage and the hardships of labour itself, such sexual abuse provides another of the main perspectives from which Nichols explores the slavewoman's lot, though she tends initially to approach the topic with a striking circuitousness. In 'One Continent / To Another', for example, the threat of rape is not so much directly confronted as eerily foreshadowed, as memories of the black woman's idyllic existence in Africa before her enslavement are retrospectively sullied by a sense of later vulnerability, particularly in the anxious image of the 'jigida' which 'guard[s] the crevice / the soft wet forest / between her thighs' (p. 6). In 'Ala', similarly, the slave-mother who murders her child is graphically represented in a posture suffused with suggested violation: she is punished for her infanticide by being positioned 'Face up' on the ground, her 'naked body' 'coat[ed] ... in sweet / molasses' (p. 23) for 'ants [to] feed' (p. 24) on, with her 'arms and legs spread-eagle' and 'each tie with rope to stake' (p. 23). But the most complex and sustained engagement with rape occurs in 'Your Blessing' and 'In my Name', a diptych of poems appearing at the beginning of Part Four of the text. Taken together, these poems explore the black woman's ambivalent response to the mixed-race child whose advent is the living sign of white male sexual violence and, in so doing, recall and develop Charles's 'Sugar Cane Man', with its fleeting and uneasy glance towards miscegenation.

In 'Ala', the killing of the slave-child by means of a 'pin' stuck into 'the soft mould' of its head is an outrageous act of maternal resistance. It is designed to deliver the infant from the horrors of the future awaiting it by allowing its soul to wing 'its way back / to Africa' and hence claim precisely the freedom – from slavery and from the body itself – whose negation is symbolized by the disciplinary plight to which its mother, the ironically spread-eagled 'rebel woman' (p. 23), is condemned. In 'Your Blessing', by contrast, infanticide is imagined as something to be carried out not in the name of resistance, but for the sake of the violated black mother, who yearns, initially at least, 'to retch / herself / empty' (p. 52) of her unborn child and thus symbolically expel the 'guilt' with which she feels her rape has 'tainted' her. This ritualized self-cleansing is allied to the slave's desire not only to be rid of her own impending motherhood but also to repress all vestige of the child's white paternity, a wish which requires the intervention of an ancestral African divinity and is articulated in images of shame, regression and possible cure:

Cover me with the leaves of your
blackness Mother

shed tears

for I'm tainted with guilt and
exile

I'm burden with child and maim

Heal me with the power of your blackness
Mother

shed tears

for I'm severed by ocean and
longing

I'm mocked I'm torn I fear

Cover me
Heal me
Shield me

With the power of your blessings. (p. 53)

Although the slave receives the redemption for which she clamours in the poem's repetitious closing lines – 'Mother I need I have your blessing / Mother I need I have your blessing' (p. 55) – this is not before she has been enjoined to embrace the progeny she once spurned, simultaneously also embracing her own maternal identity: as the Mother advises, she must 'Clasp [her] child to [her] bosom' and 'cast [her] guilt to the wind' (p. 54). Such reconciliations are duly effected in the counter-statement of 'In my Name', which records and celebrates the child's birth, while at the same time striving to maintain the disavowal of its origins in white male sexual violence, particularly in the insistent use of the possessive: 'my bastard fruit / my seedling / my sea grape / my strange mulatto / my little bloodling' (p. 56). But it is not just the signs of the father which are to be eradicated here, washed away in the purifying moment of parturition – 'For with my blood / I've cleansed you': he himself is under threat. In a triumphant reversal of 'Eulogy''s desolate images of slaves 'swallowing [their] tongues / cold and still on [their] chains', it is now the white man who is to suffer such a fate: 'Let the evil one strangle on his own tongue', the mother urges her infant, 'even as he sets his eyes upon you' (p. 57).

The multiple forms of black female oppression dramatized in *I is a Long Memoried Woman* (the Middle Passage, labour, rape) are complemented by multiple forms of resistance, some of which have already been considered, whether they be the acts of slave suicide celebrated and mourned in 'Eulogy' or the infanticide of 'Ala'. In addition to these, however, there is one further form of resistance available to the slave, which involves her in a kind of strategic duplicity and emerges, specifically, in the course of her negotiation of the master's desire. In 'Your Blessing' and 'In my Name', the slave's identity is that of sexual victim, but elsewhere in the text she is accorded a more defiant role, appearing to comply with and fulfil the master's sexual and racial fantasies in order to prosecute what turn out to be her own murderous ends. This reversal in the disposition of power between master and slave, male and female, white and black is played out in the series of linked poems which brings Part Three of Nichols's text to a close. To some extent, the power shift is enabled by a use of obeah, as indicated in 'Night is her Robe', where the black woman 'gather[s] strange weeds' and 'wild root', together with 'leaves' which themselves possess the equivocal 'property / both to harm and to heal' (p. 46), but, in the main, it is effected by means of the slave's capacity for seduction. The mutually supportive arts of obeah and seduction the slave cultivates are brought together in 'Old Magic', which defines the sexual encounter it anticipates as a scene of misreading, ironically underlining the gap between what the slave pretends to be for the master and what she is for herself by drawing attention to her singularity: 'the one you going / sleep with / the one you going / think is kind' (p. 47). The encounter itself is staged in 'Love Act', the poem which follows on directly from 'Old Magic'. Here the titular pun ('Act' meaning 'action' but also 'charade') reflects the slave's own double-dealing, which takes in not only her sexually promiscuous owner but his family as well:

Soon she is the fuel
that keep them all going

He / his mistresswife / and his
children who take to her breasts
like leeches

he want to tower above her
want her to raise her ebony

haunches and when she does
he thinks she can be trusted
and drinks her in. (p. 48)

In these lines the slave reorders the 'Great House' she has 'enter[ed]' (p. 48), usurping the position of the white woman within the domestic economy: she becomes both surrogate mother to the master's vampiric 'children', who turn her milk to blood as they 'take to her breasts / like leeches', and sexual partner to the master himself, who 'drinks her in' with the same oral zeal. Yet if the slave is not the acquiescent subject she seems to be but a subversive one, then the master is not quite himself either: the phallic domination and white superiority displayed in his towering desires are illusory, tokens of a sexual and racial hauteur entirely without foundation. Such an inversion of the master–slave hierarchy is explicitly signalled in the poem's concluding lines. Here the quintessential symbol of white rule and black oppression changes hands – 'Her sorcery cut them / like a whip' – even as the plantocratic family whom the slave bewitches remains oblivious to its own deadly predicament, dispossessed of power and knowledge alike: 'She hide her triumph / and slowly stir the hate / of poison in' (p. 49).

As well as taking over the roles of surrogate mother and wife in 'Love Act', the slave becomes a kind of instructress in 'Skin Teeth', the bite-sized poem which completes Part Three. In this direct sequel and coda to 'Love Act', she provides her literal-minded oppressor with an elementary lesson in how to decipher the black female body, schooling him in the arts of antithetical reading: 'Not every skin-teeth / is a smile "Massa"', she explains, just as her 'bending' at his request is not a sign of weakness, compliance or respect, but a ruse by which she places herself in a position 'only the better / to rise and strike' (p. 50). Such duplicitous strategies look back to the epigraph to the text, whose eponymous speaker is distinguished as much by Nichols's typographic choices as by her own vernacular idiom:

From dih pout
of mih mouth
from dih
treacherous
calm of mih
smile
you can tell
i is a long memoried woman (p. 1; bold in original)

Here it is not just that the black woman needs, like the slave of 'Skin Teeth', to be read antithetically in order to be read aright, but that she says as much, openly admitting that the 'calm of [her] / smile' is 'treacherous', a kind of mask for an inner agitation which the text as a whole sets out to chart.

The slave's doubleness not only constitutes one of the strategies by which she resists the master, but also mirrors the dissemblance of the sugar cane on which the master's power is based, thus adding a new dimension to the analogical relationships discussed earlier in the context of work. Nowhere is such dissemblance more conspicuous than in the remarkable 'Sugar Cane', a poem from Part Two of the text, in which the slave temporarily suspends her labours in the cane-field in order to contemplate the curious properties of the plant (or grass) surrounding her:

> There is something
> about sugarcane
>
> He isn't what
> he seem –
>
> indifferent hard
> and sheathed in blades
>
> his waving arms
> is a sign for help
>
> his skin thick
> only to protect
> the juice inside
> himself. (p. 32)

While the slave conceals her rebellious potential beneath a mask of docility, the cane's apparent invincibility is a cover for an inner weakness. Its stems may be 'indifferent hard' but in fact contain 'juice', just as its leafy tops seem like 'blades' but turn out to be 'arms' 'waving' for 'help'. Nor is it any wonder that the phallic cane should feel so vulnerable, since, as in Grainger, it is not only heir to a range of complaints – 'shiver[ing] / like ague / when it rain' (pp. 32–33) and 'suffer[ing] / from bellywork / burning fever / and delirium' – but also always at risk from natural disaster, in the shape of 'the hurricane' which 'strike[s]' and 'smash[es]' it 'to pieces'. Even were the cane to escape these forms of destruction, it is destined, in the end, to be undone, as the slaves who 'groom and weed' it do so only until such time as it has 'grow[n] tall', when they 'feel the / need to strangle / the life / out of [it]' (p. 33). Perhaps it is for this reason that, as it ripens, the cane comes to assume the 'aura / of jaundice' (p. 32)?

Either way, the duplicity of 'sugarcane' the crop is shared by 'Sugar Cane' the poem, as content is replicated in form:

Slowly
pain-
fully
sugar
cane
pushes
his
knotted
joints
upwards
from
the
earth
slowly
pain-
fully
he
comes
to learn
the
truth
about
himself
the
crimes
committed
in
his
name. (p. 34)

As these words and broken parts of words (in the special case of 'pain- / fully') file out onto the page, they establish a striking visual effect, imitating the columnar shape of the cane itself – tall, slender and upright. Yet this impression is a typographic *trompe l'oeil*, designed to foster an illusion of mimesis where none exists. The words resemble the cane in terms of their vertical arrangement, it is true, but their descending movement runs counter to the trajectory they describe, as the cane clambers 'upwards / from / the / earth' into a shameful self-consciousness precipitated by the 'crimes / committed / in / [its] / name': the duplicity of Nichols's slave is reflected in the dissimulation of the cane, which is mirrored, in its turn, in the poem's formal masquerade.[21]

In its emphasis on black female rather than male experience, *I is a Long Memoried Woman* marks out a critical distance from the treatment of slavery in Brathwaite and Charles, according a central role to what is absent in 'Labourer' and 'Sugar Cane Man'. Nichols's 'Sugar Cane' itself, however, suggests a degree of debt to the work of her predecessors, especially Charles's poem of the same title, which forms another of his contributions to the *Breaklight* volume. In this poem, as in Nichols's, the cane is reimagined as the opposite of what it appears to be, a process of reassessment Charles extends to encompass the sugar the cane produces. The shifts in definition and perception the poem puts in play are most readily evinced in the contrast between its opening lines, in which the cane figures as a 'succulent flower' with 'sweet stalks',[22] and the lapidary slogans with which it ends:

> Cane is sweet sweat slain;
> cane is labour, unrecognized, lost
> and unrecovered;
> sugar is the sweet swollen pain of the years;
> sugar is slavery's immovable stain;
> cane is water lying down,
> and water standing up.
>
> Cane is a slaver;
> cane is bitter,
> very bitter,
> in the sweet blood of life.[23]

In one respect, these lines advance a vision of things significantly at odds with Nichols's, whose perspective on the cane is unusually sympathetic, stressing its vulnerability and suggesting that it should not be held directly responsible for the offences which have blossomed around it. For Charles, on the other hand, the sense of incrimination (and recrimination) could hardly be more intense, giving rise to a series of abrupt metaphorical transformations culminating in the spectacular accusation that 'Cane is a slaver', a phrase which in itself is appropriately duplicitous, suspending cane's true identity somewhere between slave ship and slave-master. Despite this difference of view, though, the overlap with Nichols's poem comes in the way Charles's similarly privileges and deploys the practice of reading against the grain: at the start of the poem, the cane may seem particularly juicy and, by the mid-point, has even reduced its 'reapers', who 'come at noon, / riding the cutlass-whip', to drooling over the prospect of its consumption, their own 'saliva sweeten[ing] everything',[24] but, by the poem's conclusion, it has become 'bitter, / very bitter', souring 'the sweet blood of life' with its unpalatable history. Yet if the sense of cane's duplicity is what links Nichols and Charles together, it ultimately ties them both back to the abolitionists, one of whose favourite rhetorical strategies is to expose the pleasures of sugar for the sham they are, bringing to light the suffering and violence on which they feed and to which Charles bears witness: 'sweat', 'labour' and 'swollen pain'.

Returning to Rape: Sugar Men and Sugar Women in Dabydeen's *Slave Song*

Slave Song represents an attempt to mediate between the conflicting gender-biases which characterize the work of Brathwaite and Charles, on the one hand, and Nichols, on the other, accommodating both black male and black female perspectives as it shuttles back and forth between the time of slavery and the contemporary Guyana where Dabydeen (like Nichols) was born. Yet although Dabydeen's text allows the black woman considerably more space than she enjoys in the work of his male predecessors, the white male sexual violence which she suffers and to which Nichols gives prominence remains something it rarely confronts in any sustained or systematic manner. *Slave Song* may be a more formally nuanced and adventurous project than *I is a Long Memoried Woman*, but it is unable either to match or to develop the insights into black female sexual trauma explored in the earlier work.

Slave Song's 'Introduction' opens by briefly revisiting the early phases of Guyana's colonial history, glancing back to the era of its exploration by Sir Walter Raleigh in 1595. For Raleigh, as for the Spanish conquistadors before him, the region's principal attraction lies in its mythical status as 'the land of El Dorado, the country of the Golden City of the Prince of Manoa' (p. 9). For the Guyanese subject of the postcolonial period in which *Slave Song* is written and published, by contrast, the English quest for gold gives way to an altogether different, if ultimately no less fabulous pursuit. As Dabydeen comments:

> We are, in literature anyway, creatures of peasant flesh squelching through mud and cane-field, bearing about us the stench of fish and fresh blood. In the moment of our rawness there is recoil, the cry for transfiguration is heard which to the Guyanese is the cry for 'whiteness', for the spiritual qualities of Raleigh's Elizabethan Empire. 'England' is our Utopia, an ironic reversal, for Raleigh was looking away from the 'squalor' of his homeland to the imagined purity of ours whereas we are now reacting against our 'sordid' environment and looking to 'England' as Heaven. All is a criss-cross of illusions, a trading in skins and ideals. (p. 9)

Despite the initial qualification restricting it to the domain of 'literature', this passage possesses a much wider resonance. What is crucial amid the flurry of scare quotes by which the passage is marked is the notion of the 'cry for "whiteness"', a formulation pointing in a number of different directions. As is clear from its immediate context, the phrase denotes, first and foremost, a yearning on the part of the native for the values supposedly exclusive to the erstwhile colonizer – a desire tied, in its turn, to a 'recoil' from a '"sordid" environment'. Yet the Guyanese who 'look[s] to "England" as Heaven' (or 'Utopia') charts a migrant path akin to sugar's own: he or she aspires towards a metaphorical recasting of self not unlike the material changes sugar itself undergoes, as it is partially refined in the Caribbean before being further purified in Britain and its colour alters from the brown of raw muscovado to the white of the crystals beloved of the metropolitan consumer.

As well as evoking sugar's self-improving path from colony to metropole, Dabydeen's 'cry for "whiteness"' is articulated in the experimental double-take of *Slave Song*'s formal design, as the fourteen poems the collection contains first appear in Guyanese Creole and then reappear translated into standard English, with all but one of the translations prefaced by critical commentaries of varying depth and range. In the 'Postscript' to the second edition of *Slave Song*, Dabydeen at once adds to and reflects upon the already supplementary 'apparatus' of the volume's 'Introduction, notes and translations', suggesting that this paraphernalia is a subtle reminder of *The Sugar-Cane*, whose own composition involves 'masses of notes and explanations' (p. 67).[25] At the same time, however, *Slave Song*'s movement from Creole to English, from the language of the slave to the language of the master, enacts, albeit with an ironic self-consciousness, the identification with the white other in which the Guyanese subject is caught up.

In addition to its resonances with both the production of sugar in general and the production of *Slave Song* in particular, the notion of the 'cry for "whiteness"' has an intertextual dimension most easily illustrated by 'Two Cultures', the final poem in the volume. Here a young male Guyanese returning from a sojourn in England is ridiculed by an elderly peasant for uncritically adopting the foreign values to which he has been exposed:

'Hear how a baai a taak
Like BBC!
Look how a baai a waak
Like white maan,
Caak-hat pun he head, wrist-watch pun he haan!' (p. 36)

As Dabydeen puts it in his gloss, 'The young man affects white manners and white speech in a show of superiority', even as the old peasant 'sees through the fraud' and remains stubbornly convinced that 'no Guyanese can ever evolve into "whiteness"' (p. 64).

The situation 'Two Cultures' portrays is not without precedent in the annals of black Caribbean writing, specifically recalling the insights into the colonial condition elaborated by Frantz Fanon in *Black Skin, White Masks* (1952). Taking black male subjectivity in the context of post-war French Martinique as his touchstone, Fanon writes, in a clear prefigurement of Dabydeen: 'The black man wants to be like the white man. For the black man there is only one destiny. And it is white. Long ago the black man admitted the unarguable superiority of the white man, and all his efforts are aimed at achieving a white existence.'[26] Such an identification with the white other and concomitant alienation from the black self are not surprising, given how the signs of racial difference are codified: whiteness bespeaks 'beauty and virtue'[27] and is linked to all things civilized and human, while blackness, conversely, 'is the symbol of Evil and Ugliness'[28] and is linked to all things primitive and bestial.

As Fanon demonstrates, these processes of identification and alienation also work in the opposite direction, as the white man turns to his black counterpart as the embodiment of the sexuality he has repressed: 'Projecting his own desires onto the Negro', Fanon observes, 'the white man behaves "as if" the Negro really had them'. Such supposed 'sexual potential' makes the black man attractive to the white, yet it can transform him, equally, into a figure of terror and threat. As Fanon notes, parodying voices from the archive of white fear, 'The Negro symbolizes ... biological danger' and 'is fixated at the genital; or at any rate ... has been fixated there',[29] just as, in the most extreme example of such discursive parody, he becomes synonymous with sexual violation itself: 'Whoever says *rape* says *Negro*'.[30] The colonial encounter in *Black Skin, White Masks* is thus a richly pathological one, fraught with mutual misrecognition, its nature no better captured, in fact, than in Dabydeen's own words: 'a crisscross of illusions, a trading in skins and ideals'.

While the status of the black man as rapist is no doubt just as much an ideological fabrication for Dabydeen as it is for Fanon, it is none the less precisely in such a sensational guise that he features in a number of poems in *Slave Song*. In his 'Introduction', Dabydeen suggests that Creole is a language perfectly suited to the labour out of which it grows: it is an idiom 'angry, crude [and] energetic' in which 'English diction is cut up' (p. 13), just as the cane is slashed and chopped by the worker in the field. But if Creole's 'brutality' (p. 14) does violence to the English tongue, its own verbal body is a wounded one too, represented by Dabydeen in terms of a certain 'brokenness'. This in turn mirrors the physical if not psychological condition of Creole's 'original users' (p. 13), one of whom is depicted in 'Slave Song', the collection's title-work:

Tie me haan up.
Juk out me eye.
Haal me teet out
So me na go bite.
Put chain rung me neck.
Lash me foot tight.
Set yu daag fo gyaad
Maan till nite –

Bu yu caan stap me cack floodin in de goldmine
Caan stap me cack splashin in de sunshine!

Whip me till me bleed
Till me beg.

Tell me how me hanimal
African orang-utan
Tell me how me cannibal
Fit fo slata fit fo hang.
Slice waan lip out
Waan ear an waan leg –

Bu yu caan stap me cack dippin in de honeypot
Drippin at de tip an happy as a hottentot! (p. 26)

Here the slave is exposed to two different but interrelated forms of violence, the first of which is discursive and constructs him, in the tradition of Long and Edwards, as both 'African orang-utan' and 'cannibal'. The second, enabled and legitimated by the first, is corporeal and fleshed out in the polymorphous torments to which the slave is subjected, as he loses 'eye', 'teet', 'lip', 'ear' and 'leg' at the master's whim. But the slave has a savagery of his own to impart, countering his disfigurements and dismemberments with a priapic sexual violence whose object is the master's wife. In the lines cited above, the rape of the colonial mistress is represented in terms which are oddly innocent and exuberant, as the slave's 'cack' variously 'flood[s] ... de goldmine', 'splash[es] in de sunshine' and 'dip[s] in de honeypot' of the white woman's vagina, her body transformed into his own private El Dorado. Yet at the end of the poem, the rape is rather less playfully described, as the slave basks in an obscene sexual pleasure which atomizes the body of his victim just as much as his own is atomized by his oppressor: 'Is so when yu dun dream she pink tit, / Totempole she puss, / Leff yu teetmark like a tattoo in she troat!' (p. 27).

This last image of the 'teetmark ... in she troat' suggests that the slave has taken the master at his word and become the very 'cannibal' he is said to be. As 'dream' makes clear, though, black male sexual violence in 'Slave Song' is merely a profane fantasy, leaving no anatomical impression on the white woman whatsoever. As well as emphasizing this point in his gloss on the poem, Dabydeen argues that the fantasy is none the less a vital strategy of resistance, helping the slave to survive 'in the face of utter suffering and cruelty' (p. 49). While this may be true, what is notable about 'Slave Song' is how it positions the (imaginary) rape of the white woman as an act of revenge for the pain endured by the enslaved male rather than female body, which the master freely violates, of course, for real. The master himself escapes any direct retribution for his rapacity in the poem, just as the sexual plight of the black woman remains not simply unavenged but unacknowledged.

'Slave Song' is immediately preceded in the text by 'The Canecutters' Song', a poem which concerns itself with slavery's legacies as they are manifested in the Guyana of the present. Despite the distance separating the historical moments on which these two poems respectively focus, it is evident that, in one sense, little has changed in the interim between them: the slave's sexual fantasies live on and repeat themselves in the reveries of the 'solitary canecutter' who speaks all but the poem's last four lines (chanted by his fellow-workers as a lewd chorus). It is equally clear, however, that the canecutter's longing for the white woman has a very different motivation to the slave's. It is not so much an act of revenge arising from the pain inflicted upon the black male body, that is, as an attempt to break through the barriers of race and class dividing him from the object of his desire. The dramatic levelling of position to which the canecutter aspires is textually marked in the poem's shifts of tone and language. In its first movement (lines 1–17), 'The Canecutters' Song' is lyrical and poignant, as the speaker praises the aureate charms of his paramour while lamenting her unattainability: 'Yu puss-mouth glow, mesh wid light, sun a seed an sprout deh / Me too black fo come deh' (p. 24). In its second movement (lines 18–32), on the other hand, the distance between black man and white woman suddenly collapses and images of beauty and delight yield to those of violence, domination and pain:

> Bu when night come how me dream …
> Dat yu womb lie like starapple buss open in de mud
> An how me hold yu dung, wine up yu waiss
> Draw blood from yu patacake, daub am all over yu face
> Till yu dutty like me an yu halla
> Like when cutlass slip an slice me leg, an yu shake
> Like when snake twist rung me foot, when we cut cane. (pp. 23–25)

Earlier in the poem, the speaker posits sex with the white woman as magically cleansing and elevating, an experience with the capacity to bring him up to her exalted racial and social level: 'Wash dis dutty-skin in yu dew / Wipe am clean on yu saaf white petal!', he implores. Here, though, it is the white 'hooman' who is remade in the black man's image, rather than the reverse. Her cane-like body, 'Tall, straight, straang-limb' (p. 24) at the start of the poem, is, as Dabydeen puts it, viciously 'chop[ped] … down to size' (p. 47), as it is pinioned in 'de mud' and she is forced to resemble her attacker's 'dutty' look by being smeared with 'blood' from her own womb. The blurring of identities is further registered in the way the white woman's terrified response to her assault becomes mixed up with the hazards of the black man's occupation, whether they be physical wounds or mental trepidations: 'yu halla / Like when cutlass slip an slice me leg … yu shake / Like when snake twist rung me foot, when we cut cane'.

The most sinister and provocative aspect of the doubling between victim and assailant comes in Dabydeen's contention that the white woman is weirdly complicit in her own violation. While the poem itself does not obviously support this claim, the penultimate paragraph of the detailed commentary

Dabydeen provides for it is adamant that this is the case, reading the poem's female figure against the grain of her own apparent innocence. Like the sugar-cane in Nichols, this figure, who 'walk tru de field fo watch we canecutta' (p. 24), is not what she seems, no disinterested observer of labouring black male bodies but their voyeur:

> The fact that she comes to the canefield to watch the canecutters at their brutal work suggests that she is as fascinated by them as they are by her. She wants to be degraded secretly ... to be possessed and mutilated in the mud. The tragedy is as much hers [as theirs] for her desires too are prevented by social barriers. She can only stand and watch and fantasise, then go away. (p. 47)

This 'warped mentality' (p. 55) is evident elsewhere in *Slave Song*, particularly the graphic (or even pornographic) 'Nightmare', which features a white woman who dreams of being raped by a 'gang' of 'sweat-stink nigga' with 'cane-stiff cack' (p. 31), only to awaken from her sleep in a state of 'surreptitious sexual arousal' rather than the 'terror' (p. 55) the poem's title might lead a reader to expect.

Such a mentality is also another sign of the continuities between Dabydeen and Fanon, for whom desire similarly wears a mask of fear. As Fanon infamously declares in chapter 6 of *Black Skin, White Masks*, at the conclusion to his analysis of white female psychosexuality: 'when a [white] woman lives the fantasy of rape by a Negro, it is in some way the fulfillment of a private dream, of an inner wish'.[31] For this assertion he has been predictably castigated by a number of white feminist critics, including Diana Fuss, who finds Fanon's reading of 'white women's rape fantasies' to be 'deeply troubling'.[32] As Fuss goes on to argue, however: 'Ultimately, what may be most worrisome about the treatment of interracial rape in *Black Skin, White Masks* is not what Fanon says about white women and black men but what he does *not say* about black women and white men'.[33] This is a criticism which can be directed towards 'The Canecutters' Song' as well, where the rape performed by the white man upon the black woman is not just erased from the text (as is also the case in 'Slave Song'), but turned into its opposite: the roles of rapist and victim are transposed across the lines of race, and history returns to the text in the shape of fantasy.

As is abundantly clear from his 'Introduction', Dabydeen is well aware of the doubly oppressed condition of the black woman, sketching the ways in which she has served historically as libidinal resource for the white man, himself oppressed by the 'burden of having to appear decent' (p. 10). The examples Dabydeen gives in support of his claims run back to the early eighteenth century, ranging from the familiar to the obscure:

The white man desired the freedom to indulge in a bestial, fevered sensuality – in what Defoe in the 18th Century described as 'unspeakable acts of copulation'; in what Lawrence in the 20th Century described as the 'hot, fecund darkness of the African body'. The fantasy of dominance, bondage and sado-masochism, of sensual corruption and disintegration, could be enacted upon the submissive, inferior black female. Hence Jonathan Corncob is initiated into the sensual, tropical degradation of taking a 'Negress' straight from the cane-fields, hot, dirty and drenched in rank sweat. (p. 10)[34]

Similar assertions about the violent and opportunistic nature of white male sexuality under colonialism are made in the critical gloss to 'Brown Skin Girl', in which Dabydeen notes how the 'white man, in the days of colonial rule, took Guyanese women for his mistress or his whore, at his leisure' (p. 62). Paradoxically, though, the openness of these critical statements finds no echo in the poems to which the statements are attached: these are far more evasive, unwilling or unable to accommodate within themselves the historical truth of the black woman's sexual suffering. This is something already demonstrated by 'Slave Song', 'The Canecutters' Song' and 'Nightmare', where the imaginary rape of the white woman works to mask the genuine violation of her black counterpart, but it is also evident in poems in which black women feature in their own right.

One of these is 'Slavewoman's Song', a poem striking not least for its anomalous status as the only piece within the collection to appear without critical supplement, as if Dabydeen, in contrast to his usual practice of generous exposition, were somehow reluctant to consider it in any detail or furnish the reader with any clues as to its potential meaning. Yet as much as it is out of step with the rest of *Slave Song*, this seemingly capricious withdrawal of interpretative guidance is in direct accord with the enigmatic nature of the poem itself, which dramatizes a one-sided call and response between the black woman who gives the poem its title and the gender-neutral figure listening sympathetically to her song. As is immediately apparent, the song is not in fact a song at all, but merely an asymbolic 'howl' (p. 34), which the slavewoman refuses (à la Dabydeen) to gloss, thus obliging the speaker to propose a series of speculations as to the possible sources of its inspiration:

Pickni?
Dem tek pickni way?
Wha dem do wid pickni
Mek yu knaack yu head wid stone
Bite yu haan like daag-bone?

Is husban mek yu halla gal?
Wha dem do wid maan
Mek yu daub yu face wid cow dung

Juk yu eye an chap yu tongue?
Dem trow am Demerara, feed am alligata?

Muma? Pupa? Africa?
Belly big wid Massa? (p. 34)

Perhaps the slavewoman cries for the loss of her children or husband, the speaker suggests, signalling her grief for these departed figures not only vocally but also in the hectic pantomime of the bodily harm she inflicts upon herself? Perhaps, alternatively, it is the separation from her own mother and father or even Mother Africa which is the ground of her distress? Or perhaps, in yet another scenario, the slavewoman's hysteria is occasioned by interracial rape, figured in the grotesquely homuncular vision of a 'Belly big wid Massa'? Whatever the answer to these questions, it is noticeable that it is the last of them which brings the poem to a sudden halt, sealing it up in a loop of repetition as its final four lines exactly echo those with which it opens: 'Ya howl – / Hear how ya howl – / Tell me wha ya howl foh / Tell me noh?' (p. 34). In *Slave Song*'s 'Postscript', Dabydeen semi-comically figures his 'Introduction, notes and translations' as 'peculiar midwives to the poems, seeking to strangle them at birth' (p. 67), but 'Slavewoman's Song' requires no such malign obstetrics because it is a poem which seems already to have strangled itself.

In 'Slavewoman's Song', the abuse of black woman by white man is raised by the poem as a possibility only to be swiftly choked away. In 'Song of the Creole Gang Women', on the other hand, it is given an ampler and more subtle treatment, even as, in the end, the results are just as evasive. Like 'The Canecutters' Song', this poem has a contemporary setting, transforming the inarticulate and mysterious cries of the howling slavewoman into a polyphonic exchange between five black female cane-workers bemoaning their stifled existence in present-day Guyana. At the poem's outset, the white man emerges, once again, as an oppressor-figure, his tyranny writ large in the impersonal shape of Bookers, the British company which, until its nationalization by the Guyanese government in 1976, monopolized the country's sugar industry. As is implicit in the language used at this juncture by the first of the gang-women, the behaviour of this particular sugar-giant bears comparison to that of a slave-master, with each laying claim to the labouring black female body as a form of property:

Wuk, nuttin bu wuk
Maan noon an night nuttin bu wuk
Booker own me patacake
Booker own me pickni.
Pain, nuttin bu pain
Waan million tous'ne acre cane.
O since me baan – juk! juk! juk! juk! juk!

So sun in me eye like taan
So Booker saach deep in me flesh
Kase Booker own me rass
An Booker own me cutlass –
Bu me dun cuss … Gaad leh me na cuss no mo! (p. 17)

As Dabydeen notes, the process of planting the cane to which these lines allude is a 'vicious' one, 'a repeated stabbing into the soil' (p. 12), aggressively articulated in the poem by the 'juk! juk! juk! juk! juk!' of its seventh line. But as the toiling woman pierces Bookers' earth with her exclamatory hoe, all the while complaining at the 'wuk' and 'pain' she must endure, it becomes evident that she is possessed by the company as much sexually as economically. Bookers owns both her 'patacake' and her 'rass' (respectively and uncompromisingly rendered by Dabydeen as 'cunt' and 'arse' [p. 39]) and even subjects her to a symbolic corporate rape as it penetrates the *terra incognita* of her body: just as the 'sun' blinds her 'eye like taan [thorn]', 'So Booker saach deep in [her] flesh'.

Yet while the poem begins by constructing the white man as sexual aggressor to the black woman as sexual victim, it goes on to trouble and complicate the conventional postures of interracial rape, particularly in the uncomfortable questions asked by the fourth gang-woman:

Everyting tie up, haat, lung, liva, an who go loose me caad? –
Shaap, straight, sudden like pimpla, cut free
An belly buss out like blood-flow a shriek?
Or who saaf haan, saaf-flesh finga?
Or who go paste e mout on me wound, lick, heal, like starapple suck? (p. 18)

As in the passage cited above, the violence of white male sexuality is once more present in these lines, figured as a 'pimpla', or, as Dabydeen clarifies in his note, 'a gigantic white thorn [which is] a menace to the countryside of Guyana' (p. 37). But the point about this thorny sexuality is that it is precisely not represented as a 'menace' or threat here, but rather as something the black woman actively desires and regards as unexpectedly liberating. The white man will 'loose [the] caad' in which the clothes around the woman's working body are tied and 'cut [her] free', his 'mout' no longer to be feared as if it were that of flesh-eating piranha ('pirae' [p. 17]), but welcomed for its ability to 'lick, heal [and] suck' the very 'wound' he has created. Such a terrifying revision of rape as an event not to dread but to desire aligns the fourth gang-woman with the white female fantasists who appear in 'The Canecutters' Song' and 'Nightmare', making her part of a strange and pathological sisterhood. At the same time, though, it places her seriously at odds with those other black women, whether enslaved or free, for whom the depredations of the white man are no perversely alluring daydream but an all too painful truth.

In the reduction of that truth, as in 'Slavewoman's Song', to nothing more than a traumatic 'howl', Dabydeen signals an essential difference between the project of his collection as a whole and that elaborated by Nichols in *I is a Long Memoried Woman*, dodging the questions of white male sexual violence (and answering black female suffering) which she confronts. Such questions are taken up in Caryl Phillips's *Cambridge*, albeit with an ambivalence which seems, in effect, to combine the more resolute nature of Nichols's approach with Dabydeen's evasiveness. As the subsequent chapter demonstrates, it is in the course of exploring these issues that Phillips's novel also engages with other texts besides *The Sugar-Cane* (the common point of reference for all the poets considered here), opening up a new and complicated set of dialogues.

Notes

1. Eliot, 'Brother Jacob', p. 87 (italics in original).
2. The ur-text to this important work (co-winner of the Booker Prize for Fiction in 1992) is Unsworth's own *Sugar and Rum* (1988), a novel in which the central character is a writer from Liverpool whose creative powers become tellingly blocked as he struggles to complete a historical fiction on the city's slave trade. *Sacred Hunger* itself has been the harbinger to other historical novels in the white British tradition with a similar focus on themes of sugar and slavery, most notably Philippa Gregory's *A Respectable Trade* (1995) and James Robertson's *Joseph Knight* (2003).
3. This is a topic which has to date received very little critical attention, but for a brief if sketchy preliminary analysis, which also extends to include an appreciation of the Cuban poet Nicolás Guillén, see Keith Ellis, 'Images of Sugar in English and Spanish Caribbean Poetry', *ARIEL: A Review of International English Literature*, 24.1 (1993), 149–59.
4. As well as meeting with initial acclaim from the literary establishment, *I is a Long Memoried Woman* was the inspiration for a film directed under the same title by Frances-Anne Solomon (LedaSerene/Women Make Movies, 1990), but critical response to the text remains fairly limited, in both quantity and quality. For some of the more searching analyses, however, see Alison Easton, 'The Body as History and "Writing the Body": The Example of Grace Nichols', *Journal of Gender Studies*, 3.1 (1994), 55–67; Jan Montefiore, *Feminism and Poetry: Language, Experience, Identity in Women's Writing*, second edition (London: Pandora, 1994), pp. 224–34; and Denise deCaires Narain, *Contemporary Caribbean Women's Poetry: Making Style* (London and New York: Routledge, 2002), pp. 182–86. For detailed readings of individual poems included in Nichols's volume, see Elfie Bettinger, 'Grace Nichols's "Sugar Cane": A Post-Colonial and Feminist Perspective', *Anglistik und Englischunterricht*, 53 (1994), 117–27; and Döring, pp. 68–71 (also on 'Sugar Cane').
   If anything, Dabydeen's *Slave Song* has been critically even less well served than Nichols's text, though there are none the less some perceptive contributions. See Mark McWatt, 'His True-True Face: Masking and Revelation in David Dabydeen's *Slave Song*'; Sarah Lawson Welsh, 'Experiments in Brokenness: The Creative Use of Creole in David Dabydeen's *Slave Song*'; and Benita Parry, 'Between Creole and Cambridge English: The Poetry of David Dabydeen', all in *The Art of David Dabydeen*, ed. Kevin Grant (Leeds: Peepal Tree, 1997), pp. 15–25, 27–46 and 47–66, respectively. See also the selective but trenchant remarks on the text in Lee M. Jenkins, *The Language*

of Caribbean Poetry: Boundaries of Expression (Gainesville, FL: University Press of Florida, 2004), pp. 68–75.

5. Grainger, III. 533–37.

6. Grainger, II. 123.

7. Grainger, p. 184.

8. Grainger, III. 167–68.

9. Edward Kamau Brathwaite, 'Labourer', in *Breaklight: The Poetry of the Caribbean*, ed. Andrew Salkey (Garden City, NY: Doubleday, 1972), p. 239.

10. Brathwaite, p. 240.

11. For an exhaustive and illuminating account of the rise and fall of Three-fingered Jack, his association with the practice of obeah and the multiple literary reconstructions to which his story was subjected throughout the fifty years or so after his death, see Srinivas Aravamudan, 'Introduction' to William Earle, *Obi; Or, The History of Three-Fingered Jack*, ed. Srinivas Aravamudan (Peterborough, ON: Broadview, 2005), pp. 7–52.

12. Brathwaite, p. 240.

13. David Dabydeen, *Slave Song*, second edition (Leeds: Peepal Tree, 2005), p. 51. Subsequent references to this work are incorporated in the text and given by page number in parenthesis after quotations.

14. Faustin Charles, 'Sugar Cane Man', in Salkey, p. 88.

15. Charles, 'Sugar Cane Man', p. 89.

16. Charles, 'Sugar Cane Man', p. 88.

17. Charles, 'Sugar Cane Man', p. 88.

18. Charles, 'Sugar Cane Man', p. 89.

19. Charles, 'Sugar Cane Man', p. 89.

20. Grace Nichols, *I is a Long Memoried Woman* (London: Karnak House, 1990), p. 27. Subsequent references to this work are incorporated in the text and given by page number in parenthesis after quotations.

21. Nichols briefly revisits 'Sugar Cane' in 'Yes, through it all', one of the poems in her recent *Startling the Flying Fish*. In this new context, the cane is once more gendered as male, though its most salient feature is not now duplicitousness so much as irrepressibility: 'No matter how we / burn and chop', 'crush and boil', or even 'curse and blame him', Nichols writes, 'Next year he up again / hands in the air / waving fresh-fresh as ever'. This gift for indefatigable self-renewal is echoed in the metaphorical movement of the text, which constantly refigures the cane's identity, turning it first from 'carefree carnival character' into 'Mr Midas, the man / with the golden touch' and thence into an 'original alchemist'. In this last guise, the cane enjoys the unique privilege of occupying the roles of transformer and transformed at the same time, changing itself into sugar for consumption, as it 'spill[s]' its 'crystal-seed / [its] tiny jewels / of transformation / at our weeping feet'. See Grace Nichols, *Startling the Flying Fish* (London: Virago, 2005), p. 61.

22. Faustin Charles, 'Sugar Cane', in Salkey, p. 185.

23. Charles, 'Sugar Cane', pp. 185–86.

24. Charles, 'Sugar Cane', p. 185.

25. Between the critical reflections included in *Slave Song*'s first edition and the 'Postscript' to its second, there are several other occasions when Dabydeen adopts the role of critic to himself, contextualizing and analysing his purposes in the composition of the text. See his 'On Writing "Slave Song"', *Commonwealth Essays and Studies*, 8.2 (1986), 46–48; 'On Not Being Milton: Nigger Talk in England Today', in *The State of the Language*, ed. Christopher Ricks and Leonard Michaels (London and Boston: Faber and Faber, 1990), pp. 3–14; and 'Hogarth and the Canecutter', in *'The Tempest' and its Travels*, ed. Peter Hulme and William H. Sherman (London: Reaktion Books, 2000), pp. 257–63.

Also relevant are Dabydeen's interviews with Wolfgang Binder (1989) and Frank Birbalsingh (1991), reprinted in Grant, pp. 159–76 and 177–98, respectively.

26. Frantz Fanon, *Black Skin, White Masks*, trans. Charles Lam Markmann, Foreword by Homi K. Bhabha (London: Pluto Press, 1986), p. 228. Dabydeen's debt to Fanon in *Slave Song* is briefly noted by Parry, pp. 54–55.

27. Fanon, p. 45.

28. Fanon, p. 180.

29. Fanon, p. 165.

30. Fanon, p. 166 (italics in original).

31. Fanon, p. 179.

32. Diana Fuss, *Identification Papers* (New York and London: Routledge, 1995), p. 156.

33. Fuss, p. 156 (italics in original). Fuss's position echoes that of Mary Ann Doane, who contends that by shifting the focus away from rape as 'the white man's prerogative as master/colonizer to the white woman's fears/desires in relation to the black male', Fanon 'effectively eras[es] the black woman's historical role'. See Mary Ann Doane, *Femmes Fatales: Feminism, Film Theory, Psychoanalysis* (New York and London: Routledge, 1991), p. 222.

34. The final sentence of this passage entails something of a distortion of the anonymous late eighteenth-century novel to which Dabydeen refers, since Corncob in fact refuses each of the thirty or so 'hen negroes' offered up to his sexual pleasure by the old acquaintance turned planter whom he encounters during a sojourn in Barbados, preferring instead 'a very pretty mulatto girl' later presented to him by the same 'gentleman' as an alternative. See *The Adventures of Jonathan Corncob, Loyal American Refugee. Written by Himself*, ed. Noel Perrin (1787; Boston, MA: David R. Godine, 1976), p. 70.

6

'Daughters Sacrificed to Strangers': Interracial Desires and Intertextual Memories in Caryl Phillips's *Cambridge*

What [the slave] could propose to himself by telling a lie which must be so soon detected, I cannot conceive; but I am assured, that unless a negro has an interest in telling the truth, he always lies – in order to keep his tongue in practice.
> – Matthew Lewis, *Journal of a West India Proprietor*

You ... become aware of the possibility of being somebody who can ... perhaps do something about redressing the imbalance of some ills and false-hoods that have been perpetrated by others about your own history.
> – Caryl Phillips, interview with Carol Margaret Davidson

'Wordy War': Rewriting the Archive

Like much other postcolonial literature, including the poetry examined in the previous chapter, *Cambridge* is a work in which intertextuality plays a vital role. As Lars Eckstein has shown, the novel incorporates into itself a dizzying array of sources, drawing chiefly on white and black first-person accounts of Caribbean slavery produced during a period from the 1770s to the 1840s.[1] Prominent among these writings are Lewis's *Journal* and Equiano's *The Interesting Narrative*, texts respectively discussed in detail and more briefly earlier in this book. The first of these works is integral to Part I of the novel, which consists of the diary of Emily Cartwright, a thirty-year-old middle-class English spinster, deputed by her father to inspect his West Indian sugar estate at an unspecified moment after abolition. *The Interesting Narrative*, on the other hand, is exploited as intertext in Part II, providing the primary model for the confession of the African-born male slave who belongs to the estate and after whom the novel is titled. As if to mirror the arrogance of empire and the discrepancies of power between white and black at the time when the novel is set, Emily's journal occupies by far the greater space in this slender though formally sophisticated text, with the story told by the elderly Cambridge condensed into just thirty-five pages. The two narratives are circumscribed by other materials written in third-person voices, which augment *Cambridge*'s polyphonic effect still more. Together with a brief Prologue and Epilogue, these include (as Part III) a seemingly authoritative report on the violent death of the estate's self-appointed overseer, Arnold Brown, which Phillips grafts into his novel, almost verbatim, from Mrs Flannigan's *Antigua and the Antiguans* (1844).

Despite its constitutive nature, however, *Cambridge*'s 'larger intertextual dimension' has, as Eckstein observes, 'gone practically unacknowledged'[2] by criticism, perhaps not least because Phillips himself gives no obvious clues as to its existence: in contrast to *Slave Song*, the novel is not attended by convenient glosses or explanations to guide the reader in his or her path through the text. As a consequence, most critics tend to focus on intra- rather than inter-textual strategies, exploring the two key narratives around which *Cambridge* is organized, together with the nuanced counterpoint between them.[3] There is, though, a certain irony to this critical emphasis, since, far from being mutually exclusive, the novel's intra- and intertextual elements are complementary, with Cambridge's response to Emily paralleled in the broader dialogue the novel conducts with its white archive, and Lewis's *Journal* especially. Viewed in terms of race, the stories told by white woman and black man exist in predictable tension: notwithstanding some initial bouts of anti-slavery sentiment, Emily offers an intractably negative portrait of the racial other, which is subsequently debunked by Cambridge. Yet Cambridge's narrative not only discredits Emily's wayward assumptions about blackness (as a slave might rebel against a master or a mistress), but also serves as a kind of hermeneutic supplement to the tale she tells, filling out the gaps and silences in her text and resolving its enigmas. What it discloses, above all, is the hidden history of sexual violence inflicted upon Cambridge's second wife, Christiania, by Brown, the 'good *cane-man*'[4] who, in addition to his other transgressions, has the distinction of becoming Emily's eventual, if finally indifferent, lover.

The revisionary effects of Cambridge's narrative are not limited to Emily's journal, however, but reach far beyond this to encompass Lewis's, thus both crossing and questioning the generic boundaries between fictional and historical forms. As suggested in chapter 3, the sexual violence the white man directs towards the black woman is something almost entirely eradicated from the representation of slavery in Lewis's text: it is rewritten or masked in the figure of black male rape which dominates 'The Isle of Devils', and can only really manifest itself in whispered and occasional forms. When it comes to such violence, Lewis's colonial memoir is driven, in other words, by an aesthetics of refinement – for which the processes of sugar-making can stand as allegory – while Phillips's postcolonial response puts the allegory into reverse. What his novel develops instead is an aesthetics of contamination, operative in relation both to Emily's fictional text and to the major historical document underlying its composition.

From Mastery to Mystery

Towards the end of her journal, Emily records an exchange in which Cambridge is accused by 'a young overseer' of having 'purloin[ed]' some 'meat' from the estate. The 'huge negro' denies that his removal of this item can be deemed 'stealing' because 'come Sunday he intended to replace the meat with stock from his own provisions', adding that were 'permission ... sought for every insignificant act ... there would be precious little time for work on the plantation' (p. 112). In the context of the 'constant war' (p. 128) fought between Brown and Cambridge, such a case of unacknowledged theft might indeed seem trivial, though it remains notable, even so, for the rhetorical cunning by which the slave promotes the pursuit of his own immediate interests as ultimately conducive to the master's economic well-being. From an intertextual perspective, however, this petty controversy takes on a genuine importance, functioning as a parable for the novel's own compositional methods, which are precisely marked by the clandestine appropriation of property – albeit textual rather than edible – belonging to others.

A representative instance of the strategies of appropriation on which *Cambridge* is built occurs when Emily takes an introductory trip around her father's 'sugar plantation', observing its 'principal scenes of life' with Brown as chaperon. At first regarded by Emily as wholly charmless, Brown by this juncture has begun to find favour, even to the degree that Emily becomes intrigued by 'the technical procedures employed in the cultivation of the cane' it is her escort's task to supervise. Recognizing that without the charismatic existence of '*King Sugar* none would be here, neither black nor white' (p. 82; italics in original), Emily recalls how her inspection of the paternal holdings begins:

> The method of sugar-cane production, upon which all tropical wealth depends, formed the elementary lesson of my day with Mr Brown. First, explained my master, the ripe canes are cut in the field and brought in bundles to the sugar mill, where the cleanest of the black women are employed to deliver the canes into the machines for grinding, while a solitary black woman draws them out at the other end once the juice has been extracted. She then throws the emaciated cane through an opening in the floor, where a pack of negroes is employed in bundling up this *trash* for use as fuel. The precious cane-juice gushes out of the grinding machine through a wooden gutter, and becomes quite white with foam. It streams into the boiling house, and enters a siphon where it is heated by the boiler.

It is slaked with lime to encourage it to granulate. The scum rises to the top, while the purer and more fluid juice flows through another gutter into a second siphon or copper. When little but the scum on the surface remains, the gutter communicating with the first copper is blocked off. The remaining waste travels through a final gutter, which conveys it to the distillery. Here the solution is mixed with molasses or treacle to become rum.

    … Under the guidance of Mr Brown I was able to observe all the tools, utensils and instruments employed in this industry, but it not being the season I was unable to see the process in full operation. However, Mr Brown's explanation was so thorough that not only do I feel confident that I might explain the mysteries of this process to any stranger, but I am persuaded that I must myself have observed it in action! (pp. 82–83; italics in original)

A reader might be forgiven for finding something strangely familiar about this scene of instruction, because it is heavily indebted to Lewis's journal entry for 11 January 1816, in which he evokes 'the whole process of sugar-making'.[5] Yet not only is this account of the labours of the plantation laden with intertextual echoes, but its derivativeness is echoed in turn by the second-hand nature of the knowledge whose acquisition it describes. As the penultimate sentence makes clear, the 'elementary lesson' Emily receives from her 'master' at this point does not involve direct experience: under Brown's tutelage, she 'observe[s] all the tools, utensils and instruments employed' in the creation of sugar, even as, 'it not being the season', she is 'unable to see the process in full operation'. Despite its secondary status, Emily's understanding of how sugar comes into being is nevertheless sufficiently informed as to appear authoritative. Complete with his muscovado-coloured name, Brown is sugar's grasping nonpareil,[6] since, as Emily puts it, 'there is [no]body who knows more than [him] about the business of squeezing profit from a moderately sized plantation in the tropical zone' (p. 82), but she herself can 'explain the mysteries of [the] process to any stranger'.

    Emily's excitement at mastering sugar's secrets has its correlate in the frisson the reader gains from identifying Lewis as source here, an experience available to a greater or lesser extent on almost every page of the novel, whether in relation to Lewis himself or to other colonial traveller-diarists, who (besides Flannigan) include Janet Schaw and Mrs Carmichael – as well, of course, as the ex-slave, Equiano. At the same time, Emily's mastery is part of a more general programme by which she strives to comprehend and so control the 'new world' she has 'crossed the ocean to discover' (p. 18). Despite its Columbian pretensions, this programme can sometimes seem fairly modest and mundane, as when Brown takes 'the trouble to explain to [Emily] the mysteries of two fruits' – the shaddock and the mango – 'which regularly grace [their] table' (p. 81), or 'label[s] a tree or shrub whose colour or particular grace … attract[s]' his visitor's 'eye' (p. 85). On the other hand, though, the programme can be more ambitious, mobilizing more sophisticated strategies than just the play of question and answer in which Emily participates, whether with Brown himself or with Stella, the 'ebony matriarch' (p. 36) appointed as her personal slave. One of these strategies entails translating what is new and exotic into the already known and is to be observed, for example, in two events Emily records while her journal is still in its infancy. The first of these in fact takes place even before she leaves the ship which has transported her to the unnamed island where the novel's action largely unfolds and involves her initial sighting of the 'infamous sugar canes, whose young shoots' seem to be 'billow[ing] in the cooling breeze like fields of green barley' (p. 18). The second occurs after disembarkation, as she travels towards her father's estate and 'marvel[s] at the riches of the fields' around her, noting how they are 'divided into cane-pieces by different species of hedge, some of which … resemble [the English] hawthorn'. As she adds, in a still more strikingly down-to-earth domestication of difference: 'These West Indian fields were all neatly dressed as though preparing for turnip husbandry as practised in England' (p. 23).

Of all the strategies at her disposal, though, the one on which Emily's sense of interpretative mastery (and racial superiority) most depends is that of the stereotype. As Homi K. Bhabha has argued, the stereotype is an indispensable element of colonial discourse: it is designed to turn the other into a fixed and knowable entity, even as its constant repetition is, ironically, the symptom of an anxiety that the truths it seems to usher in and guarantee may, in the end, be nothing more than self-serving illusions.[7] Such a nervous logic is entirely characteristic of Emily's journal, which works tirelessly to construct and maintain the black subject in a position of 'self-evident inferiority' (p. 35), invoking a panoply of well-worn formulas in order so to do. If the slaves whom Emily encounters can be peremptorily and uniformly dismissed as being 'addicted to theft and deceit at every opportunity' (p. 39) and figured as 'cannibals' as they eat their '*souse*' (p. 44; italics in original), they additionally possess an animality manifesting itself not only in terms of bodily appearance ('broad negro paws' [p. 111]) and sexual mores ('the brutish gratification of … desire' [p. 39]), but also the nature of their speech. Perhaps more than any other, it is this particular aspect of the 'negro stock' (p. 38) to which Emily most frequently returns in the course of her narrative, portraying moments of black utterance in ways which make the subjects from whom it emanates seem scarcely human. The sound of Stella's voice as she awakens Emily from her first day's siesta on the plantation is likened to the 'mooing of a cow' (p. 29), just as the black talk the mistress hears around her more generally is variously marked by an 'enervating yawn and drawl' (p. 95), 'all-too familiar bray' (p. 110) and 'incoherent slobber' (p. 123).

Such is Emily's growing faith in her own discursive authority that it leads her in due course to consider the possibility of making her experiences and opinions known to the public at large. She resolves, on returning from her colonial sojourn, to undertake 'a small lecture tour' (p. 85) which, she trusts, 'might be of interest' to 'ladies' associations' back home and further entertains the idea of 'compos[ing] a short pamphlet framed as a reply to the lobby who, without any knowledge of life in these climes, would seek to have us believe that slavery is nothing more than an abominable evil' (p. 86). As this phantom tract suggests, Emily travels just as far politically as she does geographically in the novel, arriving at a position directly opposed to that with which she at first aligns herself, as articulated in the breezy hope that her 'adventuring will encourage' her 'Father' to submit to 'the increasingly common … English belief in the iniquity of slavery' (p. 8). While such a shift in political ground is both consistent with and no doubt influenced by the sea-change in Emily's feelings towards Brown, the assumptions on which it is based are problematic to say the least, and no more so than from the perspective of Cambridge himself, one of those slaves whose essential nature Emily professes to have deciphered. Itself 'framed as a reply' to Emily's narrative, Cambridge's text dismantles the menagerie of stereotypes by which she (like most other white characters in the novel) seeks to encage blackness, showing them to apply more properly to the oppressor than to the oppressed. At the same time, the narrative reveals how the traits supposedly unique to the oppressor's culture – civilization, Christian faith, sexual virtue, intellect, literacy, humanity – can just as easily be appropriated by the black subject. Although, as Cambridge puts it, he will always be 'a little smudgy of complexion', he can lay claim, none the less, to the exalted and seemingly antithetical title of 'Englishman' (p. 147).[8]

In thus casting the stereotype into doubt, Cambridge's tale contests the mastery Emily arrogates to herself. Yet the unsettling of Emily's authority is something revealed in her own white writing just as much as in the black counter-statement succeeding it, as can be shown from considering three scenes of misreading in which she becomes characteristically implicated at different moments in the novel. The first of these takes place early on as she leaves Baytown – 'the point' where her 'residence in the West Indies' (p. 102) begins – and 'set[s] forth' towards the family estate, situated some 'three or four miles to the north-west' (p. 21) of the island-capital:

> Just after we turned off the *island road*, and into a small ascending lane, a number of pigs bolted into view, and after them a small parcel of monkeys. This took me by surprise, and I … jumped some considerable space … However, on resettling my position, I discovered that what I had taken for monkeys were nothing other than negro children, naked as they were born, parading in a feral manner to which they were not only accustomed, but in which they felt comfortable. (pp. 23–24; italics in original)

Part of the significance of the swift play of vision and revision occurring here is its status as an ironic comment on the more rigid patterns of taxonomic error which typify Emily's journal as a whole: in this particular instance, the misconstruing of black child for monkey no sooner happens than it is corrected, even as it is just such kinds of misprision which ordinarily go unquestioned as Emily moves and writes from day to day, prosaically invoking a language of the bestiary in her negotiation of the black subjects she meets, whether enslaved or free. At the same time, this incident is important for the way in which it threatens to bring about a textual or rather an intertextual version of the perceptual mistake to which Emily herself at first succumbs. After all, to a reader ungrounded in the archive of colonial materials on which Phillips constantly draws, Emily's encounter with those briefly simianized 'negro children' will inevitably be taken to be the product of authorial invention, rather than seen for what it is – an episode reworked from the second chapter of Schaw's *Journal of a Lady of Quality* (1776). Arriving in Antigua and proceeding, like her fictional avatar, to her 'lodgings', Schaw writes: 'Just as we got into the lane, a number of pigs run out [*sic*] at a door, and after them a parcel of monkeys. This not a little surprized me, but I found what I took for monkeys were negro children, naked as they were born'.[9] But whether or not this passage is identified as the precursor to the classificatory error in Phillips, the error itself offers a preliminary indication that Emily is not the most reliable of narrators and, while her confusion is quickly resolved, it is just as quickly followed by a new gaffe. She describes the 'blacks' as 'native people' (p. 24) and has to be 'corrected on [this] count' by the Lewis-like 'book-keeper' (p. 25) who is the white companion on her journey.

The second scene of misreading is located rather later in the text as Emily takes up Brown's 'unexpected and generous offer to spend a day touring with him', moving beyond the plantation into the island at large in order to 'taste fully each hidden corner' of the new realm she has come to 'inhabit'. Like the mix-up en route to the estate, this incident turns upon an encounter with naked black bodies, though here they do not belong to children but are fully grown. Accepting Brown's invitation with 'a light heart and eager anticipation', Emily writes (p. 100):

> Just beyond the village known as *Butler's*, Arnold drew the carriage to a halt beside a broad stream which coursed through the cane-pieces. He did so in order that I might have the opportunity to observe some negroes engaged in washing clothes. The negro men … did no more than stand and watch as their women performed the domestic ritual, pounding clothes against stones, and then rinsing these rags in the turbid water. The appearance of the females was truly disgusting to me, for without a single exception their arms were drawn out of their sleeves and from the waist upwards they were in a state of unashamed nakedness. One woman, her hair matted with filth,

and, I imagine, her flesh host to countless forms of infestation, stood in a condition of total nudity in the centre of the stream. Long encrusted with dirt by her labours, she now scrubbed away at the small rolls of grease with her soapless hands. Eventually she stepped clear of her muddy brown bath, and as the water beaded on the shining surface of her newly bright skin she merely lifted her head to the heavens and imbibed the heat of the sun, which would soon dry her ebon hide. Arnold informed me that such habits of cleanliness were uncommon in these people, who prided themselves on their infrequent use of water. (pp. 101–102).

This passage involves a borrowing neither from Lewis nor from Schaw, but from Carmichael's *Domestic Manners and Social Condition of the White, Coloured and Negro Population of the West Indies* (1833).[10] Although it begins as a description of half-clad black women 'engaged in washing clothes', the passage alters tack in midstream, so to speak, directing attention towards one female figure in particular, who is not just semi-naked but 'in a condition of total nudity' and busy cleansing not so much her garments as herself. The drifting of narrative focus towards this black Aphrodite – rising 'Eventually' from her 'muddy brown bath' with 'newly bright skin' – is paralleled in the drifting of meaning beneath the textual surface. Emily herself explicitly frames her encounter in innocently anthropological terms: it is for her merely an 'opportunity to observe' how a common 'domestic ritual' is 'performed' by women who are black rather than white. But is this really why her suitor-guide 'halt[s]' the 'carriage' between the 'cane-pieces'? Or is he serving his own interests rather than those of his 'disgust[ed]' companion, a possibility made all the more likely by what later emerges with regard to his sexual exploitation of Christiania? While the 'negro men' may indifferently 'stand and watch … their women' carrying out their 'labours', the suggestion is that the women themselves are being appropriated as erotic objects for the 'handsomely attired' (p. 100) white male voyeur, whose desires remain imperfectly laundered between the lines of Emily's prose.

To miss the intertextual provenance of the earlier incident when Emily mistakes human bodies for their simian counterparts is to replicate her error in a different form, misconstruing what is a copy for an original, Schaw for Phillips. In this episode, by contrast, to recognize the desire underlying Brown's ostensibly objective interest in the washerwomen is to gain an insight Emily lacks and so secure the hermeneutic upper hand against her. But Phillips's colonial ingénue is herself capable of tentatively questioning her own interpretative competence, as illustrated in the third and final scene of misreading, played out as Emily continues her circuit of the island and incurs, on returning to Baytown, 'a slight misfortune to the heel of [her] right shoe'. This obliges her (together with Brown) to visit the 'hovel' (p. 104) of a free black cobbler, who responds to the presence of his lofty white callers by 'prostrat[ing] himself

... in a gesture of base supplication'. But far from affirming Emily's sense of racial superiority, the cobbler's self-abasement constitutes a 'performance' from which she is surprisingly anxious to escape, 'beat[ing] a hasty retreat, determined if need be to hobble all day'. This sudden withdrawal is in part literal but partly also metaphorical, as Emily dissolves the strange particulars of her encounter with the cobbler into generalized reflections on the 'sooty tribe' to which he belongs. She reads his behaviour as a synecdoche for the 'belief' of black people as a whole 'in their own degradation and inferiority', which, she argues, is both 'the greatest impediment' to their uplift and 'one of the ugliest consequences' of their history of oppression. Despite her seemingly adamantine conclusions, 'the case of this *sambo*' seems none the less to elude her grasp, leaving Emily nonplussed as to the real meaning of 'negro civility': 'truly ... I was unsure', she writes, 'whether or not he was making sport of us, for I detected about his free person touches of wit which he appeared to be only partly concealing, but to what purpose I could not fathom' (p. 105; italics in original).

Enigmatic Bodies

These three scenes of interpretative uncertainty are located outside the environs of the paternal estate and, taken together, bear out Emily's Conradian sense that, in travelling to the West Indies, she is 'entering a dark tropical unknown' (p. 22) where mastery yields to mystery. Yet it is on the plantation itself that the sense of enigma is at its most intense, reaching resolution only in the apocalyptic forms of Brown's death and that of Cambridge, who, adjudged to be his murderer, is 'hanged and gibbeted' by way of 'punishment', his 'whitened bones' left to 'glisten in the moonbeams' (p. 174): Emily might possess a hand-me-down expertise with regard to the rites and riddles of sugar-making and be able to impose a carapace of meaning on her experiences by dint of the stereotype, but her status as an absentee slave-owner's daughter accords her no privilege when it comes to excavating the plantation's secret history. One reason for this is that those with the ability to shed light on the subject are not inclined to use it, with the book-keeper who accompanies Emily on her journey to the estate providing a tone-setting instance of such evasiveness. He is quite content to school his charge in racist myths concerning the true identity of the 'native people' of the Caribbean (he tells Emily they are cannibals) and to offer instruction 'on the question of colour', but falls silent when asked about 'Mr Wilson, the manager of the estate', whose position Brown has usurped. As Emily notes, the book-keeper 'seem[s] unable to give [her] a clear and acceptable answer on this topic' (p. 25).

Emily's 'faithful Stella' is similarly selective in what she will and will not say, as, for example, on the supposedly 'recuperative walk' she and her mistress take one 'evening', just as the 'negroes in the field' are beginning to look forward to 'the end of their day's labour'. As the two women make their rounds during this transitional time between 'work and play', Stella provides a 'suitable commentary' on the slaves' 'behaviour' (p. 40), with much of the information she imparts directly taken by Phillips from Lewis's journal entry for 6 January 1816. But while she helps Emily comprehend the oblique sexual meanings of the various 'dances' the slaves perform once work is done – 'courtship … marriage … being brought to bed' – Stella is pointedly unwilling 'to offer … assistance' in decoding 'the songs … about *massa*' (p. 43; italics in original). She is even less forthcoming concerning the exact reason for the untimely whipping Brown inflicts upon Cambridge, 'with all the severity of vindictive malice' (p. 41),[11] just before the slaves begin their 'revelry' (p. 43). In contrast to Cambridge's fellow labourers, 'trudg[ing]' back 'towards the village' from the cane-fields and 'reluctant to turn their heads for fear of what they might witness', both Emily and Stella are subjected to the disturbing spectacle of colonial violence in all its immediacy and excess, as Brown repeatedly 'raise[s] and crack[s] his cattle-whip' across the back of the 'grey-haired *blackie*' (p. 41; italics in original). But if they are united by the burden of a shared witness, white woman and black do not share the same knowledge with respect to the origins of the cruelty enacted before them. Just as the administration of the master's power only redoubles the slave's resistance – Cambridge 'stare[s] up' at the sun 'in defiance' (p. 41) of Brown and 'steadfastly refuse[s] to flinch away' (p. 42) – so Emily's desire to master what she sees by discovering and articulating its meaning elicits its own kind of opposition in the shape of her maid's grudging and fragmentary disclosures. As Emily puts it: 'Stella … seemed loath to answer my questions as to the cause of this brutality. All I could obtain from her was the intelligence that the black has a history of insubordination, and that *massa* foolishly seeks to make him more ruly by inflicting stripes' (pp. 41–42; italics in original).

This refusal to be drawn on the precise 'cause' of Brown's 'brutality' towards the unruly Cambridge is a stance maintained throughout the novel, not only by Stella herself – '"You no know what dat man suffer"' she later tells Emily, in her 'grotesque lingo' (p. 119) – but by other major characters as well. Mr McDonald, the 'slave-doctor' (p. 181) who is also Emily's physician, fails to answer her directly when examined on the question of the beating, merely venturing the truism 'that when two strong wills cross one must expect trouble' (p. 94). For his part, Brown advances an explanation for his actions which is as abstruse as it is self-justifying, setting the whipping in the context of the so-called '*deficiency* laws' (p. 58; italics in original) and the increased need to uphold colonial 'discipline' as both the number and 'quality of the whites' on the estates diminishes and the threat of 'insurrection' (p. 59) grows accordingly.[12] Even the remembering Cambridge does not seem entirely sure about the motive for the flogging he receives, betraying his uncertainty in the belated version of the event appearing towards the end of his narrative:

> The … day [after Christiania's rape] Mr Brown found weak pretext to inflict upon me a severe beating in the presence of an English female. Whether this was some customary ritual to ensure easier access next time he should choose to visit my *wife*, or due punishment for the defiance I had chosen not to hide, I could not tell. But upon my back, in a series of random patterns, were markings that cut deep into the flesh. (p. 162; italics in original)

It is evident from this that the violence of the master can be just as equivocal in its way as the 'civility' of the 'negro', suspending meaning between alternative possibilities: is the 'severe beating' 'inflict[ed]' upon the enslaved male body to be linked to the violation suffered by its female counterpart, or should it be connected to Cambridge's 'defiance' of Brown when he publicly refuses the prestigious 'title of Head Driver' (p. 161)? Whatever his purposes, Brown conceals them with a 'weak pretext', even as they escape Cambridge too. The 'markings … cut deep into [the slave's] flesh' thus disintegrate into a meaningless spectacle, reminiscent of the 'hideous pattern of weals' 'sculpted', as Emily puts it, on the 'broad black backs' of Cambridge's 'fellow field-workers' by the 'application of the lash' (p. 41).

Shortly after bearing witness to the 'unnecessary savagery' (p. 62) of Cambridge's whipping, Emily describes the 'white populace' on her father's estate as 'secretive', fashioning herself as a kind of colonial heroine-detective, whose mission is 'to unravel' the 'mysteries' with which she is faced and pinpointing Brown as 'the chief enigma' (p. 45) on which to work. As the examples of Stella's self-censorship and Cambridge's ambiguously scarred body suggest, however, the plantation's black populace proves to be just as obscure as its white. This is most strikingly evidenced in Christiania, the psychologically disturbed 'coal-black *ape-woman*' (p. 73; italics in original),[13] whose intrusions into the text, fleeting though they be, constitute for Emily a constant source of vexation and bafflement. These disruptive and distracted cameos frequently take place in the dining room of the Great House where Emily and Brown eat together, and are viewed by the former with growing consternation as a serious flouting of the racial conventions which should keep white and black bodies apart. But if Emily is offended both by Christiania's disregard for plantation protocols and by Brown's open complicity with 'this slattern's presence' (p. 58) during meals, it is not least because the table at which the slavewoman mysteriously appears is a symbolically charged space, where appetites of the stomach stand in for sexual cravings and hence also a space where the 'social evil of miscegenation' (p. 52), as McDonald calls it, disports itself in coded form.

The connection between the two kinds of bodily appetite, the literal and the figurative, is first implied in the slippage marking the words with which

Stella informs Emily that Brown has requested her presence at dinner on the evening of her arrival at the estate. Arousing her mistress from slumber, Stella exclaims, "'Missy! Missy! You must hurry, hurry quick! Mr Brown, he hungry and he no wait too long for you'" (p. 28) – as if Emily were a dish to sate a desire which has as much to do with sex as with food and is quite possibly even cannibalistic. Yet while Stella's message ominously prefigures the eventual liaison between white woman and white man, Emily herself is more preoccupied with the possibilities of sexual intimacy as they occur across the lines of racial difference, speculating that the 'strange and haughty black woman' (p. 73) whom Brown 'desire[s] to have ... share his table' (p. 75) might also be the companion of his bed. As so often with Emily, however, the problem is one of misreading: although correct in sensing the existence of a secret desire between master and slave, she errs radically in assuming that it is mutual, attributing to Christiania a mercenary sexual agency which runs precisely counter to the truth of her lot as sexual victim. It is consequently no surprise that when Emily cross-examines Stella about the personal goals of the 'inky wench, who ... dare[s] publicly to preside at [her] table' (p. 76), she should meet with so affronted a reaction:

> It appeared that [Stella] took offence at the manner in which I portrayed the ambitions of black womanhood, but she manifested her rage not by overt onslaught, but by covert smouldering. I asked her if it were not true that young black wenches are inclined to lay themselves out for white lovers, and hence bring forth a spurious and degenerate breed, neither fit for the field nor for any work that the true-bred negro would relish. She would not answer. I asked her if it was not entirely understandable that such women would become licentious and insolent past all bearing because of their privileged position? Again, she would say nothing in response. I informed her that I have even heard intelligence that if a mulatto child threatens to interrupt a black woman's pleasure, or become a troublesome heir, there are certain herbs and medicines, including the juice of the cassava plant, which seldom fail to free the mother from this inconvenience. At this point Stella seemed ready to quit my chamber. (p. 76)

In the encounter with the free black shoe-maker considered earlier, Emily moves from the particular to the general, classing his behaviour as racially typical, but in this passage (adapted from Schaw)[14] the trajectory is reversed, as she strives to account for Christiania's attendance at the dining table in terms of what she has gathered concerning local 'custom' (p. 75), figuring her as the embodiment of the 'ambitions of black womanhood' at large. Yet it could be argued that Emily's analysis of the politics of Caribbean sexuality discloses as much about the 'covert smouldering' of her own desires as it does about the longings of the 'young black wenches' whose scheming she condemns, just as

McDonald will later anxiously conceal his attraction to Emily by displacing it onto Cambridge (pp. 93–94). Either way, the effect this escalating series of innuendoes has on Stella – 'She would not answer', 'she would say nothing in response', '[she] seemed ready to quit my chamber' – tells its own story, silently marking out the interpretative limits beyond which Emily's journal is unable to move.

By way of direct sequel to the interrogation of Stella, Emily turns angrily to Brown himself for clarification of Christiania's exact 'status' (p. 76), tracking him down to a 'denuded cane-piece', where he is overseeing the 'Sisyphean labours' of her father's slaves, only to find her own hermeneutic efforts meeting once more with defeat. Yet the cane-field is not only a site stripped of enlightenment but also a place which offers a crude symbolic commentary on the thwarting of the quest for 'meaning' (p. 77) itself. Although the 'sun [is] high' (p. 76) when the infuriated heroine-detective sets out for the 'fields', it comes to be 'darken[ed] for a few seconds', as she draws nearer to Brown, by a 'flight of birds' which 'cast[s] a shadow like that of a cloud', just as Brown's own 'hand' is later 'raised … to block' the light 'from his face' (p. 77) as Emily questions him. The scene's conspicuously symbolic elements are allied to its equally salient ironies. Earlier in the text, Emily's stormy confrontation with Christiania leads her to demand, albeit unsuccessfully, that a 'black retainer … escort the negress from [her] table' (p. 73), even as here it is she who is to be removed from the scene, as Brown quietly instructs one of the slaves 'to bear [her] back to the Great House'. This order leads to a more visceral sort of removal, as Emily responds hysterically to the 'nigger' who lays 'his black hands upon [her] body', her 'stomach turn[ing] in revulsion' as its 'contents [are] emptied upon the ground' (p. 78).

While they may be ineffective at first, the 'entreaties' (p. 80) of 'the wild Englishwoman' (p. 77), as Emily calls herself, appear eventually 'to have borne fruit': Christiania is 'forbidden' by Brown 'to sit at the dining table' and indeed 'confined' altogether 'to the negro village', along with the 'primitive obeah' in which she is generally thought to be adept. This 'profound change in the heart and soul of Mr Brown' (p. 80) signals the seemingly arbitrary reorientation of his desire away from Christiania and towards Emily, who becomes the object of 'an intimate interest' (p. 163) culminating in her seduction at Hawthorn Cottage, a fate itself anticipated in the revealingly carnal terms she uses to dramatize the cane-field contretemps: 'For some time we stood, toe to toe, two solitary white people under the powerful sun, casting off our garments of white decorum before the black hordes, each vying for supremacy over the other' (p. 77). But it is not long before Christiania returns to the plantation, bringing with her a set of practices even less accountable (though more disquieting) than her mealtime appearances. As Emily reports:

Outside my window, I began to discern nocturnal scratching noises. At first I was too frightened to properly investigate, in fear that some strange beast might be waiting for an opportunity to assault and devour me body and soul. Eventually, on the third night, I pulled back a corner of the blind and peered into the darkness, whereupon I observed the re-entry into the drama of my life of the arrogant black wench, Christiania. Squatting down on her hams, she appeared to be scratching at the dirt, to what purpose I knew not. Furthermore, she was uttering sinister sounds which I did not wish to hear repeated throughout the night. (p. 89)

This passage contains a cluster of verbal traits quite characteristic of Emily's journal as a whole, combining a familiar rhetoric of detection (and equally familiar split infinitive) – 'I was too frightened to properly investigate' – with a customary language of perplexity ('to what purpose I knew not'). What is most significant about the passage, though, is the image of the 'strange beast' and, in particular, Emily's fear that it is to 'devour' her, 'body and soul'. This baleful creature turns out, of course, to be non-existent, just as the 'small parcel of monkeys' featured earlier in the novel metamorphoses, on reflection, into a group of 'negro children'. None the less, the fact that it is endowed with hunger is appropriate, since, as Cambridge's narrative later makes clear, Christiania is not just 'scratching at the dirt' here but consuming it, a detail subtly linking her 'nocturnal' activities outside Emily's window to the dinner table scenes in which the two women have previously clashed. For Emily, Christiania's 'scrabblings and croakings' (p. 90) simply provide further proof of the stereotypical nature of the black subject as a hideous mix of the bestial and the demonic: Christiania 'whin[es] like a dog in the filth, making noises as if she were communing with the devil himself' (p. 91), she writes. For Cambridge, however, his wife's 'dirt-eating' is construed in different if also contradictory ways. On the one hand, it seems to be as repellent to him as it is to Emily herself, leading him to condemn the habit as a 'filthy behaviour' and sign of a 'paganism' anathema to the Christian faith he has assimilated from his exposure to the English. On the other, though, it elicits a more sympathetic definition as an effect specifically produced by Christiania's subjection to the sexual appetites of Brown. As Cambridge contends, his wife's night-time rituals can be 'traced … to a *sickness* brought on by Mr Brown's hunger' (p. 163; italics in original), the implication being that she has been impregnated by Brown and is engaging in geophagy as a way of making good a dietary deficiency.[15]

It would not be unreasonable to suggest that Christiania's pregnancy, no less than the tropical advent of Emily, is one of the factors contributing both to Brown's loss of interest in the slavewoman as sexual object and to her concomitant relegation from the dining table, just as the latter event produces the grounds on which her geophagy becomes necessary. It might be similarly suggested that Christiania's condition helps retrospectively to explain the sense of anger occasioned in Stella by Emily's remarks on the natural resources black women use to dispose of 'a mulatto child' whose existence threatens their 'pleasure', since Christiania is doing the exact opposite, struggling to nourish herself in a bid to nourish her unborn baby. Either way, it would seem that Christiania's dramatic fall from the grace and favour of the Great House to the humiliation of 'crawling' (p. 91) in the soil outside it is something adumbrated in the text long before it comes to pass. This at least is the burden of Emily's first encounter with Brown, which occurs in the 'dining room' and finds him 'sitting at the head of [a] broad table, his feet upon a chair, engaged in digging out mud from the soles of his boots with, of all implements, a dining fork'. But if Christiania's fate is prefigured in these unlikely actions – themselves assisted by those of the 'black boy', who 'catch[es]' the mud and 'hurr[ies]' to toss it out of the window so that it might not lay where it fell' (p. 30) – her destiny itself broadly anticipates what happens to Emily. The latter in her turn is abandoned by Brown to become, in the novel's Epilogue, the mother to his stillborn child, finally entering the spaces of a delirium not unlike those 'zones of illogicality' (p. 164) into which Christiania has already strayed. These parallels between the sexual fates of slavewoman and slave-mistress throw into relief the irony underlying their mutual antagonism, since, far from being adversaries, Emily and Christiania are more properly one another's doubles. Given this fundamental affinity, it is no wonder that Brown should contemplate the spectacle of Emily indignantly hurtling towards him across the cane-field as if steeling himself for confrontation with a disgruntled slave: 'He … turned and watched, waiting, hands upon hips and whip in hand, for my approach' (p. 77).

Just as the prefigurative aspects of Brown's shoe-cleaning habits can hardly be said to announce themselves with any great obviousness, so Emily's confession that she is carrying Brown's child is delivered with a similar discretion, emerging only in her journal's closing pages in the aside referring to 'a brief and disturbing visit' from McDonald and the desperate hope that 'Arnold will not consider abandoning [her] now', especially given the suggestion that all is not well with her 'weak womanly body' (p. 127). Both of these soft-voiced textual details demand from the reader, in other words, the same kind of attentiveness required from the doctor himself, as he performs his 'auscultations' (p. 178) in the course of helping his patient through the travail of the stillbirth. Yet the 'lamentable condition' (p. 127) in which Emily finds herself is as much ideological as it is physical. As well as annulling the programmatic narrative of lucrative marriage to Thomas Lockwood, 'a fifty-year-old widower with three children', which Emily's father originally arranges for her West Indian return, the daughter's predicament disrupts the norms of early nineteenth-century middle-class English femininity altogether. As the Prologue makes clear, these are nothing if not constraining, allowing 'A woman' merely to 'play upon a delicate keyboard, paint water-colours, or sing' (p. 3) and fastening her body 'into backboards, corsets and stays to improve her posture' (p. 4).

A History of Sexual Violence: *Cambridge contra* Lewis

The seduction, pregnancy and abandonment of the Englishwoman who voyages to the colonial margin is, to use her own phrase, likely to appear 'a major scandal' in the eyes of the patriarchal regime holding sway at home. As Cambridge's story illustrates, however, there are a variety of other scandals to consider too, one of which arises from the very existence of the story itself and, in particular, its positioning within the narrative sequence of the novel as a whole. By the time the reader comes to learn Cambridge's tale, its author is already dead: as Emily reports, 'he is hanged from a tree' and hence 'no longer able to explain or defend' the 'treacherous act' (p. 128) he is alleged to have committed. But by placing Cambridge's story after Emily's, Phillips creates the disconcerting impression that it is being related posthumously. It is as if the 'man strung up' with 'mouth agape' and 'tongue protruding' were indeed explaining and defending this supposed 'act' and in so doing had been oddly exempted from the usual laws of life and death, unable, as the ministering doctor asks of his patient, to '"keep still and stop talking"' (p. 183). For Emily, the decorous and sophisticated style in which Cambridge recounts his tale would no doubt also scandalize, since it undermines her assertions about the animalistic nature of black expression, providing a written complement to the '*lunatic* precision' which seems, as she earlier notes, to govern Cambridge's 'dealings with … English words' and leads her to suspect that he 'imagine[s] himself to be part of [her] white race' (p. 120; italics in original).

Beyond the outrage of Emily's identity as fallen woman and that of Cambridge as verbally meticulous textual revenant or '"dead man's jumby"' (p. 174), there lies the scandal of Christiania's rape, carried out on the 'evening' when Brown appears at Cambridge's 'hut', 'consumed with passion' and demanding crudely phallic entry with his 'pistol'. Although the rape takes place 'after dark', there is nothing covert about it, either for Cambridge himself, who has 'no doubt' that Christiania is 'the object of [Brown's] … desire' (p. 161), or for the 'fellow-slaves' who gather at the scene and dumbly condemn the white man 'as a disgrace to his own people and their civilization'. Nor is Brown's brutal 'act' designed simply to provide its perpetrator with sexual pleasure, additionally functioning as a double-sided form of power. It enables him not only to humiliate Christiania for the grandiose delusions which lead her to sit at his table and play at being 'mistress of the Great House' (p. 162) but also to punish Cambridge for his equally '*haughty*' defiance of the 'swaggering authority' invested in the whiteness of the master's 'skin' (p. 161; italics in original).

Brown's 'violation' (p. 162) of Christiania is not an isolated event but part of a larger pattern of white male sexual cruelty towards the black female. This pattern cuts back across the whole of Cambridge's brief but sweeping tale and links its different phases, as they take him first from Africa to England (via the Middle Passage) as an illegally captured slave and thence to the Caribbean, via a failed return to Africa as a Christian missionary. During the 'decade' or so spent in England, for example, Cambridge recalls how his 'criminal' master organizes the libidinal economy of his 'Pall Mall home', contrasting Anna, the 'sturdy Englishwoman' who will eventually become Cambridge's first wife, with Mahogany Nell, 'a woman of [Cambridge's] own clime and complexion'. In a clear inversion of Cambridge's own interracial preferences, the white servant is 'deemed' by the master to be 'unworthy of fleshy explora-tion', while the black is 'frequently admitt[ed] ... to his bed' and forced to meet his sexual 'needs' (p. 141), perhaps even '"performing the rites of Venus as they are done in the Carib seas"' (p. 143). Betraying the extent to which he does not merely 'Wash[ ] and clothe[ ]' himself 'in the English manner' (p. 140), but actively internalizes England's racially supremacist culture, Cambridge writes: 'Although [Nell's] pigmentation might not be as engaging as that of the fair daughters of Albion, my master clearly derived much comfort through his actions, for they were frequent and, if my ears did not deceive me, brutal in their lengthy pleasure' (p. 141). These abusive domestic arrangements look back in their turn to the Middle Passage, recalled by Cambridge as an experience of unprecedented racial hatred and evoked by Phillips by means of direct intertextual echoes of *The Interesting Narrative*:

> The white men came below with eatables. Those who found the strength to refuse were lashed, often to death. It appeared that bitterness and cruelty were sterner masters than mere avarice. Such malice as these men of very indifferent morals exhibited, I had never witnessed among any people. Their most constant practice was to commit violent depredations on the chastity of female slaves, as though these *princesses* were the most abandoned women of their species. (p. 138; italics in original)

Reworking and combining scenes from two different moments in Equiano's text,[16] this passage confirms Cambridge's earlier diagnosis of 'the slave trade' as a 'national madness' (p. 134) on the part of the English, crazily capable of privi-leging 'bitterness and cruelty' above 'avarice' by destroying the bodies which are the very source of profit. But the equally sinister symptom of such a collective pathology is the sexual exploitation of the black female, which, as Cambridge's experiences everywhere attest, is indeed a 'constant practice', repeating itself even after 'English law' has 'decreed trading in human flesh illegal' (p. 141).

Cambridge's narrative produces uncanny effects, exposing a history of sexual violence which would remain otherwise hidden amid the leaves of

Emily's journal and is all but elided in Lewis. In his descant on 'the *deficiency laws*', Brown berates the deterioration in the abilities of the white people who are attracted to the West Indies and with whom he is obliged to make a living, the objects of his vitriol ranging from 'the poorest sort of tradesmen and clerks, unqualified in any type of plantation work' to '*Carpenters* who knew not a saw from a chisel, *bricklayers* who knew not wood from stone [and] *book-keepers* who were illiterate and innumerate' (p. 59; italics in original). Yet while he himself can boast the skills and knowledge this unpromising gaggle of expatriates does not have, he is lacking in a more urgently moral sense and in the end to be numbered with those 'degraded white people' McDonald figures as the 'offscum ... offscouring [and] indeed ... very dregs of English life' (p. 51) – terms harking back to the Lewis-based account of 'sugar-cane production' with which this chapter began. Seen in the light of McDonald's typically strident but also strikingly saccharine language, the way in which Brown is dispatched to his death thus seems strangely appropriate: it involves a 'heavy blow' (p. 173) delivered to the head from 'an old copper skimmer (used in boiling sugar)', which Cambridge has 'sharpened' for this precise 'purpose' (p. 171).

Or at least this would be so, were the idiosyncrasies of Cambridge's *modus operandi* to be believed. As it happens, however, they cannot claim credence by being part of his own narrative – which makes no mention of a skimmer as the instrument of Brown's death and represents the death itself simply as the result of self-defence rather than an act of murderous vengeance (p. 167) – and stem in fact from another account of the novel's violent climax. This takes the form of the anonymous three-page report which is sandwiched between Cambridge's text and the novel's Epilogue and which presents itself to the reader as an official colonial document. Yet this document, cursory, imposing and sensationalist at once, not only rewrites the manner and the nature of Brown's demise but also alters other crucial aspects of Cambridge's story, thoroughly recasting its dramatis personae. Cambridge himself reappears in the official record as an 'insane man', while Brown is tricked out with the epithets 'Christian' (p. 171) and 'good' (p. 173). Brown's abuse of Christiania is reinscribed in turn as an 'innocent amour', 'carried ... on with a woman' who is identified not as Cambridge's wife but merely as 'belonging to the property' (p. 171) Brown oversees.

The identities of these three figures thus become disguised beneath the very document which purports to tell their true story, even as the document itself engages in a certain generic masquerade, appearing to form an authentic part of Phillips's fiction but belonging, it should be recalled, to Flannigan's text.[7] But whether taken at face value as Phillips's own invention or seen more accurately as a piece of historical writing conscripted into *Cambridge* from elsewhere, the official account of Brown's 'untimely death' (p. 171) needs to be read as much for what it does not say as for what it does. In this it has a good deal in common with both Emily's chronicle of her Caribbean encounters and Lewis's *Journal*, the text from which Phillips borrows so freely and deliberately and from whose silences the rapacious '*massa*' is finally brought to book.

Yet while *Cambridge* readily illuminates the violence of white male desire, it is (like *Slave Song*) clearly less willing to acknowledge the black female suffering such desire provokes. Austin Clarke's *The Polished Hoe*, by contrast, not only provides a more graphic insight than Phillips's novel into the systems of sexual oppression bred by plantation culture but also does so from the perspective of the woman who is caught up in them. At the same time, Clarke's novel shifts perspectives in another but equally important sense, elaborating its own distinctive black version of the analogies between sugar and text examined earlier in this book in the white writing of Grainger, Lewis and Eliot.

Notes

1. Lars Eckstein, *Re-Membering the Black Atlantic: On the Poetics and Politics of Literary Memory* (Amsterdam and New York: Rodopi, 2006), pp. 63–115. Eckstein's is by far the most comprehensive analysis of intertextuality in *Cambridge* to date, showing how Phillips manipulates more than twenty source-texts by means of the related compositional techniques of montage and pastiche. As Eckstein summarizes: 'the novel is composed of numerous, in most cases slightly modified fragments of older texts (montage); [while] at the same time, these fragments are supplemented and interconnected by passages which merely imitate the source-material stylistically while relying entirely on Phillips's own imagination (pastiche)' (p. 73). For other major readings of Phillips's novel attuned to its intertextual project, see Evelyn O'Callaghan, 'Historical Fiction and Fictional History: Caryl Phillips's *Cambridge*', *Journal of Commonwealth Literature*, 28.2 (1993), 34–47; Paul Sharrad, 'Speaking the Unspeakable: London, Cambridge and the Caribbean', in *De-Scribing Empire: Post-Colonialism and Textuality*, ed. Chris Tiffin and Alan Lawson (London and New York: Routledge, 1994), pp. 201–17; and Jenny Sharpe, *Ghosts of Slavery: A Literary Archaeology of Black Women's Lives* (Minneapolis and London: University of Minnesota Press, 2003), pp. 105–19. Almost all of the specific passages on which Phillips draws are helpfully collated by Eckstein in the appendix to his book (pp. 241–71).
2. Eckstein, p. 74.
3. For examples of this critical approach, in which *Cambridge*'s intertextual elements are either acknowledged but not emphasized or are ignored altogether, see Sylvie Chavanelle, 'Caryl Phillips's *Cambridge*: Ironical (Dis)empowerment?', *International Fiction Review*, 25 (1998), 78–88; Bénédicte Ledent, *Caryl Phillips* (Manchester and New York: Manchester University Press, 2002), pp. 80–106; and Maurizio Calbi, 'Vexing Encounters: Uncanny Belonging and the Poetics of Alterity in Caryl Phillips's *Cambridge*', *Postcolonial Text*, 1.2 (2005), < http://postcolonial.org/index.php/pct/article/view/343/121 > [accessed 16 August 2007].
4. Caryl Phillips, *Cambridge* (London: Picador, 1992), p. 124 (italics in original). Subsequent references to this work are incorporated in the text and given in parenthesis after quotations.
5. Lewis, p. 57.
6. As well as recalling the colour of the sugar whose production he oversees, Brown's appellation resonates with the pigmentation of the ubiquitous mulatto subjects who

populate Lewis's text, gathering, for example, at the racially exclusive 'ball of brown ladies and gentlemen' (Lewis, p. 106) witnessed at Montego Bay. Such a resonance is also entirely in keeping with Brown's sexual abuse of Christiania and the conception of the mixed-race child to which it leads.

7. For Bhabha's influential analysis of the workings of the stereotype, see Homi K. Bhabha, *The Location of Culture* (London and New York: Routledge, 1994), pp. 66–84. As he puts it, in terms which are directly pertinent to the tensions of Emily's journal, the stereotype 'is a form of knowledge and identification that vacillates between what is always "in place", already known, and something that must be anxiously repeated ... as if the essential duplicity of the Asiatic or the bestial sexual licence of the African that needs no proof, can never really, in discourse, be proved' (p. 66).

8. The larger effect of such an unsettling of the seemingly natural distinctions between whiteness and blackness is to unravel the essentialist ideology of race on which slavery and the slave trade are predicated. This in turn underscores the way in which Phillips's shaping of Cambridge's story is indebted to Equiano beyond the mere use of montage and pastiche, since *The Interesting Narrative* is similarly concerned to challenge and subvert conventional assumptions about racial difference. For a reading of Equiano along these lines, see my *Textual Politics from Slavery to Postcolonialism: Race and Identification* (Basingstoke and London: Macmillan, 2000), pp. 9–31.

9. Janet Schaw, *Journal of a Lady of Quality, Being the* Narrative *of a Journey from Scotland to the* West Indies, North Carolina, *and* Portugal, *in the years 1774 to 1776*, ed. Evangeline Walker Andrews (with Charles McLean Andrews), intro. Stephen Carl Arch (Lincoln, NE and London: University of Nebraska Press, 2005), p. 78.

10. For the original text inspiring Phillips here, see Mrs A. C. Carmichael, *Domestic Manners and Social Condition of the White, Coloured, and Negro Population of the West Indies*, 2 vols (New York: Negro Universities Press, 1969), vol. 1, p. 10.

11. This phrase is not Phillips's, but taken word for word from the penultimate entry in Lewis's *Journal* (for 1 May 1818), where the whipping is carried out by a 'free mulatto' (Lewis, p. 248) who is mistress to a black slave-child. The borrowing is not noted by Eckstein.

12. The legal measures to which Brown fleetingly refers are glossed in Theodore W. Allen, *The Invention of the White Race, Volume One: Racial Oppression and Social Control* (London and New York: Verso, 1994), pp. 137–38. First promulgated in the late seventeenth century in Barbados and widely adopted on other British West Indian possessions thereafter, the '"deficiency laws"' were designed, Allen writes, 'to provide quotas, as they might be termed today, according to which the plantation owners were required, under penalty of the law, to employ at least one "white" male for every so many "Negroes," the proportion varying from colony to colony and time to time, from one-to-twenty (Nevis, 1701) to one-to-four (Georgia, 1750)'.

13. The figuration of Christiania in these hybridizing terms is part of the general trend by which the novel ironically links the human and the simian for its anti-racist purposes. The earliest example of this is the misreading of 'negro children' for 'monkeys' which occurs at the start of Emily's colonial experience, while a more haunting later instance emerges in the course of Cambridge's narrative, as he recalls the '*bird and beast shops*' he sees during his time in London. In these freakish emporia, Cambridge writes, 'negro children are sold for amusement like parrots or monkeys, although the practice of decorating them with gold or silver collars has mercifully fallen from usage' (p. 151; italics in original). The pattern is completed in Cambridge's speculations as to why it is that Brown might tolerate Christiania's play-acting as colonial mistress: 'Perhaps he looked upon my comely *wife* as a visual entertainment, in the same manner that some Englishmen keep about them dwarfs or pet monkeys?' (p. 162; italics in original).

14. See Schaw, pp. 112–13.

15. For detailed information on the role of geophagy as a means of nutritional supplement during pregnancy, see Kenneth Morgan, 'Slave Women and Reproduction in Jamaica, c. 1776–1834', *History: The Journal of the Historical Association*, 91 (2006), pp. 235–36.

16. The first of these scenes occurs in the context of Equiano's evocation of his own Middle Passage in chapter 2 of *The Interesting Narrative*, while the second is located in chapter 5, when Equiano is forcibly returned to the West Indies from England to be re-enslaved. See Equiano, pp. 56 and 104.

17. See Mrs Flannigan, *Antigua and the Antiguans: A Full Account of the Colony and Its Inhabitants from the Time of the Caribs to the Present Day, Interspersed with Anecdotes and Legends. Also, an Impartial View of Slavery and the Free Labour Systems; The Statistics of the Island, and Biographical Notices of the Principal Families*, 2 vols (London: Saunders and Otley, 1844), vol. 2, pp. 89–92.

7

'Somebody Kill Somebody, Then?': The Sweet Revenge of Austin Clarke's *The Polished Hoe*

Their different instruments of husbandry, particularly their gleaming hoes, when uplifted to the sun, and which, particularly when they are digging cane-holes, they frequently raise all together, and in as exact time as can be observed, in a well-conducted orchestra, in the bowing of the fiddles, occasion the light to break in momentary flashes around them.

– William Beckford, *A Descriptive Account of the Island of Jamaica*

The weapon and the tool seem at moments indistinguishable, for they may each reside in a single physical object … and may be quickly transformed back and forth, now into the one, now into the other. At the same time, however, a gulf of meaning, intention, connotation, and tone separates them. If one holds the two side by side in front of the mind … it is then clear that what differentiates them is not the object itself but the surface on which they fall.

– Elaine Scarry, *The Body in Pain*

Unearthing the Past

The first-person narrative of sexual suffering which remains unarticulated in *Cambridge* emerges, in *The Polished Hoe*, in the tale told by Mary Gertrude Mathilda Paul, a mixed-race woman with skin 'the colour of coffee with a lil milk in it'.[1] This tale spans a period from the early 1950s, when the novel is set, to the time of Mary's childhood and recalls her systematic abuse by Mr Bellfeels, manager of the Barbadian sugar plantation on which she is born. But Mary's ability to give voice to the sexual history she shares with the muted and dirt-eating Christiania of Phillips's text is only one of several differences between the two women and the novels they inhabit. As well as attaining to the status of narrating subject, Mary takes on two other roles from which Christiania is debarred. The first of these is that of Bellfeels' reluctant mistress, a position in which she realizes what for the slavewoman are only 'flights of fantasy',[2] exchanging her body for the material comfort and social privilege Bellfeels, though himself not quite 'pure white' (p. 367), is able to provide. The second role sees Mary turn from mistress to murderess, as she assumes the sort of vengeful agency in which her enslaved counterpart is precisely lacking. In Phillips's novel, indeed, the master's wrongs are not, strictly speaking, avenged at all, since his death occurs more by accident than by design during a notably laconic scuffle with Cambridge: 'He struck me once with his crop, and I took it from him', Cambridge observes, 'and in the resultant struggle the life left his body'.[3] In Clarke's text, conversely, there is nothing remotely accidental about the demise of Bellfeels, whom Mary kills with the shining handle of the implement giving the novel its title,[4] sexually mutilating him thereafter with the hoe's sharpened blade.

Mary divulges the long history of abuse culminating in this moment of luminous violence in the form of a confession delivered over a single night to the village detective, Sergeant Percy DaCosta Benjamin Stuart, the black man who has been in love with her since he was ten years of age, but who remains separated from the object of his desire by barriers of race and class. While the confessional mode presupposes the revelation of secrets specific to the confessant, Mary's statement simultaneously possesses a collective edge which represents a departure from this pattern. In speaking and acting for herself, she speaks and acts, equally, on behalf of other oppressed women, whether they be those who suffer directly at the hands of Bellfeels – her mother, for example, or Clotelle, the young black girl hanged from a tamarind tree – or those more distant and anonymous female figures who are part of the island's slave past and whose stories Mary learns about from her maternal ancestors. The collective dimension to Mary's tale is not restricted to the ways in which it incorporates the transgenerational narratives of other women, though, but extends to embrace the oppressed black men whose histories of failed rebellion are periodically invoked in the text, particularly in Part Three. As it recalls these vanquished rebels, Mary's narrative both looks back to the bloody history of insurrection on her own plantation and moves beyond the horizon of Barbados itself – more often referred to in the novel under the soubriquet of 'Bimshire'[5] – to draw in the history of slave rebellion in the America of the early 1830s.

In so far as she stands in for and redeems the black man as failed rebel, Mary is implicitly a threat not merely to traditional hierarchies of racial difference but also to the conventions of gender identity as they are upheld in white and black communities alike. By visiting murder and mutilation upon Bellfeels, in other words, Mary obliquely unmans Percy, usurping the detective-lover's potential role as defender of female virtue and avenger of its loss. In so doing, she confronts him with those anxieties about his own masculinity which regularly surface in the course of the novel, both in the professional context of his duties as policeman and in the more private realm of his sexual life. This being the case, it is not surprising that Percy should exhibit a certain ambivalence towards Mary's confession, manifested as a tension between a desire to hear and record her story, on the one hand, and a wish to silence and erase it, on the other. The latter impulse corresponds to Percy's disavowal of the broader history of slavery in Barbados, from which Mary's account of her 'personal life' (p. 29) cannot readily be disentangled. It is also no doubt one sign of what Wilberforce, Mary's only surviving child by Bellfeels, calls 'the ironies of life' (p. 15), since it makes Percy oddly complicit with Bellfeels' own concern to silence the truths of Mary's history, not the least of which is that she is in fact Bellfeels' daughter and hence a victim of incest as well as of rape.

As Mary's narrative attests, the instruments of colonial labour so appealingly celebrated by Beckford in this chapter's first epigraph can have purposes radically different to those for which they are originally intended, as the polished hoe she uses in the North Field of the plantation – prior to her elevation to the Main House as 'servant girl' (p. 166) and Great House as mistress – turns into the weapon with which, as it were, she polishes off her oppressor. Yet even as Mary herself becomes more polished or refined as she makes the transition from field hand to mistress, her skills as a labourer are not forgotten, but rather transmuted into those she deploys as storyteller. Such an analogy between the labours conducted in the cane field and the labours of narrative is suggested towards the novel's outset, as Mary remembers the nausea of sex with Bellfeels. Here she speaks in a richly associative Creole which is both quite typical of her oral style throughout and a sharp contrast to the Standard English of the novel's third-person narrator:

> 'I don't know how I managed to stomach his weight laying-down on top of me all those years; breeding me and having his wish; and me smelling him; and him giving-off a smell like fresh dirt, mould that I turned over with my hoe, at first planting, following a downpour of rain, when all the centipees and rats, cockroaches and insects on God's earth start crawling-out in full vision and sight, outta the North Field.' (p. 39)

The turning of the soil after a 'downpour of rain' exposes a host of monstrous forms to Mary's view, just as her 'history in confession' (p. 29) unsettles the official accounts of itself the colonial plantation likes to cultivate, revealing the hideous truths aswarm beneath them. What Mary's narrative does is replicated in turn by *The Polished Hoe* itself, as it extends the aesthetics of contamination begun in Nichols and Dabydeen and developed in Phillips.

'Malice Aforethought': A Murder and its Histories

Mary's recollection of the incubus-like Bellfeels 'laying-down on top of [her]' is not disclosed to Percy himself, but to the young Constable whom Percy deputes to take her 'preliminary Statement'. As it turns out, the Constable is chosen for this task not because his superior anticipates that his 'report ... would be of much eventual help' but rather so that Percy can 'evade his duty' for as long as possible, in the hope that Mary's disturbing story, which is also in part his own, might somehow come to 'be buried' amid the 'heaps of ... memories' he prefers to leave 'untouched' (p. 85). It is for this same reason that the Constable finds himself listening to Mary as she pinpoints the moment when her hatred of Bellfeels first crystallizes. Conversing with the Constable in the elegant parlour of the Great House, Mary casts her mind back 'many-many years' to the spaces of her childhood, one of which is the 'Church Yard of Sin-Davids Anglican Church' (p. 17) on the morning of Easter Sunday. It is here as a 'lil girl, seven or eight' that she is introduced to Bellfeels by her impoverished mother, who offers her, 'out of need' (p. 16), as a potential worker on the plantation where he is then 'field overseer' or 'driver' (p. 19):

> 'Mr. Bellfeels put his riding-crop under my chin, and raise my face to meet his face, using the riding-crop; and when his eyes and my eyes made four, he passed the riding-crop down my neck, right down the front of my dress, until it reach my waist. And then he move the riding-crop right back up again, as if he was drawing something on my body.
>
> 'And Ma, stanning-up beside me, with her two eyes looking down at the loose marl in the Church Yard, looking at the graves covered by slabs of marble, looking at the ground. Ma had her attention focused on something on the ground. My mother. Not on me, her own daughter.' (p. 19)

Although the ostensible purpose of this encounter is to assess Mary's suitability for the rigours of plantation labour, the salacious movements of Bellfeels' 'riding-crop' across her body trace out an alternative and clearly sexual design, whose corrupt nature is signalled in its turn in the semi-comic corruption of 'Saint' into 'Sin'. This transformation of Mary's body into a prospective sexual geography for the master's profane delight is underscored in other features of the text, including the simile likening the crop to a 'hand' which 'crawl[s] over' (p. 29) her, seeming first to be 'taking off [her] clothes, and then ... [her] skin' (p. 31). But if Mary's fate as future sexual victim is both etched upon her person by Bellfeels' sinister crop and written into the language of the text, there is also a hint of redemption here. The time at which Mary is effectively marked out by Bellfeels as private property is, as she remembers from the Collect, a time of passage *through the grave, and the gate of hell*, but this journey leads, ultimately, to a *joyful resurrection* (p. 18; italics in original).[6]

As much as it bespeaks his own desires, Bellfeels' crop also utters a demand for silence, addressed, in particular, to Mary's mother, May. As the daughter puts it, this time in a digital rather than manual simile, the crop is comparable not only to Bellfeels' insect-like hand but also to his finger, which Mary imagines 'clasped to her [mother's] lips, clamped to her mouth to strike her dumb … to keep her peace' (p. 20). Perhaps it is for this reason – as the admonitory crop-finger presses against the mother's mouth and leaves her 'parlyzed in speech' (p. 71) – that May directs her gaze towards 'the graves covered by slabs of marble', as if it is beneath these stony surfaces that the cry of maternal protest has been entombed? This reading is supported by the language of interment and suppression in which Mary subsequently recalls the patriarchal conditions Barbadian women must negotiate during the childhood days in which her initial meeting with Bellfeels takes place. In contrast both to the 'English suffrages-women' who are their vociferous contemporaries and to the 'modern … dark-skin women' whom Mary sees 'walking-'bout [her] Village' in 'dresses of African print' and speaking 'defiant words', the early twentieth-century females of her mother's generation have a 'voice' which 'dare not' make itself known. It must instead be 'buried inside [their] hearts', just as their 'thoughts and … acts, and … wishes' remain 'concealed in [their] craw' (p. 72).

Pre-eminent among the things which cannot be disclosed by 'Ma' in this primal scene is the consanguinity of the relationship between Mary and 'the powerful man' (p. 19) to whom she is given up. The irony, though, is that the text itself seems unable to keep the truths of paternity quite secret, whispering them in apparently trivial details, as, for instance, its allusions to the 'new shoes' in which Mary is presented to Bellfeels for inspection. As it transpires, these items are not genuinely 'new' at all, since they have been previously owned by Bellfeels' 'youngest daughter', Miss Emonie, who, as Mary notes, 'was the same size as [her], in clothes and in height'. Although Mary is adamant that these 'Hand-me-downs' come to her not 'through inheritance' but as 'cast-aways', the doubling of body-sizes tells a different tale, linking the two girls in an unacknowledged kinship whose psychological discomfort is expressed by means of physical sensation: Emonie's 'shoes pinched like hell', Mary comments, 'because her feet were white feet; and very narrow' (p. 18). But this infernal footwear symbolizes something more than just the uneasy truth of the incest to come when Mary reaches puberty. It is also indicative of how, even in what is seemingly the most mundane of contexts, the association with Bellfeels induces bodily pain, just as the pain itself looks forward ironically to the novel's denouement: as the colloquialism has it, Mary's new shoes seem to be 'killing' (p. 19) her, even as it is she who will literalize the metaphor when she kills Bellfeels.

In its travels from 'chin' to 'neck' to 'waist' and 'back … again', Bellfeels' crop colonizes Mary's anatomy with his own desire, creating an experience which cannot be 'erased' (p. 397), as the novel's constant return to it would indeed suggest. Such processes are in turn writ large upon the topography of Barbados itself, as Bellfeels gradually transfers his attentions from mother to developing child and *'feast*[s] *on*' '*Mary-girl*' – as if she were a '*sweet delicious piece o' veal*' (p. 72; italics in original) – in a number of secret spaces dotted about the island. Among these sites is the 'one-mile underground tunnel' (p. 398) – running beneath the Great House and on out towards the North Field – into which Mary leads Percy in Part Three of the novel. What is striking about the strange descent into 'the belly of the land' (p. 363) which the two figures make is the way in which it works as a spatial metaphor for the narrative operations of the novel as a whole, which so often involve delving beneath the benign surfaces of things in order to recover the less than appealing truths they cover up, showing how Bellfeels is, for instance, anything but what he pretends to be: an '*exemplary character*', with '*affectionate dispositions*' and '*generosity of spirit*' (p. 445; italics in original).

Together with its function as a trope for the excavatory work performed by Clarke's novel, the movement into this subterranean space mirrors the sexual abuses suffered therein. These take place during the period in which Mary is '*groom*[ed]' by Bellfeels, until such time as, in the words of her mentor-tormentor, she '*get*[s] *more riper*' (p. 398; italics in original):

> Mr. Bellfeels brought Mary-Mathilda here into this underground tunnel, and pulled up her dress, and pulled down her cotton panties, and pushed his index finger on the left hand as high into her pussy as it would go; sometimes beyond the second joint. And then he put the same finger into his mouth; licked it dry, noisily, regardless of her time of month; and then he took the flask of rum from his khaki jodhpurs, which he always carried, and held his head back, and let the strong, burning white liquid fall into his mouth. …
>
> '*Young pussy and mature white rum, the best anecdote for a man! Eh, Mary-girl? What you say?*' (p. 398; italics in original)

Here Mary's entry into the 'underground tunnel' is paralleled by Bellfeels' insertion of his 'index finger' into the 'secret passage' (p. 371) of her vagina, before this prying member is in turn inserted into another bodily orifice, in the form of Bellfeels' mouth, and the secretions it bears are mixed with the 'burning white liquid' Mary's labours in the field help to produce. While such actions could hardly make the imbalance of power between male and female clearer, there is a simultaneous sense in which they unsettle the very mastery they seem to confer, as the '*mature white rum*' Bellfeels combines with '*Young pussy*' causes him to lose control of his language and say '*anecdote*' when presumably he intends 'antidote'. This loss of control is supplemented by the irony the malapropism brings with it, since the lurid tale of sexual connoisseurship the novel recounts at this juncture can only be considered to be the worst '*anecdote for a man*', rather than the '*best*'.

The history of Mary's '*force-ripening*' (p. 167; italics in original) is remembered by the text in another incident from her youth, which occurs when she is thirteen and Percy – who is its unseen witness – just ten, with the forty-year-old Bellfeels himself seeming to the two children to be an 'old man' (p. 168). Like the original encounter in the churchyard, this episode is keyed to the Christian festival of death and resurrection, although in this case it takes place not on Easter Sunday, but on the 'happy food-clogged Easter Monday' of the 'Sin-Davids Anglican Church Annual Outing and Picnic' (p. 181). As well as being situated at much the same point in the religious calendar as Mary's first meeting with Bellfeels, the episode's spatial location – a cave hidden away on the beach where the bank holiday revels are being held – links it to the site of her sexual grooming. As is the case with the 'passage below the ground' (p. 387), the Crane Beach 'retreat' (p. 181) both constitutes an interior space fashioned out of the island's geological substance and has a comparable figurative resonance as a symbol for the vagina. At the same time, the liaison to which the cave plays host marks a violent departure from the traditions of secluded romance which have 'been built up' around it 'over the years' (p. 180), since Mary and Bellfeels are no lovers locked in a consensual tryst, but rather victim and assailant. While the rape occurring on 'this joyful afternoon' (p. 172) escapes the general notice of the picnic-goers, it is perhaps both known about and sanctioned by the island's 'big men' who are Bellfeels' associates and who shade themselves beneath the 'beach-grape trees', 'telling dirty stories about women' (p. 173). For Percy, on the other hand, there is neither ignorance of Mary's rape nor complicity with it, but just the pain of its acknowledgement as, in a prefiguring of the detective abilities on which his professional identity will come to be based, he tracks Mary to 'the mouth of the cave' and overhears the cries which come from it: 'He heard Mary's voice [which] was tender, soft, like a soprano. It was a frightened voice; frightened as if it was coming out of the throat of a fawn … who was trying to speak; and who knew that its throat would be cut' (p. 181).

This incident is one to which this chapter will return in its next section, where it will be considered for what it says about Percy's anxieties regarding his own masculinity. For the moment, though, attention is to be focused upon the third of the clandestine spaces Bellfeels chooses for Mary's sexual exploitation. This is the space of the North Field into which she and Percy eventually surface 'at the end of the [underground] passage' and where, following in the footsteps of her maternal ancestors, Mary claims to have 'started [her] life' (p. 403). Since 'Crop-Season … is in full swing' at the time when the novel's events take place, the ground Mary and Percy traverse as they enter the field is strewn with trash burned off from the canes before they are cut down and sent to the 'Factory' for 'grinding' (p. 12), and it is this refuse which initially invests the location with feelings of comfort and security. As her 'feet strike the trash' and 'the trash responds to her weight', for example, Mary remembers the childhood rituals whereby her mother 'would shake her mattress every evening before spreading it back onto the six pieces of board' (p. 406) making up her daughter's bed. These homely customs are rehearsed by Mary in the present, as she invites Percy to lie down in the field, 'piles some trash high, to make a pillow for her back' (p. 416) and 'rearranges some more ... to make a thick, fluffy mattress' (p. 417). But even as the cane's discarded leaves furnish Mary with remembered and material comforts alike, 'the smell of the earth' rising up through her *ad hoc* bedding has the opposite effect. Compounded with the 'distant sickening fragrance of crack-liquor, the hot, sweet juice squeezed from the ground canes', it activates memories far more disquieting, which, as so often in the text, centre upon Bellfeels' 'leather riding-crop' (p. 421). In the scene in the churchyard, this instrument touches 'the neck of the cotton frock' which, by way of complement to Mary's cast-off shoes, originally 'belonged to ... Miss Euralie' (p. 397), Bellfeels' other (legitimate) daughter. In the 'deserted section of the North Field' to which Mary is 'made to follow' him, however, the crop, as she recalls, toys with her garments more boldly. It 'lift[s]' up her 'dress' in order for Bellfeels to violate her with what he quaintly calls his '"tool"', while her fellow-workers, like the Crane Beach picnickers, feed themselves obliviously, 'eating their flour bakes and drinking molasses water that had pieces of chipped ice in it' (p. 421).

The immediate result of Bellfeels' assault upon his sixteen-year-old victim is 'the excruciating pain' which, in a characteristically entomological metaphor, 'crawl[s] through [Mary's] body' for 'the rest of [the] afternoon' on which the rape takes place. Its more extended consequence, on the other hand, is pregnancy and 'the first of three abortions induced with herbs and other bushes' (p. 422) by Mary's mother and grandmother. Yet far from being unique to the daughter's history, this unholy trinity of events – rape, pregnancy and abortion – entails a startling repetition of the mother's sexual biography. As Mary tells the Constable early on in the novel, May is also violated by Bellfeels 'when no more than seventeen, or sixteen' and can only be 'release[d] from the thing that [he] sowed inside her' (p. 49) by the yet more ancestral intervention of Mary's great-grandmother, who kills the 'baby conceived in rape' by calling on a knowledge of natural 'medicines; and cures; plus a lil touch of obeah and witchcraft' (p. 48) derived from her African homeland. As the belated deathbed account of her sufferings recalls, Mary's mother wishes 'she [had been] *somebody-else*' on the 'night' the incident occurs: what she articulates, in other words, is a longing to transcend the limits of the race, class and gender identity which condemns her to the shifting status of 'field hand ... harlot [and] tool for [the] man who came into her house, small as it was, humble as it was ... And *robbed* her of her maiden' (p. 46; italics in original). Yet there is a sense in which, in still another of the novel's ironies, such a wish turns out to have been parodically realized: Mary's mother does indeed become '*somebody-else*', reliving the squalor and anguish of her own experience in that of her daughter.

At the same time, however, there remains one vital respect in which the daughter differs from rather than reincarnates her mother's history. Although the mother's rape is initially carried out in the supposed sanctuary of her own 'house', subsequent violations more often than not lead back to the canes of the North Field. The multiple abortions in which the female members of Mary's family conspire might be read as forms of material resistance to the systems of racial and sexual oppression personally embodied in Bellfeels,[7] but, amid the 'terror and … despair' (p. 471) of the canes themselves, the prospects of resistance are never anything other than imaginary:

> [May] limped home a little later than the other field hands, sore from the throwing up and down of her hands, like a machine, with the hoe in her hands; and driving it, with venom and hate, 'I going-kill yuh, I going-kill yuh … one o' these good days …' into the ground which was hard as rock, sometimes; hard as a piece of coral from the sea; sometimes hard as soft mud; and her thighs sore from Mr. Bellfeels' brutal prick which dug into her without mercy, without the lubrication of love. (p. 471)

Here, 'Barely out of sight and hearing distance of the eleven other women in the field gang' (p. 472), Bellfeels' 'brutal prick' digs into the labouring maternal body, even as the counter-violence it precipitates is not directed at Bellfeels himself but displaced elsewhere, as May 'driv[es]' the hoe she inherits from her own mother (and will bequeath to her daughter) into the 'ground'. This harmless displacement of the mother's murderous impulses – her 'venom and hate' – is mirrored in the fantasies of Bellfeels' sexual mutilation which she entertains but can never fulfil. In Mary's case, though, the possibilities of revenge which escape the mother are brought to fruition when she confronts Bellfeels, 'slouched in rum' (p. 395) in 'his favourite Berbice chairs' (p. 506), on the verandah of the Plantation Main House. At this critical moment, the family hoe is no longer plunged angrily into 'the thick black soil' (p. 471) of the cane field but turned against the oppressor, first striking him a deadly blow to the skull and then severing the 'circumcised head' of his penis in what the novel grimly calls a 'spoiled slaughtering' (p. 508).

Mary's actions are designed to make good the wrongs sustained by women besides her own mother (and herself) and the most spectacular of these supplementary figures is Clotelle, whose memory haunts *The Polished Hoe* with an intensity and ubiquity similar to that which attaches to Bellfeels' riding-crop. As her debut in the text makes clear, Clotelle has much in common with Mary and May alike, since her story is once again a harrowing tale of rape and pregnancy at predictable hands. But what is distinctive about

Clotelle's plight, or apparently so at least, is the manner in which she chooses to resolve it, resisting the sexual crimes perpetrated against her by Bellfeels not by recourse to abortifacients but by the even more radical step of suicide. As Mary recounts the circumstances of Clotelle's death to the Constable:

> 'Ma tell me when that sad tragedy happened … Ma tell me that she saw Clotelle laying down in the cane-brake, with her face washed in tears; and bleeding; and that it was later the same night, in all the rain, that Clotelle climbed up the tamarind tree; and how Clotelle had-use pieces of cloth that she rip-off from her own dress, with all the blood and all the man's semen staining it; and how Clotelle make a rope outta her own dress, and wrap-it-round the highest branch she could reach in the tamarind tree, and the rest you know. Yes. The rest you know.' (p. 23)

This version of Clotelle's demise is corroborated by the 'attopsy' (p. 22) demanded of the authorities by her mother, even as the inquiry simultaneously modifies the account by identifying the instrument of Clotelle's suicide not as the 'rope ripped from her own clothes' but as a 'butcher knife' used to slit her throat when the 'rope falter[s]' and she cannot 'die clean'. For Percy, on the other hand, the knife tells a different 'story' to the one officially ascribed to it in the post-mortem, leaving 'a red line' (p. 55) on Clotelle's flesh which he interprets as the mark not of 'suicide' but of 'murder' (p. 59). This counter-reading of Clotelle's 'dead-body' finds its echo in the chorus to the 'sweet calypso' (p. 22) which 'remembers Clotelle's tragedy' (p. 23) and whose popularity – it 'climb[s] to number one on the hit parade' (p. 22) – matches her own suspension from the 'highest, most convenient limb of the tamarind tree' (p. 55): "*Who full she up, / And tie she up, / Could cut she down*" (p. 23; italics in original). It is further supported in the 'rumours that blow through the Village whispered by the Plantation's servant-women' (p. 356), which similarly debunk the authenticity of Clotelle's suicide by claiming it to have been staged. Clotelle's story thus not only offers one more typically graphic incrimination of Bellfeels but also encapsulates the equally typical tensions in the novel between official and unofficial accounts of events on the 'Island of Bimshire' (p. 29), illustrating how the latter need to be exhumed from the former if the truths of history are to be properly recognized and commemorated.

In the end, though, the collective aspects of the violence Mary metes out to Bellfeels involve more than a desire to avenge either her own sufferings or those of her mother and Clotelle, linking also to the untold stories of those women who, like Mary's unnamed great-grandmother, were once slaves. Such transhistorical solidarity is not surprising since, in Mary's eyes, there is little difference between her own experience and that of the female slave placed at the beck and call of her masters. As Mary tells Percy as they pick their way through the 'underground tunnel' (p. 490):

'it was common practice on most plantations for the overseer, the driver, the bookkeeper, and don't mention the manager, to breed the slaves, any slave-woman, from age ten to forty, fifty, sixty … we were common preys; you snap your finger and a slave-woman come running, and end-up laying down under you … "*Hey-you!* … *Cumm-ere!*" Yes!' (p. 490; italics in original)

Here the sense of continuity between Mary and those her own memory summons back into the present is articulated in the pronominal slippage of 'we were common preys', just as the 'slave-woman' who punctually 'come[s] running' can herself be easily exchanged for 'any' other and the identities of her oppressors become similarly indistinguishable as a result of a 'common practice'. The blurring of historical epochs – the post-emancipation period and the time of slavery – finds its parallel in a certain blurring of spaces, as the sexual conduct characterizing 'plantations in Bimshire' merely reproduces that already prevalent on the 'ships leaving Africa' for the Middle Passage: on these benighted vessels, there is yet 'more rape', even as, in this context, there is nothing fake about the 'suicides' such maltreatment brings about, as female slaves 'decide to jump overboard, and face the broiling green waves of the Deep' (p. 490).[8]

Bellfeels' death and, in particular, the genital mutilation which is its grisly coda work to redress the sexual pain both he and the system he represents have historically inflicted upon the mixed-race and/or black female body. But it is important to remember that it is not only women but also men who are subjected to the cruelties of the plantation system in this text and that Mary's assault upon the unmentionable 'manager' is an act of vengeance carried out in their name as well. At times, such cruelties can have their own sexual element, as in Bellfeels' beating of Golbourne, an assault sparked by the outraged discovery that the latter is amorously involved with the 'nursemaid to the Plantation thrildren' (p. 24) Bellfeels himself desires. Although this attack occurs under the cover of a 'dark night', the body which sustains it bears daily witness to its ferocity, as the 'kicks' Bellfeels gives Golbourne in his 'two groins' (p. 25) result in a permanent testicular swelling, turning a former 'model of manhood' into a monstrous cripple: after the beating, as Mary observes, Golbourne becomes a pitiable grotesque, 'walking-'bout Flagstaff Village, with his goadies … meaning his two enlarge testicles, the size of two bread-fruits, wobbling-'bout inside his oversize pants, built specially by the tailor to commodate [his] two things' (p. 24).

The violence the plantation levels at the male body is not always either sexually motivated or genitally inscribed, however, but can also arise as a means of containing the workers when they 'rebel' against their lot by 'ask[ing] for a couple-more pennies-a-week' (p. 375). This violence is an aspect of the plantation's past which displays itself in what Mary describes as a 'pageantry of blood' and about which she gradually learns as it 'leak[s]-out' – in her appropriately fluid figure – 'through various cracks and crevices' in Bellfeels' dinner-table 'conversations'. Yet as the metaphor of secretion changes and she puts together the 'pieces of this history' (p. 378) for Percy, the underground tunnel where she tells her tale is itself re-membered, duly altering from a site of sexual violation to a place of supererogatory colonial discipline. While the workers' agitation for an increase in their 'wages' (p. 375) is in truth but a 'little disturbance' (p. 391), the punishment it calls down upon the three 'ring leaders' (p. 375) – one of whom is Golbourne's father – is anything but trivial. As Mary recalls, they are 'disfigured … almost beyond recognition' (p. 377) by the 'rhythm' of the 'cowskin' which 'tear[s]-into [their] flesh, *plax! plax! plax!*' (p. 375; italics in original), before being drowned at sea.

The discursive correlates to the excesses in this 'administration o' violence' (p. 376) appear in the ways in which those who are its victims come subsequently to be mythologized by islanders on both sides of the colour-line. For Mary's mother, who is enjoined 'to bind the wounds and clot the blood' covering the workers' lacerated bodies, the scene she confronts seems less like the consequences of a whipping in an 'underground cellar' than 'a tableau-type picture of the three men on the Cross, on Golgotha Hill, in Biblical times', with Golbourne senior as Christ and the 'forty slashes going in all directions' on his back resembling the 'Star of Bethlehem' (p. 377). For the 'Plantation-people' themselves, on the other hand, the older Golbourne and his two associates – 'Pounce father, and Manny grandfather' (p. 380) – are far from Christ-like figures. Rather the three are demonized as 'insurrection-aries' (p. 383), whose ultimate aim is nothing so modest as an improvement in pay, but the wholesale destruction of the estate – an event which, in Mary's heavy irony, is to occur despite 'all the good things that the Plantation do for the Village and the labourers and the poor and the cripple' (pp. 380–81). Yet the 'chaos' (p. 381) into which the paternal Golbourne and company allegedly threaten to plunge the plantation is as much a repetition of the past as it is a future danger, reviving memories of slave unrest played out in an American rather than a Caribbean context and concentrated, specifically, in the legendary figure of Nat Turner, leader of a short-lived but major uprising in Southampton, Virginia in August 1831.

While the links between this 'Amurcan Nigg-rah' (p. 381) and the 'three men' who dare to 'rais[e] their voice' (p. 380) against the economic status quo are deliberately exaggerated by the estate, there is certainly something Turneresque about Mary, just as *The Polished Hoe* itself constitutes a response to the work in which Turner's insurgency is recorded, Thomas R. Gray's *The Confessions of Nat Turner* (1831), with Clarke's fiction rewriting its historical pre-text from a female/feminist perspective. Both Mary and Turner have, for example, a tendency to search for the portents of their fate amid the everyday. Mary waits for 'years' for a 'sign to tell [her when] the correct time' for action 'ha[s] come', 'counting … down' to a 'fraction of a second!' (p. 119) and, in the period prior to the decisive assault on her oppressor, contemplates an '*L* … in the clouds', which, as she speculates, could stand 'for *Luck*' or '*Love*' (p. 368; italics in original), but is also oddly hoe-like in its shape. Turner, for his part, experiences grander though less equivocal celestial visions: he beholds 'white spirits and black spirits engaged in battle' as 'the sun [becomes] darkened … thunder roll[s] in the Heavens, and blood flow[s] in streams'.[9] In addition to this, both figures translate their revelations into violence, with Mary destroying Bellfeels and Turner spearheading a revolt which claims around sixty white victims during the two days for which it lasts.[10]

Alongside such similarities, there also exist some important differences between the female rebel and her male counterpart. Although there is, as already suggested, a strong collective element to Mary's revenge, she finally acts alone, whereas Turner operates as part of a larger (and exclusively male) body, following a path which, in another difference from Mary, possesses no overtly sexual ground.[11] But the most significant of the distinctions between fictional avatar and historical prototype emerges in relation to the shared practice of confession. For Mary, one of the central purposes behind her speech is redemptive, her narrative unfolding, as she tells Percy, in a bid to 'save [her] soul'. Yet the salvation Mary seeks is not the religious or spiritual kind traditionally associated with the confessional genre, but hermeneutic. What she wants to leave in conversing first with the Constable and then with Percy is a 'legacy of words' in which 'the pure history of [her] act' (p. 116) can be preserved, thus escaping the 'various interpretations' (p. 117), both spoken and written, which threaten to distort it from a range of quarters: 'word of mouth … the *Bimshire Daily Herald*; and … Village gossip' (p. 116; italics in original). For Turner, on the other hand, such discursive purity is necessarily compromised by the status of his amanuensis as a slave-holding local lawyer: in this capacity, Gray both inflects and frames the voice he claims merely to be transcribing with his own, delivering a version of events which is coloured by racial prejudice and brands Turner a 'gloomy fanatic'.[12]

Questions of Gender

In contrast to the acts of infanticide and suicide to which the novel intermittently alludes, the murder of Bellfeels represents a more direct strategy of resistance, which, as the parallels with Turner suggest, identifies Mary with a heroic black masculinity: in killing Bellfeels, in other words, Mary figuratively takes on the very manhood she literally removes from her oppressor turned victim in the immediate wake of the homicide. This identification of female violence with the masculine is part of a broader pattern of gender reversal in the text, the first signs of which emerge during the sequence where Mary recalls how she methodically prepares the instrument of Bellfeels' death for the moment of its 'destiny' (p. 67). While the hoe whose 'handle' is made from the wood of the 'clammy-cherry tree' (p. 64) is a kind of matrilineal heirloom passed down from grandmother to mother to daughter, the chemicals Mary wishes to apply to it to make it 'shine' (p. 65) take her into a space firmly defined as masculine. In such 'sacred territory' (p. 70), as she tells the Constable, Mary can only seem like an amusing interloper:

> 'I went one morning, when he wasn't too busy, to see Mr. Waldrond the Joiner and Cabinetmaker. Mr. Waldrond makes the most beautiful furnitures in this Village, in this whole Island, if you ask me! And I respectfully asked Mr. Waldrond for a drop of oil and a daub of the stain or polish he uses on mahogany. Mr. Waldrond look at me, and laughed. "Never," Mr. Waldrond say, "in all my born-days, and during my time as joiner and cabinetmaker to this Plantation, plying my trade in this Village, have a girl, a woman, axe me to lend she the tools of my trade!"' (p. 65)

But it is not only the handle of Mary's hoe which comes to acquire the sheen of masculinity, as it is assiduously rubbed and cleaned with the 'linseed oil ... Hawes Lemon Oil ... and homemade polish' (p. 65) procured from the joiner. The blade similarly assumes such a quality, honed as it is, 'every evening' for 'three months' (p. 66), on a greased whetstone, until it is 'Sharp as a iron cane bill for cutting canes' (p. 68) or 'a Gillette razor!' (p. 66).

Mary's appropriation of traits conventionally defined as masculine is not restricted to the violent revenge exacted upon Bellfeels but is evident in other respects as well. At one typically unhurried moment in this most dilatory of novels, she breaks off from the business of confession to invite Percy to dance with her to the sound of 'Miss Ella Fitzgerald's powerful voice' (p. 188) singing 'A-Tisket, A-Tasket' (1938) on the 'large Victrola grammaphone' (p. 152) and, in so doing, draws the sergeant into an embrace where gender roles are inverted and it seems that 'She is the man' and 'He ... the woman, being led'. As the narrator comments, this strange *pas de deux* is something 'more than a dance' (p. 189), allowing itself to be read, in the first instance, as a figure for the choreography of confession in the novel as a whole, with Mary's disclosures about her troubled past encouraging Percy to revisit his own painful history, recalling incidents he sometimes openly verbalizes but more often leaves unsaid. At the same time, however, the dance serves as a symbolic shorthand for the transgressiveness of Mary's sexuality. To Bellfeels, of course, '*Mary-girl*' is merely and routinely the means to the gratification of a violent lust and there are even times in the text when she is viewed in similar terms by Percy himself, whose waking dreams about his beloved are occasionally and uncomfortably marred by an 'impetus to rape' (p. 352). Mary's own sense of herself, on the other hand, is radically at odds with the rough schemas, whether real or imaginary, which reduce her to the status of sexual possession. Far from being the passive object of Percy's sometimes violent erotic reveries, for example, Mary maintains a long-standing 'sexual interest' in him, which she 'wants him to be able ... to detect' by 'dig[ging]' beneath her words for meaning' (p. 144). Such interest is confirmed in its turn by the curious rituals of surveillance in which Mary indulges, 'train[ing] a powerful spying glass on the front door of [Percy's] house', in order secretly to observe his daily activities from 'her bedroom' (p. 111).

Mary's status as desiring subject governs not only her habits of surveillance but also her reading practices, even as the story on which she comes to dwell is itself concerned with questions of seeing and being seen. On one of the frequent occasions when she 'wander[s]-off' (p. 22) from the path of her confession, Mary becomes caught up with Percy in a serio-comic scriptural exegesis:

> 'The Holy Bible says that it was David who was peeping at Bathsheba bathing, spying on the poor woman's nakedness, without her knowledge. But I have a different version, giving the interpretation that says that it was *Bathsheba*, knowing that her husband was away at the front in the Wars of Ammon and Rabbah, fighting battles and killing other women's husbands, she, Bathsheba, start feeling a lil peckish for the absence of her husband's warm body side-o'-her, in her bed, got her maid to move the basin with the water she was washing her face-and-hands with, more closer to the window where King David could see her more clearer. Naked as she was born.' (p. 419; italics in original)

Like Waldrond's workshop, the biblical text Mary glosses here (II Samuel xi. 1–5) represents another 'sacred territory' which she metaphorically enters and turns to her own account, recasting it as a testament to the resourcefulness of female desire rather than just another episode in the archive of female exploitation. Mary's ability to rival divine authority with a 'different version' of the story of 'Bathsheba the woman! And David the man!' (p. 419) is at the same time consistent with the revisionist historiography she brings to bear in the secular context of her own experience.

From these examples it is clear that Mary is, as the Constable silently reflects, 'a woman to fear' (p. 40), posing a threat to the hierarchies of race and the norms of gender alike. Further signs of Mary's classically masculine qualities might be adduced and could include the superior bodily strength enabling her to lift 'bundles of cane that would break the back of the average man' (p. 143) or the force of character exhibited in her 'determination, tough-ness [and] iron discipline' (p. 454). What needs to be emphasized, instead, at this stage is the ways in which Mary's manliness dovetails with the femininity of the detective-confessor who is her lover *manqué*. At first glance, there would seem to be little feminine about Mary's undeclared 'suitor' (p. 255), as he snaps his 'overproofed dark Mount Gay Rum' in the 'rum shop' (p. 50) owned by Mandeville White (grandson to one of the rebel-workers executed by the plantation) and exchanges notes on sexual idiosyncrasy. Nor is it only in the shop belonging to his oldest friend and confidant that Percy is able to indulge his manhood, but also among the canes from which Manny's rum is derived. Here he finds an equally intoxicating pleasure in Mary's maid, Gertrude, 'handl[ing] her too roughly ... and too hastily' on the 'thick, brown trash' (p. 146) whose colour matches that of Gertrude's 'soft ... skin' (p. 145).

As the narrator brusquely remarks, Percy likes to think of himself as 'a man of action. A man of deeds. A man of force. And drive. And hardness. Even in his fooping' and it is this ideal self-image which the regular cane field rendez-vous with Gertrude helps to nourish and sustain: 'In. *And* two flings. With his eyes shut. And *bam*! Climax. Done with that! And out' (p. 408; italics in original). This self-image is similarly bolstered in Percy's professional guise as 'big Crown-Sargeant in His Majesty's Royal Constabulary Force of Bimshire' (p. 58), diligently tracking down criminals always assumed, in a revealing irony, to be male:

> Many nights, moving along the narrow track that separates the North Field from the South Field, he would pause often, imagining that he hears the sound of a man moving in the canes, trampling the dried trash; and this would make him grip his truncheon round its thick brown girth, its leather strap wrapped tight round his fingers, as he grips it now; and his body would become tense as steel; and so, stunted by fear, he would listen to the swishing sounds of footsteps deep within the vast, dark bowels of the thick cane fields, swaying in the South Field and the North Field; wondering all the time how he will apprehend this man who intrudes upon his peace, and who delays the pause for refreshment at the rum shop, for the shot glass of Mount Gay Rum whose taste is so enticing. (pp. 51–52)

Here the 'man ... in the canes' moves according to the rhythms not of passion but of crime, even as he is merely a phantom, confected out of a combina-tion of nocturnal 'sounds' and a 'fear' which 'stunt[s]'. Elsewhere in the text, however, the criminal presence is all too real, as in the anecdote Percy tells about his pursuit and capture of the elusive Boysie-Boys, who, despite his name's childish chimes, is famed for having 'terroriz[ed] the whole Island' some 'five year[s] ago' (p. 234). But whether they be imaginary or dangerously real, the criminals Percy confronts in the course of his work always serve his purposes. They allow him both to restore 'peace' to the community he polices and to affirm his own manliness, with both achievements mixed together and celebrated in a refreshing glass of rum.

The gendering of crime as a male pursuit is underlined by the array of phallic accoutrements with which Percy equips himself in order to prosecute his duties. In the passage cited above, he carries a 'truncheon' which he 'grip[s]

... round its thick brown girth', just as, in the fevered moments before the arrest of Boysie-Boys, he 'hold[s]-on-more-tighter on [his] bull-pistle. All eighteen inches of it' (p. 234). In addition to these simulacra, Percy possesses a 'searchlight ... almost two feet long' (p. 53), a 'Watermans fountain pen' (p. 131), which he uses for 'writing-up ... Confidential Reports and Statements' (p. 130) and 'won't be caught dead without' (p. 131), and a Baton of Honour, awarded to mark his graduation from police cadet to full officer. Yet far from creating an impression of virility and power, the proliferation of such accessories implies a sexual lack, as if their overloaded bearer were not quite the 'big man' (p. 416) he aspires to be. The origins of this lack are to be found in two episodes drawn from Percy's 'young adolescence' (p. 161), both of which, in their way, are just as traumatic (and just as formative) as the incidents of sexual exploitation defining Mary's own early years.

The first of these episodes takes place when Percy is newly apprenticed to the Garrison Savannah Tennis Club as 'Assistant Gardener and Chief Water Boy' (p. 161) and witnesses the spectacular fall of a white woman, who 'slip[s]' on the freshly watered grass surface' on which she is playing a game of mixed doubles, slamming 'her body ... against the tall green-painted fence' enclosing the court. Repeatedly exhorted not to assist the injured woman by the 'high-pitched feminine voice' (p. 162) of the man who is her partner, but merely retrieve the '*bloody ball!*' (p. 163; italics in original), Percy finds himself unable to answer the imperious demand. He is transfixed, instead, by what the accident reveals to him:

> And the voice comes at him again, speaking with a heavy English accent.
> '*What the dickens, boy? Boy!*'
> The voice is shrieking now. The voice wants to rouse the staring black eyes from their examination of this young beautiful girl's private parts. To protect her. To remind the 'boy' that this is a closeness, this staring, which is *infra dig*; this is an assault, this is a kind of rape by eyes. (p. 163; italics in original)

Percy's gaze here is specifically constructed by the 'voice' of the white man as a sexual threat or scopic 'assault'. As the 'feminine' tenor of that voice suggests, however, this scene has as much to do with emasculation as with male sexual violence and it is in these terms that Percy's petrified response to the sight of the fallen woman can be read. After all, the act of looking at the woman's disarrayed body is not deliberately voyeuristic but leaves Percy 'blinded by what his eyes have chanced upon' (p. 163): it results not in sexual pleasure, that is, but in a random sexual terror, with blindness serving as a familiar Freudian trope for castration, in the same way that looking functions as a figure for rape. What Percy thus sees reflected in 'this young beautiful girl's private parts' is an admonitory vision of the punishment in which, historically speaking, black male desire for the white female body so often results. Such a reading is confirmed by the way in which the white man conflates Percy's 'desire' with 'Emmett Till's, "up in America"', where 'these kinds of staring boys are lynched' (p. 164).[13]

The trauma of metaphorical castration recurs during the sequence relating to the events in the cave on Crane Beach, where Mary is raped by Bellfeels. In contrast to the hysterical male tennis player who seems oddly 'incapable' of 'knowing how to "be a man"' (p. 162), Percy evidently possesses such knowledge in abundance. This he has absorbed from 'storybooks' (p. 181) awash with images of heroic masculinity – 'Richard the Lion-Hearted, Hercules, Charles Atlas' (p. 182) amongst others – identifying himself, especially, with 'men who ... fought duels for the women they loved' (p. 179). Yet at the critical time when the 'sagas of bravery and chivalry' he has internalized need to be translated into concrete action, Percy necessarily falls short of the mark. His 'assault on the cave' and on Bellfeels ends only in the humiliation of defeat, as his 'puny strength' is easily repulsed by the 'might' in 'the bigger man's body' and the 'Bible story of David and Goliath' is turned on its head: as the narrator poignantly observes, the 'defence of little Mary's honour' is a 'task' which is simply 'too epic for him' (p. 182).

Percy's failure to rescue Mary – a damsel in much greater distress than the female tennis player who merely loses her footing – corresponds to his subsequent failure to raise the alarm on her behalf, as empty corporeal protest gives way to similarly futile vocal complaint:

> returning from Mary's cave ... he held the conch shell up to the full blast of the sun [and] made an attempt to put the ... shell to his lips, to blow it, like a trumpet, to send the sound that fishermen made along the beach, when there was a tragedy at sea, into the ears of all. When a man had drowned ... (p. 182)

Here the vocal power on which the conquered boy 'attempt[s]' to call is strangely displaced onto a 'sun' turned synaesthetically to 'full blast'. Yet the irony is that even were Percy able properly 'to blow' his 'conch', the 'tragedy' it would broadcast 'into the ears of all' would not be that of the sexually abused female body, but of 'a man ... drowned' at sea. It is beneath the image of this haunting figure that Mary's narrative is thus itself submerged, just as the original imprint of her path to Bellfeels' hideaway is obliterated by Percy's own returning tread: 'he walked back down the beach ... trying to memorize the number of her footsteps stamped into the sand that he had followed, and that were now shifting under the weight of his weight' (p. 182).

In his capacity as Mary's confessor on the night of Bellfeels' murder, Percy is noticeably less keen to let her story be heard or even told than he is in his childhood role as the outraged but voiceless witness to her sufferings. While

Mary applauds him as 'a man trained and schooled in the art of listening' (p. 137), Percy is arguably just as adept at not listening, as he 'go[es] over things' in his mind in a way which supplants Mary's memories with his own. Such periodic deafness to his interlocutor – 'You haven't heard a word I been saying to you for the last five minutes, haven't you, Percy?' (p. 155) – is a trait he shares with the Constable who is his harbinger and who twice contrives to fall asleep during the opening phases of Mary's confession (pp. 43 and 79). It is also something complemented by a certain will to censorship, articulated, for instance, in the moment when Percy informs 'Miss Mary' that she does not 'need to tell the full story' of her 'act' and that, in any case, her narrative is one for which there is no appetite, whether private or communal: 'You don't have to tell me. It is my duty to hear it, but I don't really want to hear it. The powers-that-be don't. The public don't. And the Village don't' (p. 115). Mary herself has some sympathy for this position, entering into her own series of detours and deferrals along the way, but she remains committed, none the less, to the completion of her statement. Nowhere is her resolution made clearer than in the exasperated representation of her relationship to Percy, female speaker to male listener, as an erotic power struggle in which traditional gender roles are again reversed. As she comments:

> 'It doesn't seem like I can come to the point, at all. You shift-away from assisting me to come. When I think it is time to come, take blame, admit, confess, and have you warn me that what I say will be taken down and use against me, you veer-away, and postpone my coming.' (p. 349)

Percy's resistance to the *jouissance* of confession projected here is partly explicable on the grounds that the tale Mary wants to tell confronts him with episodes in his own personal history, like those occurring at the tennis club and on Crane Beach, which he would prefer to forget. But it arises, equally, because the act of murder forming the climax to her narrative both fulfils Percy's own wish to 'make [Bellfeels] disappear ... off the fecking face of the earth' (p. 411) and functions as another figurative castration at the same time. The problem for Percy, however, in what is perhaps the novel's bitterest twist, is that by variously turning a deaf ear to Mary's voice, covering it up with his own memories and ultimately proposing that she censor her narrative, he in effect colludes with Bellfeels, the very figure who is their mutual enemy and who himself strives to seal the truth of things in silence. Bellfeels' parting words to Mary following her molestation in the underground tunnel, for instance, are *'Don't tell you mother'* (p. 398; italics in original), while the mother herself is left in no doubt as to the discursive constraints upon her when she blackmails him into providing for her daughter. No sooner does she threaten Bellfeels with the public exposure of his incest than she is subjected to 'the biting tongue of the riding-crop across her back, *whap!-whap!*' and then warned: 'You ever whisper *that* one-more-time, and I fecking kill you, like shite!' (p. 473; italics in original).

The evasiveness Percy displays towards the disclosures Mary makes in the course of the novel ultimately broadens out beyond the realms of the personal into a more general if unsustainable disavowal of Barbadian slavery itself. While Percy would like ideally to believe that 'Slavery never touch Bimshire' (p. 388), his more qualified and supposedly realistic position is that its presence on the island was of a lesser order in comparison to the regimes established elsewhere, a claim based on the assumption that their excesses are somehow un-English: 'But whole-scale slavery like what they have in Amurca, *no!* Not in a English colony, Jesus Christ. I know the English. The English won't do a thing like that. You know what I mean?' (p. 365). Yet just as Mary turns her own deaf ear to Percy's entreaties that she censor her story, so she counters his denials by arguing not only that slavery was a *bona fide* historical reality in Barbados and the Caribbean as a whole but also that there is 'no difference between those brutes who enslave us here in the Wessindies, and the ones that enslave other coloureds in Amurca' (p. 389). As she explains to her defensive auditor, both Caribbean and American slave histories are marked by modes of bodily and discursive violence which are mutually exportable: 'a lash is a lash. Whether it be delivered by a cowskin, a balata, a bull-pistle, here in Bimshire; or by a cat-o'-nine tail, as they did to Nat Turner in Southampton. Or with a lash from their tongue' (p. 390). The relatively abstract terms in which Mary puts her case are fleshed-out in their turn in the 'narratives' of extreme white cruelty she inherits from her foremothers and which include, *inter alia*, the story of slaves 'carried out in the sea, to feed to the sharks' (p. 400) when the plantation deems them to be 'no longer any use' (p. 399).

Towards the end of Clarke's novel, Mary and Percy improvise between themselves what they call a 'play-play Court' (p. 439), with the one put on imaginary trial by the other for 'Murder in the first degree!' (p. 440). This regressive mock-tribunal is perhaps another glance in the direction of Gray's *Confessions* (which closes with its own brief resumé of Turner's arraignment, together with a transcription of the death sentence passed upon him) and it is certainly designed to lampoon the system of colonial law operating outside the text as itself a mockery of justice. But the pretend prosecution is also self-consciously treated by Clarke as an occasion on which to underscore his distance from the traditional symbolic values of the seemingly unremarkable implement at his novel's heart, looking back, in particular, to the painters of the European Renaissance. As Percy asseverates in his make-believe role as Solicitor-General, the hoe as it appears in the work of these artists stands for '*industry …. bounty and … honest labour*' (p. 441; italics in original). Yet when the same tool reappears amid the sugarscapes of the 'tropical New Whirl' (p. 194) which Europe created, it becomes something rather different and rather less noble, functioning, at least for those compelled to use it, as a sign of racial and sexual oppression. In Clarke's early twenty-first-century handling, however, the hoe Mary polishes so lovingly and wields so lethally is refashioned as an instrument not of oppression but of liberation, just as his novel breaks free from the whitewashed plantation visions offered in Grainger and Lewis, digging up all they would have buried.

Notes

1. Austin Clarke, *The Polished Hoe* (Birmingham: Tindal Street Press, 2004), p. 367. Subsequent references to this work are incorporated in the text and given in parenthesis after quotations. While Clarke's novel met with immediate acclaim at the time of its publication, winning both the Giller Prize in 2002 and the overall Commonwealth Writers' Prize for Best Book the following year, it has gone on to elicit little sustained critical attention. The one notable exception to this somewhat surprising rule occurs in the work of Judith Misrahi-Barak, who – to make matters more curious still – has written on the text on two separate occasions. See Judith Misrahi-Barak, 'Skeletons in Caribbean Closets: Family Secrets and Silences in Austin Clarke's *The Polished Hoe* and Denise Harris's *Web of Secrets*', in *Family Fictions: The Family in Contemporary Postcolonial Literatures in English: Proceeds of an international conference, hosted by the Department of English, University of Gröningen, the Netherlands, 17–19 November 2004*, ed. Irene Visser and Heidi van den Heuvel-Disler (August 2005), pp. 53–64, < http:// irs.ub.rug.nl/ppn/297597558 > [accessed 16 August 2007]; and 'Tilling the Caribbean Narrative Field with Austin Clarke's *The Polished Hoe*', in *Cultures de la Confession: Formes de L'Aveau dans le Monde Anglophone*, ed. Gilles Teulié and Sylvie Mathé (Aix-en-Provence: Presses Universitaires de Provence, 2006), pp. 127–42. In an interesting recent development, the novel has also been adapted for the stage and was first performed by Canada's Obsidian Theatre Company in Toronto from 22 February to 4 March 2007, under the direction of Colin Taylor.
2. Phillips, p. 162.
3. Phillips, p. 167.
4. As Elizabeth Walcott-Hackshaw points out in a review of the text, the title of Clarke's novel is a *double entendre*, exploiting the manner in which meanings change as they travel across linguistic and geographical borders: 'a hoe in Standard English is a plantation tool', she notes, 'but in the English Caribbean "hoe" is another word for whore. The polished hoe is then both subject and object of a crime as Bellfeels has been murdered by his polished whore with the farm instrument'. See Elizabeth Walcott-Hackshaw, '*The Polished Hoe*', *Callaloo: A Journal of African-American and African Arts and Letters*, 29 (2006), p. 680. This semantic slippage between hoe-as-tool and hoe-as-whore is something on which the text itself twice comments quite explicitly (see pp. 135 and 441).
5. The origin of 'Bimshire' as an alternative (and generally affectionate) name for Barbados is uncertain, with some commentators giving the word an English and others an African provenance. For an illuminating historical perspective on these competing claims, see Sean Carrington, Henry Fraser, John Gilmore and Addinton Forde, *The A-Z of Barbados Heritage* (Oxford: Macmillan Education, 2003), p. 25. For the novel's own account of the island's nomenclature, see p. 321.
6. At a slightly earlier juncture in the novel, Mary informs the Constable that her 'memory is fading' and that her 'mind [is] not sharp no more' (p. 12) and this is borne out in the discrepancy between the Collect as she recites it here and how it is set

down in its ecclesiastical source, which refers to a spiritual passage through the 'gate of death' rather than 'hell'. Though slight, the error in Mary's memory is none the less significant, evoking a sense of the living torment she endures prior to Bellfeels' murder. For the original text which Mary misquotes, see *The Book of Common Prayer and Administration of the Sacraments and other Rites and Ceremonies of the Church according to the use of the Church of England together with the Psalter or Psalms of David pointed as they are to be sung or said in Churches and the form or manner of making, ordaining and consecrating of Bishops, Priests and Deacons*, enlarged edition (1662; Cambridge: Cambridge University Press, 2004), p. 126.

7. The status of abortion as a mode of resistance in *The Polished Hoe* is another sign of the novel's continuity with the slave era. For an informative and balanced discussion of the practice, see Morgan, pp. 244–46.

8. This sense of conflation between the spaces of the plantation and those of the slave ship is also implicit in the novel's rhetorical habits and, in particular, its tendency to figure the terrestrial in terms of the aquatic, as in its sublime assertions that the 'fields of sugar cane' where Mary and other women are abused are as 'wide as the Carbean sea' and 'vast as the Atlantic Ocean itself' (p. 396). Such amphibious rhetoric even seeps into Mary's description of the secret world beneath the fields to which she is taken by Bellfeels and in which personal and collective histories collide. As she remarks to Percy: "And here I am. In this underground tunnel, just like on one of those ships, reeling in the middle of two waves, in a trough of the ocean, with the wave over my head, waiting to swallow-me-up and drown me"' (p. 490).

9. *The Confessions of Nat Turner and Related Documents*, ed. Kenneth S. Greenberg (Boston and New York: Bedford/St Martin's, 1996), p. 46.

10. For these figures, see Greenberg, p. vii.

11. While this may be true of the rebellion as represented by Gray, Turner is provided with a sexual life – and a sexual motivation for his violent actions – in William Styron's *The Confessions of Nat Turner* (1967), the most famous and most controversial rewriting of the original. For a useful overview of the controversy generated by the novel, see Greenberg, pp. 28–31.

12. Greenberg, p. 41.

13. The allusion here is to the lynching of fourteen-year-old Emmett Louis 'Bobo' Till on 28 August 1955 for allegedly whistling at a white woman four days earlier, while visiting relatives in Mississippi. For a comprehensive account of this case, see Stephen J. Whitfield, *A Death in the Delta: The Story of Emmett Till* (New York: Free Press, 1988).

Bibliography

Allen, Theodore W., *The Invention of the White Race, Volume One: Racial Oppression and Social Control* (London and New York: Verso, 1994).

Anon., *The Adventures of Jonathan Corncob, Loyal American Refugee. Written by Himself*, ed. Noel Perrin (1787; Boston, MA: David R. Godine, 1976).

Anon., *Jamaica, a Poem, In Three Parts. Written in that Island, in the Year MDCCLXXVI. To which is Annexed, A Poetical Epistle From the Author in that Island to a Friend in England*, in *Caribbeana: An Anthology of English Literature of the West Indies, 1657–1777*, ed. Thomas W. Krise (1777; Chicago and London: University of Chicago Press, 1999), pp. 326–39.

Aravamudan, Srinivas, 'Introduction' to William Earle, *Obi; Or, The History of Three-Fingered Jack*, ed. Srinivas Aravamudan (Peterborough, ON: Broadview, 2005), pp. 7–52.

Beckford, William, *A Descriptive Account of the Island of Jamaica: With Remarks upon the Cultivation of the Sugar-Cane, throughout the different Seasons of the Year, and chiefly considered in a Picturesque Point of View; Also Observations and Reflections upon what would probably be the Consequence of an Abolition of the Slave-Trade, and of the Emancipation of the Slaves* (London: T. and J. Egerton, 1790).

Beeton, Isabella, *The Book of Household Management; Comprising Information for the Mistress, Housekeeper, Cook, Kitchen-maid, Butler, Footman, Coachman, Valet, Upper and under house-maids, Lady's-maid, Maid-of-all-work, Laundry-maid, Nurse and nurse-maid, Monthly, wet, and sick nurses, etc. etc. also, sanitary, medical, & legal memoranda; with a history of the origin, properties, and uses of all things connected with home life and comfort* (1861; Lewes: Southover Press, 2003).

Behn, Aphra, *Oroonoko: Or, The Royal Slave. A True History*, ed. Lore Metzger (1688; New York and London: Norton, 1973).

Benítez-Rojo, Antonio, *The Repeating Island: The Caribbean and the Postmodern Perspective*, second edition, trans. by James E. Maraniss (1992; Durham, NC and London: Duke University Press, 1996).

Bettinger, Elfie, 'Grace Nichols's "Sugar Cane": A Post-Colonial and Feminist Perspective', *Anglistik und Englischunterricht*, 53 (1994), 117–27.

Bhabha, Homi K., *The Location of Culture* (London and New York: Routledge, 1994).

Birkett, Mary, *A Poem on the African Slave Trade: Addressed to Her Own Sex* (London: J. Jones, 1792).

Blackburn, Robin, *The Overthrow of Colonial Slavery, 1776–1848* (London and New York: Verso, 1988).

Bohls, Elizabeth A., 'The Planter Picturesque: Matthew Lewis's *Journal of a West India Proprietor*', *European Romantic Review*, 13 (2002), 63–76.

The Book of Common Prayer and Administration of the Sacraments and other Rites and Ceremonies of the Church according to the use of the Church of England together with the Psalter or Psalms of David pointed as they are to be sung or said in Churches and the form or manner of making, ordaining and consecrating of Bishops, Priests and Deacons, enlarged edition (1662; Cambridge: Cambridge University Press, 2004).

Boswell, James, *Life of Johnson*, ed. R. W. Chapman, intro. Pat Rogers (1791; Oxford: Oxford University Press, 1998).

Brathwaite, Edward Kamau, 'Labourer', in *Breaklight: The Poetry of the Caribbean*, ed. Andrew Salkey (Garden City, NY: Doubleday, 1972), pp. 239–40.

Brontë, Charlotte, *Jane Eyre*, ed. Margaret Smith (Oxford: Oxford University Press, 1998).

Burn, Andrew, 'A Second Address to the People of Great Britain: Containing a New, and Most Powerful Argument to Abstain from the Use of West India Sugar. By an Eye Witness to the Facts Related' (London: M. Gurney, 1792).

Burnard, Trevor, *Mastery, Tyranny and Desire: Thomas Thistlewood and his Slaves in the Anglo-Jamaican World* (Chapel Hill and London: University of North Carolina Press, 2004).

Byron, Lord George Gordon, *Byron's Letters and Journals*, ed. Leslie A. Marchand, 13 vols (London: John Murray, 1973–94).

Calbi, Maurizio, 'Vexing Encounters: Uncanny Belonging and the Poetics of Alterity in Caryl Phillips's *Cambridge*', *Postcolonial Text*, 1.2 (2005): <http://postcolonial.org/index.php/pct/article/view/343/121> [accessed 16 August 2007].

Carey, Brycchan, Markman Ellis and Sarah Salih (eds), *Discourses of Slavery and Abolition: Britain and its Colonies, 1760–1838* (Basingstoke and New York: Palgrave Macmillan, 2004).

Carmichael, Mrs A. C., *Domestic Manners and Social Condition of the White, Coloured, and Negro Population of the West Indies*, 2 vols (New York: Negro Universities Press, 1969).

Carretta, Vincent, *Equiano, The African: Biography of a Self-Made Man* (Athens, GA and London: University of Georgia Press, 2005).

Carrington, Sean, Henry Fraser, John Gilmore and Addinton Forde, *The A-Z of Barbados Heritage* (Oxford: Macmillan Education, 2003).

Charles, Faustin, 'Sugar Cane', in Salkey, pp. 185–86.

—, 'Sugar Cane Man', in Salkey, pp. 88–90.

Chavanelle, Sylvie, 'Caryl Phillips's *Cambridge*: Ironical (Dis)empowerment?', *International Fiction Review*, 25 (1998), 78–88.

Clarke, Austin, *The Polished Hoe* (Birmingham: Tindal Street Press, 2004).

Coleman, Deirdre, 'Conspicuous Consumption: White Abolitionism and English Women's Protest Writing in the 1790s', *English Literary History*, 61 (1994), 341–62.

Coleridge, Samuel Taylor, 'On the Slave Trade', in *The Abolition Debate*, ed. Peter J. Kitson, vol. 2 of *Slavery, Abolition and Emancipation: Writings in the British Romantic Period*, ed. Peter J. Kitson and Debbie Lee, 8 vols (London: Pickering and Chatto, 1999), pp. 209–20.

Craton, Michael, *Searching for the Invisible Man: Slaves and Plantation Life in Jamaica* (Cambridge, MA and London: Harvard University Press, 1978).

Cumberland, Richard, *The West Indian: A Comedy* (Belfast: Henry and Robert Joy, 1771).

Dabydeen, David, 'Hogarth and the Canecutter', in *'The Tempest' and its Travels*, ed. Peter Hulme and William H. Sherman (London: Reaktion Books, 2000), pp. 257–63.

—, 'On Not Being Milton: Nigger Talk in England Today', in *The State of the Language*, ed. Christopher Ricks and Leonard Michaels (London and Boston: Faber and Faber, 1990), pp. 3–14.

—, 'On Writing "Slave Song"', *Commonwealth Essays and Studies*, 8.2 (1986), 46–48.

—, *Slave Song*, second edition (Leeds: Peepal Tree, 2005).

Davidson, Carol Margaret, 'Crisscrossing the River: An Interview with Caryl Phillips', *ARIEL: A Review of International English Literature*, 25.4 (1994), 96–97.

Deerr, Noël, *The History of Sugar*, 2 vols (London: Chapman and Hall, 1949–50).

Defoe, Daniel, *Robinson Crusoe*, ed. John Richetti (London: Penguin, 2001).

De Sola Rodstein, Susan, 'Sweetness and Dark: George Eliot's "Brother Jacob"', *Modern Language Quarterly*, 52 (1991), 295–317.

Doane, Mary Ann, *Femmes Fatales: Feminism, Film Theory, Psychoanalysis* (New York and London: Routledge, 1991).

Döring, Tobias, *Caribbean-English Passages: Intertextuality in a Postcolonial Tradition* (London and New York: Routledge, 2002).

Dubois, Laurent and John D. Garrigus, *Slave Revolution in the Caribbean, 1789–1804: A Brief History with Documents* (Boston and New York: Bedford/St. Martin's, 2006).

Dunn, Oliver and James E. Kelley, Jr, trans. and ed., *The* Diario *of Christopher Columbus's First Voyage to America 1492–1493, Abstracted by Fray Bartolomé de las Casas* (Norman, OK and London: University of Oklahoma Press, 1989).

Dyer, John, *The Fleece, in Four Books*, in *Poems. By John Dyer* (London: J. Dodsley, 1770).

Easton, Alison, 'The Body as History and "Writing the Body": The Example of Grace Nichols', *Journal of Gender Studies*, 3.1 (1994), 55–67.

Eckstein, Lars, *Re-Membering the Black Atlantic: On the Poetics and Politics of Literary Memory* (Amsterdam and New York: Rodopi, 2006).

Edwards, Bryan, *The History, Civil and Commercial, of the British Colonies in the West Indies*, 2 vols (London: J. Stockdale, 1793).

Egan, Jim, 'The "Long'd-for Aera" of an "Other Race": Climate, Identity, and James

Grainger's *The Sugar-Cane*', *Early American Literature*, 38 (2003), 189–212.

Eliot, George, 'Brother Jacob', in *The Lifted Veil; Brother Jacob*, ed. Helen Small (Oxford and New York: Oxford University Press, 1999).

—, *The George Eliot Letters*, ed. Gordon S. Haight, 9 vols (New Haven and London: Yale University Press, 1954–78).

Ellis, Keith, 'Images of Sugar in English and Spanish Caribbean Poetry', *ARIEL: A Review of International English Literature*, 24.1 (1993), 149–59.

Ellis, Markman, '"Incessant Labour": Georgic Poetry and the Problem of Slavery', in Carey, Ellis and Salih, pp. 45–62.

Equiano, Olaudah, *The Interesting Narrative and Other Writings*, ed. Vincent Carretta (London: Penguin, 1995).

Fairer, David, 'A Caribbean Georgic: James Grainger's *The Sugar-Cane*', *Kunapipi: Journal of Post-Colonial Writing*, 25.1 (2003), 21–28.

Fanon, Frantz, *Black Skin, White Masks*, trans. Charles Lam Markmann, Foreword by Homi K. Bhabha (London: Pluto Press, 1986).

Flannigan, Mrs, *Antigua and the Antiguans: A Full Account of the Colony and Its Inhabitants from the Time of the Caribs to the Present Day, Interspersed with Anecdotes and Legends. Also, an Impartial View of Slavery and the Free Labour Systems; The Statistics of the Island, and Biographical Notices of the Principal Families*, 2 vols (London: Saunders and Otley, 1844).

Flint, Kate, 'Spectres of Sugar', in *White and Deadly: Sugar and Colonialism*, ed. Pat Ahluwalia, Bill Ashcroft and Roger Knight (Commack, NY: Nova Science Publishers, 1999), pp. 83–93.

Follett, Richard, *The Sugar Masters: Planters and Slaves in Louisiana's Cane World, 1820–1860* (Baton Rouge: Louisiana State University Press, 2005).

Foote, Samuel, *The Patron. A Comedy in Three Acts* (London: G. Kearsly, 1764).

Fox, William, 'An Address to the People of Great Britain, on the Propriety of Abstaining from West India Sugar and Rum', in *The Abolition Debate*, ed. Peter J. Kitson, volume 2 of *Slavery, Abolition and Emancipation: Writings in the British Romantic Period*, ed. Peter J. Kitson and Debbie Lee, 8 vols (London: Pickering and Chatto, 1999), pp. 153–65.

Fulford, Tim, and Peter J. Kitson, eds, *Romanticism and Colonialism: Writing and Empire, 1780–1830* (Cambridge: Cambridge University Press, 1998).

Fuss, Diana, *Identification Papers* (New York and London: Routledge, 1995).

Gilroy, Paul, *The Black Atlantic: Modernity and Double Consciousness* (London and New York: Verso, 1993).

Grainger, James, *The Sugar-Cane: A Poem. In Four Books. With Notes*, in John Gilmore, *The Poetics of Empire: A Study of James Grainger's* The Sugar-Cane (London and New Brunswick, NJ: The Athlone Press, 2000), pp. 87–198.

Grant, Kevin, ed., *The Art of David Dabydeen* (Leeds: Peepal Tree, 1997).

Greenberg, Kenneth S., ed., *The Confessions of Nat Turner and Related Documents* (Boston and New York: Bedford/St Martin's, 1996).

Gregory, Melissa Valiska, 'The Unexpected Forms of Nemesis: George Eliot's "Brother Jacob," Victorian Narrative, and the Morality of Imperialism', *Dickens Studies Annual*, 31 (2002), 281–303.

Gregory, Philippa, *A Respectable Trade*, rev. ed. (London: HarperCollins, 2005).

Hall, Kim F., 'Culinary Spaces, Colonial Spaces: The Gendering of Sugar in the Seventeenth Century', in *Feminist Readings of Early Modern Culture: Emerging Subjects*, ed. Valerie Traub, M. Lindsay Kaplan and Dympna Callaghan (Cambridge: Cambridge University Press, 1996), pp. 168–90.

Hall, Stuart, 'Old and New Identities, Old and New Ethnicities', in *Culture, Globalization and the World-System: Contemporary Conditions for the Representation of Identity*, ed. Anthony D. King (Minneapolis: University of Minnesota Press, 1997), pp. 41–68.

Harkin, Maureen, 'Matthew Lewis's *Journal of a West India Proprietor*: Surveillance and Space on the Plantation', *Nineteenth-Century Contexts*, 24 (2002), 139–50.

Heiland, Donna, 'The *Unheimlich* and the Making of Home: Matthew Lewis's *Journal of a West India Proprietor*', in *Monstrous Dreams of Reason: Body, Self, and Other in the Enlightenment*, ed. Mita Choudhury and Laura Rosenthal (Lewisburg, PA: Bucknell University Press, 2002), pp. 170–88.

Henry, Nancy, *George Eliot and the British Empire* (Cambridge: Cambridge University Press, 2002).

Hochschild, Adam, *Bury the Chains: The British Struggle to Abolish Slavery* (London: Pan, 2005).

Hulme, Peter, 'Columbus and the Cannibals', in *The Post-Colonial Studies Reader*, ed. Bill Ashcroft, Gareth Griffiths and Helen Tiffin (London and New York: Routledge, 1995), pp. 365–69.

Irlam, Shaun, '"Wish You Were Here": Exporting England in James Grainger's *The Sugar-Cane*', *English Literary History*, 68 (2001), 377–96.

Jacobs, Harriet, *Incidents in the Life of a Slave Girl*, ed. Nellie Y. McKay and Frances Smith Foster (1861; New York and London: Norton, 2001).

James, C. L. R., *The Black Jacobins: Toussaint L'Ouverture and the San Domingo Revolution*, intro. James Walvin (1938; London: Penguin, 2001).

Jenkins, Lee M., *The Language of Caribbean Poetry: Boundaries of Expression* (Gainesville, FL: University Press of Florida, 2004).

Johnson, Samuel, *Critical Review*, xviii (October 1764), 270–77.

Jones, Donald, *Bristol's Sugar Trade and Refining Industry* (Bristol: Bristol Branch of the Historical Association, 1996).

Kowaleski-Wallace, Elizabeth, *Consuming Subjects: Women, Shopping, and Business in the Eighteenth Century* (New York: Columbia University Press, 1997).

Krise, Thomas W., *Caribbeana: An Anthology of English Literature of the West Indies, 1657–1777* (Chicago and London: University of Chicago Press, 1999).

Lambert, David, *White Creole Culture, Politics and Identity during the Age of Abolition* (Cambridge: Cambridge University Press, 2005).

Ledent, Bénédicte, *Caryl Phillips* (Manchester and New York: Manchester University Press, 2002).

Lenman, Bruce P., 'Colonial Wars and Imperial Instability, 1688–1793', in *The Eighteenth Century*, ed. P. J. Marshall, volume 2 of *The Oxford History of the British Empire*, editor-in-chief Wm. Roger Louis, 5 vols (Oxford: Oxford University Press, 1988), pp. 159–67.

Lewis, Matthew, *Journal of a West India Proprietor, Kept during a Residence in the Island of Jamaica*, ed. Judith Terry (Oxford and New York: Oxford University Press, 1999).

Ligon, Richard, *A True & Exact History of the Island of Barbadoes. Illustrated with a Map of the Island, as also the Principal Trees and Plants there, set forth in their due Proportions and Shapes, drawn out by their several and respective Scales. Together with the Ingenio that makes the Sugar, with the Plots of the several Houses, Rooms, and other places, that are used in the whole process of Sugar-making; viz. the Grinding-room, the Boyling-room, the Filling-room, the Curing-house, Still-house, and Furnaces; All cut in Copper*, second edition (1673; London: Frank Cass, 1976).

Long, Edward, *The History of Jamaica. Or, General Survey of the Antient and Modern State of That Island: With Reflections on Its Situation, Settlements, Inhabitants, Climate, Products, Commerce, Laws, and Government. In Three Volumes. Illustrated with Copper Plates* (London: T. Lowndes, 1774).

McDonald, D. L., 'The Isle of Devils: The Jamaican Journal of M. G. Lewis', in Fulford and Kitson, pp. 189–205.

McDonald, Roderick A., ed., *Between Slavery and Freedom: Special Magistrate John Anderson's Journal of St. Vincent during the Apprenticeship* (Philadelphia: University of Pennsylvania Press, 2001).

Mackay, Rebecca, 'Women and Fiction in George Eliot's "Brother Jacob"', *George Eliot Review*, 31 (2000), 31–36.

McWatt, Mark, 'His True-True Face: Masking and Revelation in David Dabydeen's *Slave Song*', in Grant, pp. 15–25.

Martin, Samuel, *An Essay upon Plantership, Humbly inscrib'd to all the Planters of the British Sugar-Colonies in America*, second edition (Antigua: T. Smith, 1750).

Martineau, Harriet, 'Demerara', in *The Empire Question*, ed. Deborah Logan, volume 1 of *Harriet Martineau's Writing on the British Empire*, ed. Deborah Logan, 5 vols (London: Pickering and Chatto, 2004), pp. 69–141.

—, *Harriet Martineau's Autobiography*, ed. Maria Weston Chapman, 2 vols (Boston: James R. Osgood, 1877).

Meer, Sarah, *Uncle Tom Mania: Slavery, Minstrelsy, and Transatlantic Culture in the 1850s* (Athens, GA and London: University of Georgia Press, 2005).

Menard, Russell R., *Sweet Negotiations: Sugar, Slavery, and Plantation Agriculture in Early Barbados* (Charlottesville and London: University of Virginia Press, 2006).

Meyer, Susan, *Imperialism at Home: Race and Victorian Women's Fiction* (Ithaca and London: Cornell University Press, 1996).

Mintz, Sidney W., *Sweetness and Power: The Place of Sugar in Modern History* (New York: Viking, 1985).

Misrahi-Barak, Judith, 'Skeletons in Caribbean Closets: Family Secrets and Silences in Austin Clarke's *The Polished Hoe* and Denise Harris's *Web of Secrets*', in *Family Fictions: The Family in Contemporary Postcolonial Literatures in English: Proceeds of an international conference, hosted by the Department of English, University of Gröningen, the Netherlands, 17–19 November 2004*, ed. Irene Visser and Heidi van den Heuvel-Disler (August 2005), pp. 53–64: < http://irs.ub.rug.nl/ppn/297597558 > [accessed 16 August 2007].

—, 'Tilling the Caribbean Narrative Field with Austin Clarke's *The Polished Hoe*', in *Cultures de la Confession: Formes de L'Aveau dans le Monde Anglophone*, ed. Gilles Teulié and Sylvie Mathé (Aix-en-Provence: Presses Universitaires de Provence, 2006), pp. 127–42.

Montefiore, Jan, *Feminism and Poetry: Language, Experience, Identity in Women's Writing*, second edition (London: Pandora, 1994).

Morel, Genaro Rodríguez, 'The Sugar Economy of Española in the Sixteenth Century', in *Tropical Babylons: Sugar and the Making of the Atlantic World, 1450–1680*, ed. Stuart B. Schwartz (Chapel Hill and London: University of North Carolina Press, 2004), pp. 85–114.

Morgan, Kenneth, 'Slave Women and Reproduction in Jamaica, c. 1776–1834', *History: The Journal of the Historical Association*, 91 (2006), 231–53.

Morton, Timothy, 'Blood Sugar', in Fulford and Kitson, pp. 87–106.

Narain, Denise deCaires, *Contemporary Caribbean Women's Poetry: Making Style* (London and New York: Routledge, 2002).

Nichols, Grace, *I is a Long Memoried Woman* (London: Karnak House, 1990).

—, 'Yes, through it all', in *Startling the Flying Fish* (London: Virago, 2005), p. 61.

O'Callaghan, Evelyn, 'Historical Fiction and Fictional History: Caryl Phillips's *Cambridge*', *Journal of Commonwealth Literature*, 28.2 (1993), 34–47.

O'Connell, Sanjida, *Sugar: The Grass that Changed the World* (London: Virgin Books, 2004).

Oldfield, J. R., 'Transatlanticism, Race and Slavery', *American Literary History*, 14 (2002), 131–40.

Ortiz, Fernando, *Cuban Counterpoint: Tobacco and Sugar*, trans. Harriet de Onís, with a new Introduction by Fernando Coronil (1940; Durham, NC and London: Duke University Press, 1995).

Parry, Benita, 'Between Creole and Cambridge English: The Poetry of David Dabydeen', in Grant, pp. 47–66.

Peck, Louis F., *A Life of Matthew G. Lewis* (Cambridge, MA: Harvard University Press, 1961).

Phillips, Caryl, *Cambridge* (London: Picador, 1992).

Plasa, Carl, *Textual Politics from Slavery to Postcolonialism: Race and Identification* (Basingstoke and London: Macmillan, 2000).

Reddie, Richard S., *Abolition! The Struggle to Abolish Slavery in the British Colonies* (Oxford: Lion, 2007).

Rice, Alan, *Radical Narratives of the Black Atlantic* (London and New York: Continuum, 2003).

—, '"Who's Eating Whom?" The Discourse of Cannibalism in the Literature of the Black Atlantic from Equiano's *Travels* to Toni Morrison's *Beloved*', *Research in African Literatures*, 29.4 (1998), 106–21.

Richardson, David, 'The British Empire and the Atlantic Slave Trade', in *The Eighteenth Century*, ed. P. J. Marshall, volume 2 of *The Oxford History of the British Empire*, editor-in-chief Wm. Roger Louis, 5 vols (Oxford: Oxford University Press, 1988), pp. 440–64.

Richardson, Tim, *Sweets: A History of Temptation* (London: Bantam Books, 2003).

Robertson, James, *Joseph Knight* (London: Fourth Estate, 2003).

Salkey, Andrew, ed., *Breaklight: The Poetry of the Caribbean* (Garden City, NY: Doubleday, 1972).

Sandiford, Keith A., *The Cultural Politics of Sugar: Caribbean Slavery and Narratives of Colonialism* (Cambridge: Cambridge University Press, 2000).

Scarry, Elaine, *The Body in Pain: The Making and Unmaking of the World* (New York: Oxford University Press, 1985).

Schaw, Janet, *Journal of a Lady of Quality, Being the* Narrative *of a Journey from Scotland to the* West Indies, North Carolina, *and* Portugal, *in the years 1774 to 1776*, ed. Evangeline Walker Andrews (with Charles McLean Andrews), intro. Stephen Carl Arch (Lincoln, NE and London: University of Nebraska Press, 2005).

Shakespeare, William, *Othello*, ed. E. A. J. Honigmann ([Walton-on-Thames]: Nelson, 1997).

—, *The Tempest*, ed. Stephen Orgel (Oxford: Oxford University Press, 1987).

Sharpe, Jenny, *Ghosts of Slavery: A Literary Archaeology of Black Women's Lives* (Minneapolis and London: University of Minnesota Press, 2003).

Sharrad, Paul, 'Speaking the Unspeakable: London, Cambridge and the Caribbean', in *De-Scribing Empire: Post-Colonialism and Textuality*, ed. Chris Tiffin and Alan Lawson (London and New York: Routledge, 1994), pp. 201–17.

Sheller, Mimi, *Consuming the Caribbean: From Arawaks to Zombies* (London and New York: Routledge, 2003).

Sloane, Sir Hans, *A Voyage to the Islands Madera, Barbados, Nieves, S. Christophers and Jamaica, with the Natural History of the Herbs and Trees, Four-footed Beasts, Fishes, Birds, Insects, Reptiles, &c. of the last of those Islands*, 2 vols (London: Printed by B. M. for the Author, 1707–25).

Solomon, Frances-Anne, dir., *I is a Long Memoried Woman* (LedaSerene/Women Make Movies, 1990).

Southey, Robert, 'Poems on the Slave Trade', in Wood, *The Poetry of Slavery*, pp. 216–18.

Steele, Richard, '*The Spectator*, no. 11', in *English Trader, Indian Maid: Representing Gender, Race and Slavery in the New World, An Inkle and Yarico Reader*, ed. Frank Felsenstein (Baltimore and London: Johns Hopkins University Press, 1999), pp. 81–88.

Stein, Mark, 'Who's Afraid of Cannibals? Some Uses of the Cannibalism Trope in Olaudah Equiano's *The Interesting Narrative*', in Carey, Ellis and Salih, pp. 96–107.

Sterne, Laurence, *A Sentimental Journey and Other Writings*, ed. Ian Jack and Tim Parnell, intro. Tim Parnell (1768; Oxford: Oxford University Press, 2003).

Styron, William, *The Confessions of Nat Turner* (London: Vintage, 2004).

Sussman, Charlotte, 'Women and the Politics of Sugar, 1792', *Representations*, 48 (Fall 1994), 48–69.

Teale, Isaac, 'The Sable Venus; An Ode', in Edwards, vol. 2, pp. 27–33.

Thomas, Helen, *Romanticism and Slave Narratives: Transatlantic Testimonies* (Cambridge: Cambridge University Press, 2000).

Thomas, Steven W., 'Doctoring Ideology: James Grainger's *The Sugar Cane* and the Bodies of Empire', *Early American Studies: An Interdisciplinary Journal*, 4 (2006), 78–111.

Three Tracts on West-Indian Agriculture, and subjects connected therewith (Kingston, Jamaica: Alexander Aikman, 1802).

Unsworth, Barry, *Sacred Hunger* (London: Hamish Hamilton, 1992).

—, *Sugar and Rum* (London: Hamish Hamilton, 1988).

Von Sneidern, Maja-Lisa, '"Monk" Lewis's Journals and the Discipline of Discourse', *Nineteenth-Century Contexts*, 23 (2001), 59–88.

Walcott-Hackshaw, Elizabeth, review of *The Polished Hoe*, *Callaloo: A Journal of African-American and African Arts and Letters*, 29 (2006), 680–82.

Weekes, Nathaniel, *Barbados: A Poem* (London: R. and J. Dodsley, 1754).

Welsh, Sarah Lawson, 'Experiments in Brokenness: The Creative Use of Creole in David Dabydeen's *Slave Song*', in Grant, pp. 27–46.

Whitfield, Stephen J., *A Death in the Delta: The Story of Emmett Till* (New York: Free Press, 1988).

Wiley, Michael, 'Consuming Africa: Geography and Identity in Olaudah Equiano's *The Interesting Narrative*', *Studies in Romanticism*, 44 (2005), 165–79.

Williams, Eric, *From Columbus to Castro: The History of the Caribbean 1492–1969* (1970; New York: Vintage, 1984).

Williamson, Karina, 'West Indian Georgic', *Essays in Criticism*, 52 (2002), 81–89.

Woloson, Wendy A., *Refined Tastes: Sugar, Confectionery, and Consumers in Nineteenth-Century America* (Baltimore and London: Johns Hopkins University Press, 2002).

Wood, Marcus, *Blind Memory: Visual Representations of Slavery in England and America, 1780–1865* (Manchester and New York: Manchester University Press, 2000).

Wood, Marcus, ed., *The Poetry of Slavery: An Anglo-American Anthology, 1764–1865* (Oxford: Oxford University Press, 2003).

Young, Robert J. C., *Colonial Desire: Hybridity in Theory, Culture and Race* (London and New York: Routledge, 1995).

Index